THE BIG TRIP REVEALED

REVEALED

A Family's Life-Changing Journey

~ A Travel Memoir ~

JENNIFER MOORE

Printed in Canada

First Printing, 2015

ISBN-13: 978-1505822922

ISBN-10: 1505822920

JAM Publishing
204-621 10 street
Canmore, Alberta, T1W 2A2

www.bigtriprevealed.com

Cover design by Jennifer Moore

TABLE OF CONTENTS

WHAT IF you could escape your job and the responsibilities you shoulder?

WHAT IF you could fly far away to live a new adventure every day?

WHAT IF, for one year, you could travel the world?

PROLOGUE

Long before our family's odyssey began, we stood at the airport ready to embark on our first journey overseas. I held Mattson, our angelic five month old son, while Ken, my husband, juggled our luggage, camera equipment and a gigantic diaper bag. We buzzed with excitement until our little angel fussed and Ken remembered he forgot our passports. While Mattson ramped up to rage like someone else's difficult child, Ken stood tall at the airline counter explaining why custom officials in London should let us in. He'd have the passports sent; they'd get them eventually.

The next day, back at the airport, the blunders continued: Our diaper bag, mistakenly checked, slid away as I zealously yelled "stop that belt!" Our camera sat forgotten on a chair and our son proved to be – no angel.

My parents waved goodbye with fear in their eyes. How would we manage five months in a strange land with their precious grandson when just leaving the airport had been so difficult? It was a bad start to our first major family adventure, but we did manage to keep our child safe and fall hopelessly in love with travel.

On the day that changed our lives, the sun's rays lazily stretched through the Coliseum's crumbling arches as we sipped wine and pondered how we could spend more time traveling. We didn't just want lots of two and three week holidays, we wanted extended real travel, wandering travel, spontaneous and free travel. By the time we stood to leave, our carafe of wine long empty, we had a plan; somehow, we'd find a way to take a year off and travel with our kids. It would be our Big Trip.

That conversation in Rome marked a change on our road of life. We had a dream – a dream that would take us off the expressway of secure and predictable living to a less traveled bumpy road. Exhilarated, we walked away, promising to keep our Big Trip a secret. What if we got caught in the traffic of life and never made it to the off ramp?

After returning to Canada for my dental school graduation, we began our careers and added a daughter named Makayla to our brood. Ken became an entrepreneur and started a medical engineering company. Getting it up and running turned out to be a gut-wrenching roller coaster ride, leaving us wallowing in debt. Finding money to travel seemed as likely as seeing rainbows in the desert.

The years passed and Ken's business started to turn around. Occasionally we found a way to feed the piggy bank, but finding the slot was tough when there were so many nice things we wanted. The couples in our dinner club had homes much more beautiful than ours. Saying no to the material was hard and staying focused on our dream even more difficult, but somehow we found the discipline to avoid our immediate wants – most of the time.

As the age of the kids increased, so did the pace of our lives. Frantically, we tried to juggle work, kids' lessons and a social life. Some days, life seemed out of control. Thinking about the Big Trip became a comforting day dream – a light at the end of a long tunnel.

When Mattson turned eleven, we started concrete trip planning, not knowing how we'd actually pull it off. When he turned thirteen, and Makayla turned eleven, we set a date.

Our parents were the first to know. Taking a year off for travel certainly didn't mesh with their "work hard to create security" ethic. My father furrowed his brow and in a strained voice questioned: "Are you crazy?! Why on earth would you want to give up everything you've worked so hard for to tramp around the world?" I tried to explain our desire for quality family time. How I longed to be catapulted far from the stressful routine of my existence.

Both sets of parents thought we were nuts.

The months before we left were a blur as we tried to find people to run our businesses and rent our house. Our departure date approached like a head-on collision and negative WHAT IFS crept into my head. WHAT IF our businesses failed while we were gone? WHAT IF the kids got sick with malaria or dengue fever and never recovered?

WHAT IF the house didn't rent? In a negative frame of mind, I spun out of control. The threat of terrorism dominated morning headlines and viruses like SARS threatened to morph into worldwide pandemics.

There were many sleepless nights before our departure, but we did leave; we did live our dream. What was it really like to globetrot through twenty-six countries and to sleep in a different place almost every night? What was the reality of travel beyond the tourist attractions and frozen smiling faces in pictures?

My stories, noted in a daily journal, tell of the day-to-day bump and grind of family dynamics, the emotional highs and lows of a year of travel and the life changing lessons learned along the way.

The Moores at their bon voyage party

Ready to fly away

JAPAN

September 4, 2003

People warned me that leaving would be the hardest part of our journey. How right they were. I wore out the road to the Goodwill Centre, dropping off unwanted stuff. Why had we accumulated so prolifically, only to purge without a second glance? Never, I swore, would I shop again. Cleaning house was a grind, but for the first time in my life, I caught a glimpse of what getting organized felt like. We worked and planned until time ran out, then ready or not, we left.

Once up in the air en route to Japan, I worried about our unrented house until Mattson poked me and asked what I thought the tofu loaf in his Japanese airplane meal was. Feeling playful, I proclaimed it a peanut butter/nougat bar. He chewed, paused, convulsed, gagged and spat, giving me my first Big Trip chuckle. It came at the expense of a son's trust in his mother, but that laugh marked the slow unraveling of my tightly strung nerves.

At Narita Airport, we met a long line to clear customs. Finally stepping up, the controller's dark eyes swung back and forth like a pendulum perusing passports and us. Not knowing whether to hold his gaze or look away, I felt uncomfortable and blushed. Guilty people blush. I turned even redder realizing the brush I was painting myself with. Only the slam of the entry stamp hitting our passports allowed the color to fade away.

Dragging our luggage outside to hail a cab, we watched in disbelief as a car resembling a dinky-toy pulled up. Medical equipment housed in two long hard golf cases for Ken's work (he planned to chase profitability and travel at the same time) couldn't possibly fit in its minuscule trunk. Ken wanted to pack those cases, but a group of taxi drivers, whose heads bobbed in animated conversation at the level of his armpit, blocked his way.

We eventually drove away with the golf cases sticking out of a popped trunk to New Chiba, a suburb of Tokyo. Stiffly stumbling out of the cab, we met our smiling and bowing hosts for the night. Before leaving Canada we'd joined an international travel group called Servas; its members welcomed travelers into their home for a two night home stay. The concept of connecting with locals sounded good back in Canada, but the reality of it left me feeling ill at ease.

Kozuko, our hostess, warmly welcomed us with an invitation for dinner. Before entering her kitchen I warned the kids to try everything she served, but when her train of food had no end, I was the one to plead "Please! No more!" while begging for much-needed sleep.

September 5

After passing out, I woke up not knowing where I was until the reality of the Big Trip washed over me. No more being a dentist and fixing teeth, no cooking, no cleaning, just new adventures for the next eleven months. I felt so free – free and hungry. Being a breakfast eater, it was time for food.

The kids and Ken shared my enthusiasm to explore and eat. We left the apartment at 8:00 a.m. to discover sleeping suburbs. With each turn came more apartments until Mattson let out a holler. Off in the distance, was the familiar sign of a 7-Eleven convenience store. The kids weren't happy to find rice balls, sushi and steamed pork buns replacing Slurpees, hoagies and muffins. Stomaching barbecued pork for breakfast would be our first Big Trip adventure.

Once fed, we looked at our watches; 9:00 a.m., now what? Coming from a highly programmed life, we weren't quite sure what to do with ourselves, but Ken quickly came up with a plan. We'd start our Big Trip exercise program on the spot.

Mattson was a gymnast and Makayla a dancer. We knew it was important to keep them fit, but I hadn't expected a workout on our first morning. Ken led our first family jog. Within five minutes, Makayla complained of a mild asthma attack, Mattson had a stitch in his stomach and the apartment keys went missing. Thankfully the lost keys forced Ken to leave us and retrace his steps. Collapsing and sprawling out on the grass after he left, the kids and I groaned. Having Ken as our daily programmer might be a problem.

After an enjoyable lunch with our hosts, we started our journey to Tokyo. Ken's medical equipment weighed a ton and pulling it to the station made our arms burn. Multiple mistakes, transfers and stairs later, we arrived in Tokyo and made our way to the Sakura Hotel.

We were trying to live on $200.00 a day, so the Sakura hotel was basic at best. Upon our arrival we connected with a fifteen year old Canadian boy named Mitchell whom we'd never met before. He would attend a gymnastics meet with Mattson in Tokyo later that week. When his accommodations fell through, his folks had called us in Calgary to ask if he could stay with us. Even though it would be awkward, we didn't feel comfortable with saying no.

Lining up in front of the lobby elevator, my jaw dropped when the door opened. This wasn't an elevator; it was a casket-sized vault crammed with compressed people. Seconds after the door opened, a mass of humanity stampeded past us, and in a blink of an eye the black box filled again. Ken and the kids forced their way in while I stalled. I was claustrophobic. Getting into that elevator was my worst nightmare. I headed for the stairs.

When we opened our hotel room door, oppressive heat enveloped us. The room was a shoe box. Feeling panicked, I noticed a narrow window across the room desperately needing to be opened. Rushing the three steps to get there, the window appeared to look into the next room. Surprised by that, I told everyone so, and then realized too late the terrible mistake I'd made. The window wasn't a window at all – it was a mirror. The kids instantly jumped on my faux pas. I back-pedaled, blaming my foggy brain on jet lag, but no matter what I said, they wouldn't let my "blonde" moment pass.

Not being clear and present is dangerous

In a heat-induced trance, I wandered down the hall to a ridiculously small bathroom. It took a bit of maneuvering, but if I slid myself diagonally, jamming my legs between the toilet and wall, I could close the door. I'd escaped the elevator, but I couldn't avoid the bathroom. Hot thick air stuck in my lungs as the walls closed in. Suddenly, a year of travel seemed like a very long time.

September 6

Lying wide awake in the top bunk of a bunk bed, I fought the urge to flee, pajama-clad, into the street for unconfined air. When morning finally arrived, bursting out into the hall, I met a row of Japanese youth lined up at sinks mounted along the wall. They embraced the porcelain in communal washing, brushing, rinsing and spitting. A line of black synchronized heads swung my way as I picked up my brush. Their eyes took me back in time. I felt like I was in grade ten – self-conscious and exposed during a post gym-class communal shower.

After another 7-Eleven breakfast, we made our way to the Imperial Palace to sightsee. We didn't get far before everyone complained of hunger. You don't realize how demanding stomachs can be until faced with five of them, all metabolizing at different rates. Yogurt and yet another pork bun from 7-Eleven was the best we could do.

Poor Mitchell appeared grumpy. This boy was going to head back to Canada with his wallet still filled with vacation money. Wanting him to like us, I tried lightening his mood with cheerful conversation, but after receiving dead end responses to my barrage of chirpy questions, I gave up.

At Denny's, after dinner that night, I was astonished to find an interesting cultural experience right in the privacy of my bathroom stall. The toilet had a control panel beside the toilet seat with rows of buttons labeled with self-explanatory icons. I timidly pushed the button showing a fountain of water, then jumped and gasped when the toilet responded in a bidet sort of way.

Inviting Makayla back to the bathroom to play with me, I insisted the boys partake in their own "butt amusement." They weren't gone long. The serious look on Mitchell's face made me wonder if toilet play amongst males wasn't cool, but come to think of it, Mitchell had maintained the same strained and serious look since we'd met. It was as if he didn't really want to be with us. Not liking that idea, I decided to try and win him over. Maybe he just needed a bit more time to realize how fun we really were.

September 7

Five people in a very small room made for an interesting symphony of night sounds. There was the heavy breather (Mattson), the snorer (Mitchell), the talker (Makayla) and the mover (Ken, trying to arrange his 6'5" body into a 5' floor space.) Throw my claustrophobia into the mix, and sleep was elusive.

In the morning, Ken and the boys went to the gymnastics club to train, leaving Makayla and me alone for the day. Venturing forth to sightsee in Ginza, without Ken to blindly follow, left me scared. Tokyo seemed like a city capable of swallowing you up and never spitting you out.

After a few wrong turns our walk turned into a bit of a marathon, but Makayla followed without question or complaint. I felt justified to reward her good nature with an upscale lunch at a cozy Italian restaurant. It was a stretch for Ken's budget, but the linguini carbonara was so worth it. Since Ken might not see it that way, I suggested we girls keep our little splurge to ourselves.

September 8

Wanting to get an early start to tour the fish market, we all let out a groan when the alarm buzzed at 5:00 a.m. The market was a smorgasbord for the senses. The reek of fish filled our nostrils as slimy eels coiled around each other in buckets. Weird sea creatures lurked everywhere. Preoccupied with it all, we almost got run over by a charging forklift carrying a towering pile of huge frozen tuna. Jumping out of the way landed us in a puddle of blood from fish being cleaned.

Makayla let out a piercing scream when a fish, erupting out of a water bin, hit her on the leg and thrashed on the ground. By 6:30 a.m., we were done and ready to follow the advice of our *Lonely Planet* guide book to go for sushi.

The kids objected to raw fish for breakfast, but if our travel book said to do it, we were doing it. Entering a small restaurant, we attempted to order five pieces of sushi, one each, just to say we did. When the waiter didn't speak English, Ken dissected the word 'five – rolling it out like a slow drum roll. The waiter understood his five alright, bringing five rolls instead of five pieces of sushi. The kid's faces distorted as the table filled with seaweed covered rolls. No need to worry, Ken calmly assured us, he'd simply explain the error to the waiter; but none of his arm flailing charades were understood.

During the exchange, we attracted the attention of an intoxicated group of Japanese in their mid-twenties who were drinking whisky at the table beside us. They helped Ken straighten out the excess sushi situation and sent over a couple of shots. Eating raw fish and drinking whiskey before 7:00 a.m. definitely qualified as our second breakfast adventure.

September 9

Being an art lover, I decided we should walk to the Imperial Palace Gardens and sketch in the park. Mitchell decided to skip art class, his serious unsmiling face instead studying the ground.

The landscape we chose turned out to be a difficult exercise in perspective. After forty-five minutes, even with wind gusts from Mitchell's repetitive sighs, we were over-heated and frustrated. Art class ended when Mattson's drawing of a path and tree turned into a tropical bird.

After reconnecting with Ken, who'd worked all morning, we made a move to a surprisingly posh looking high rise hotel. I questioned how such a nice place could offer room rates similar to the Sakura, but Ken assured me he'd confirmed that kids stayed for free.

Opening the door to our room, there sat one double bed framed with no more than a foot of floor space. There had been a miscommunication. Yes we could sleep as many kids in that room as we wanted, and yes they did have cots for no extra charge, but obviously cots weren't going to fit in the room we could afford.

If it seems too good to be true, it probably is

Knowing the tight budget we were on, Mitchell looked pale, probably imagining all five of us somehow spending the night in that room. With Ken deep in thought while looking under the bed and into the bathtub, he probably had reason for concern. Stepping up to save us all, I announced: "no way are we staying here!" Ken shrugged and growled "if you don't like it, do something about it." He and the boys had to leave immediately for gym training. I'd never been good at assertive confrontation. My face turned tomato red and sweat trickled down my back as I stood at the reception desk stammering and begging for an affordable solution. When I got what I wanted, I felt awfully proud of myself.

September 10

It was time to make Mitchell happy. After enduring a tough few days with us, we agreed to take him to the electronic district to buy an MP3 player. Skinny three story high stores, stacked side by side like dominos, went on forever. Finding the perfect MP3 player was going to take time. Lots of time.

A store with narrow aisles formed a complicated labyrinth sure to separate a family of four plus one, especially with our varied shopping interests. There was also the problem of five overfilled bladders. Our breakfast included a flat rate all you could drink juice and coffee bar. The first half of the day was spent either looking for a bathroom or Mitchell, who moved like a zombie from one MP3 player to another. Not enjoying shopping at the best of times, having no money to spend, and being more than a bit technophobic ensured a tragic crash to my three cappuccino caffeine high. It was my turn to frown.

When Mitchell finally made his purchase, it was time for the boys to catch a train to the gym. I wondered if it was safe to send them alone, but how could you not feel safe in a country where outdoor beer vending machines were never vandalized?

I guess you don't harm something you love. Walking the streets of Tokyo, we often found ourselves behind staggering disheveled Japanese men spewing out cigarette smoke. We following one such guy into a building labeled Capsule Hotel. Ken questioned the attendant about the hotel while I watched surveillance cameras mounted on the wall behind the front desk. They panned a honeycomb of closet sized rooms assessed by ladders all lined up in a row. When the camera switched location to the shower room, a naked Japanese man came into view. I snapped my head back towards Ken in time to catch him asking about a room for the night. A pinky blush from unexpected nudity turned fiery red anticipating encapsulation. Fortunately, you had to be male and over eighteen years of age to stay.

September 11

It was time for Mitchell and Mattson's gym meet. They were leaving us for the week to be billeted with Japanese families. Mitchell's time with us had come to a close.

Mitchell turned and walked out of the hotel room mumbling a barely audible goodbye. Watching him walk out the door was a relief, not because he was a bad kid, but because I'd felt a responsibility to make him happy; I'd wanted him to like us. He'd likely tell stories about the strange family he stayed with, but so be it; accommodating someone with a different agenda had been difficult. Even so, why had I cared so much about what Mitchell thought? Why did I want him to see me as a cool, fun mom? Maybe I shouldn't have worried about what I thought he was thinking and just been myself, a person at least occasionally perky and fun.

Bravely be yourself

Makayla and I took the metro train to Mattson's gym. The Japanese riding the train seemed very tired. Ken's business associate told us the average male works over twelve hours a day, six days a week. Add on a two to three hour commute and it was no wonder they couldn't keep their eyes open. Whether standing or sitting, they'd drool and bob in deep sleep, until the train door swished open, powering them back to life. How they knew which stop was theirs, I'll never know.

After arriving at the gym early, I was excited to read. Unfortunately Makayla, didn't share my passion for the written word. Wanting to chat, she went on and on about what gifts she should buy and take back for her friends in Calgary. Losing interest, I drifted back to my book. I felt bad when I finally noticed she'd left me to stretch on the gym floor. Guilt washed over me. I knew guilt well. Guilt for stealing time from being a mom to be a dentist; guilt for not being the best dentist because of being a mom.

In the end there was no welcoming party. Over tasty tempura at a restaurant with leather menus, we revisited the "what to buy" conversation and I gave it my all.

To lighten your load, leave guilt behind

September 12

Beginning the day with what was now my regular breakfast, a plate full of biscotti cookies and three cappuccinos, I munched and tried reading the morning paper while Makayla pointed out the poor nutritional quality of my breakfast. Back home, I always preached the importance of healthy eating. Since arriving in Japan, the closest we'd come to a vegetable was a sprinkle of grated carrot garnishing our rice. The guilt I'd sworn off of was back. What if we all came down with scurvy and our teeth fell out? And then there was the issue of the kids' short attention spans when writing in their daily journal. Perhaps it was caused by some diet-related attention deficit disorder? Dipping my biscotti into my cappuccino, I vowed to find healthier food for my family.

After breakfast, I had an amazing moment sending my first unaided e-mail. Inexperienced with computers (I drilled holes in teeth all day) I often needed computer help from Ken and the kids. With the boys gone and Makayla engrossed in her school work, I took a deep breath and tried to figure it out myself. What a thrill when I pushed the send button. From my breakfast "bad mother" low, I was high with a feeling of accomplishment. My family might be malnourished, but I was a techno-savvy woman of the new age.

Thinking for yourself makes you feel good about yourself

After deeming tomato sauce a vegetable, we had pizza for dinner. My justification came at a price. Feeling guilty again, I began to worry. Worrying was in my genes, passed down from my mother, her mother and, her mother's mother. There was an unspoken philosophy amongst us women. If you worried about something it probably wouldn't happen, so be darn sure you covered every possibility. I plunged in. The house still wasn't rented; what if it stayed vacant? On top of that, just before we left, Ken received a call with an offer capable of radically changing his company. It was a potential distribution deal requiring careful management and negotiation. There was no way Ken could administer such a deal from the other side of the world. He had no choice but to let his partner handle it. What if he messed up an amazing opportunity? I also worried about not being able to set up my online banking (so much for being a new millennium gal). Without the banking information, I had no idea how my dental practice was doing. And then there was the diet issue. We weren't eating well or exercising regularly. What if we waddled back to Canada as poor, fat slobs?

Snuggling in beside Makayla on the bed to watch a movie, my negative thoughts faded away. Never had I felt closer to my daughter.

Anticipating bad moments in life uses up the good moments in life

September13

Once again I ordered biscotti for breakfast. If the Italians could do it, why couldn't I? Makayla gave me a disappointed look and suddenly our roles reversed, she to the mother with the furrowed brow, and me, the defiant child pouting and continuing to dunk.

We'd been in Tokyo long enough for our suitcases to fill with dirty clothes. The time had come to do laundry. After giving the kids instructions on how to hand wash in the bathroom sink, they were keen to try. The novelty of it all wore off quickly though, as they discovered the work required to scrub out stains. One dribbled drop had them rushing to a bathroom to blot.

Our suitcases were full of quick dry clothing. Just a few pairs of Tilley underwear did the trick. Wash before bed, hang dry, and in the morning off you went, ready for the emergency ward, should that be your fate.

Makayla was desperately missing dance. When we stepped out into Tokyo's sweltering heat and humidity in nice clean clothes to find a dance studio, the wicking benefit of our shirts failed like a thumb in a leaking dike. By the time we found the studio, we were drenched. It took guts for Makayla to walk into an unfamiliar environment with fifteen Japanese girls, none of whom spoke English. She fit in like a pony at a dog show, but once the music started and dancing began, she settled into its universal rhythm.

September 14

Riding on my usual caffeine and sugar breakfast high, I set off for a run on the congested streets of Ikebukuro. I figured if I wasn't going to change my eating habits, I'd better run like hell.

When I asked the hotel clerk where I could find a park, he looked at me with a raised eyebrow. All Ikebukuro had to offer was concrete paving the ground and skyscrapers blocking the sky. Squeezing between sauntering small Japanese people, even after I sucked in my stomach, made me feel like a charging elephant. Long before the calories from my biscotti wore off, I gave up.

In the afternoon, we headed to Tokyo's high rise department stores, not because we liked shopping but because they had a food and alcohol section with free samples. Makayla found happiness lurking amongst the sweets. After peering longingly through glass display cases she talked her dad into coughing up money for a cream puff so fancy it looked like a delicate ornament. The clerk took five minutes to wrap it up like a Martha Stewart Christmas present. Makayla took five seconds to rip it open and gobble it down. From there, we separated to search for our preferred samples.

Settling in to sip sake and other concoctions, I was enjoying their burn on the way down when my family rushed up and interrupted my experience. Ken and Makayla, obviously distraught, had ping pong ball eyes in flushed puckered faces. Stepping up to speak for them, Mattson explained that a sample of sauce-covered mushrooms, turned out to be despised kidney. Much to my dismay, we had to leave and find a bathroom – pronto!

Looks can be deceiving

September 15

It was amazing how little we accomplished in a morning. How decadent to get up whenever we liked, drift down for breakfast, linger over the newspaper and eventually saunter back to the room for e-mail and home schooling.

Later in the morning we ended up in a park large enough to photosynthesize oxygen, something the smoggy skies of Tokyo desperately needed. Leisurely we strolled along, as bugs and creepy crawlers of the human type passed by. Teenagers hanging out in the park were dressed in Gothic black, with five inch platform shoes on their feet, safety pins through their cheeks and black hair styled in Mohawks. Makayla said they looked disgusting – a statement I intended to hold her to when the teen years arrived.

Harajuku, the area around the park, had many boutiques featuring bizarre fashion. I focused my camera on Makayla, spinning in silver sequenced platform heels, only to feel a tap on my shoulder. The shopkeeper mimed – no pictures.

By dinner time we ended up in Shibuya, a hip area of Tokyo verified by the presence of Starbucks Coffee. Seeing the sign for my beloved coffee shop made my heart skip a beat until I remembered our budget and what four frappuccinos would cost. Still, a visit seemed in order; I desperately needed to go to the bathroom.

A window just outside the bathroom provided a bird's eye view down to one of the busiest intersections in Tokyo. Thousands of people crossed the street in a crisscross of crosswalks. Mesmerized by the flow of ant-like people, I reached for my camera and focused only to feel a familiar tap on my shoulder. For a people who love cameras, they sure seemed to have a problem with people using them. The frowning security guard gestured no pictures and showed me to the door.

Imagine, kicked out of Starbucks – I was mortified!

September 16

It was our last day in Tokyo. It seemed we'd been there forever. What was once new and exciting was becoming old and irritating. Three weeks of population overload, people constantly staring at us and teeny tiny portions of food were taking their toll. I needed some open space, anonymity and a buffet. It was going to take some sake samples just to get through the day.

In Asakura, we wandered through some open air markets, stopping at an ice cream store for much needed sugar. Having trouble figuring out the flavors, a friendly enthusiastic English-speaking clerk came to our aid. She thought it fun to pass out samples and have us guess the flavors; risky business in a place where people happily ate what *Fear Factor* contestants were forced to choke down.

I'm not sure how, but everything in Japan, even dairy, seemed to taste like fish. Wanting to be good sports, we reluctantly took part and thankfully chestnut, taro root, and green tea ice cream weren't fishy at all.

With Mattson's gym meet over and all of his gym mates from Canada returning home in the morning, we enjoyed a last meal together. When Mattson said goodbye to his buds, I could see how hard it was to walk away. He wouldn't train with them again for the better part of a year.

Goodbyes are hard

September 17

The shrill ring of a 5:30 a.m. wake-up call jolted us from peaceful sleep. It was time to activate our Japanese rail passes and get out of Tokyo. Stumbling through tunnels in the metro, we fought to pull luggage through a solid mass of people. By the time we got to the station we were cranky and starving. I should clarify. The kids and I were cranky and starving. Ken isn't wired like us when it comes to food. If food was plentiful and cheap he'd happily chow down; if it was expensive or not available, he did without. Either way was fine by him. Going without was in no way fine by us.

Getting our tickets and making our train left only enough time to pick up containers of yogurt at a convenience store. The second the train stopped in Kyoto, a quest for food began. Ken wanted something cheap, I wanted something healthy, and the kids didn't want Japanese food; an argument was inevitable. Four starving people, a harmonious family does not make! Never again would I travel without a stash of snacks.

Be prepared

After our meal, the size of a Canadian appetizer, I was still hungry. I dreamed of my full fridge back in Calgary while my first dose of home sickness hit square in my complaining gut.

We had a home stay arranged in a town three train transfers away. To be social when we arrived seemed exhausting. Oh how I wished we could just stay in a hotel.

Travel days suck

September 18

The next morning, after spending the night in a modest two-story home, we timidly congregated as a family and ventured downstairs for breakfast. Masako, our host, warmly greeted us and laid down a plate full of neatly cut up fruit and bagels. The plate emptied as we swarmed and attacked like piranhas in a feeding frenzy.

At a national park, content and full from breakfast, we discovered a beautiful cascading waterfall. Beside the falls, seven artists sat deep in concentration trying to capture its magnificence on canvas. How I admired their talent. I'd always wished I could be an artist, but had never found the time. Jealously I gazed over their shoulders until sharp words between Ken and Makayla brought me back to reality.

Makayla wanted a drink from a soft drink vending machine, but Ken insisted she drink from her water bottle. An argument began. They went at it while Mattson and I, the passive members of the family, walked away. A short time later we glanced back to see Ken walking alone. Makayla, refusing to walk with her dad, had fallen behind. Ken said he would go back to get her, and told us to carry on. It wasn't long before Makayla and Ken stormed past, fighting like cats and dogs.

Makayla argued that her dad had deserted her and Ken insisted she got lost because she was dilly-dallying. Their animated hand gestures signaled the intensity of their debate. Every once in a while arms would deflate and Ken would try to grab Makayla's hand. He'd hold tight until she yanked away and marched ahead making him run to catch back up. After a short pause, up would go the arms as the cycle repeated itself. Mattson and I placed bets on whether she'd give in and keep hold of Ken's hand. Makayla was stubborn but Ken, patient and able to control his emotions, was the ultimate mediator. When they reconnected, I took the win.

We spent the rest of the afternoon with Masako. Even though she looked like a teenager, she was actually sixty-three years old. She didn't fit the image of an adventurer, yet told us how she passed out from lack of oxygen while climbing a mountain at the South Pole. Yes, the South Pole. And to top it off, she'd left her husband at home and gone alone.

Multitalented, she was a ceramic artist, writer and musician. I felt so blessed to have such a special woman touch my life. Remembering how I hadn't wanted to stay with a stranger after our miserable day of travel made me shudder; oh what I would have missed if we hadn't met.

Don't give in to passing emotion

September 19

Interesting conversation about politics, Japanese culture, and travel flowed during breakfast. Any worries I'd had about the kid's home schooling were subsiding. Every single day, educational moments popped up without any effort on my part.

After an interesting afternoon at the Osaka Aquarium, we joined Masako at a swanky restaurant serving a multi-course special of the day. The price was high, the food authentic Japanese and the presentation visually stunning. It seemed a shame to eat their culinary art, not because we'd be swallowing what took hours to prepare, but because we weren't sure exactly what it was we'd be swallowing.

The main course was a plate of green, slimy stuff crowned with a raw egg. Our stomachs turned as we psyched ourselves up for a bite. With forks loaded Ken saved the day. Returning from work, he'd gotten lost and needed Masako to come and find him. The second she left we scraped the green stuff into a napkin and disposed of it in the bathroom. Happily rid of it, we couldn't wait to see Ken's reaction to the meal. He absolutely hated runny uncooked eggs.

When Ken and Masako returned, we sat on the edge of our seats waiting to see Ken squirm, but unfortunately they'd run out of the set menu. Ken got to order whatever he wanted. We didn't get to watch him turn green. Instead, we were the ones green with envy as he smiled and ordered fried chicken.

Life isn't fair

September 20

I had fallen madly in love with Masako. I so admired her artistic passion and adventurous spirit. She insisted I take one of her six inch clay sculptures of a dancing Japanese devil as a gift. In Japan devils are sun gods and bring good luck. I really didn't have room in my suit case, but I didn't care. I'd be taking a bit of Masako back home with me.

We said goodbye, wiped away tears, and headed to the train station. Travel via Japanese Shinkansen trains was turning out to be quite enjoyable. Roomy isn't a word often used in Japan, but with ample leg room, even for Ken, our trip to Hiroshima passed comfortably.

Knowing Hiroshima's horrific history made disembarking from the train in a bustling modern metropolis seem strange. As we made our way to the epicenter where the atomic bomb exploded, I thought back to high school and the pictures in my social studies book; those pictures of destruction didn't seem real back then. Standing in front of the a-bomb dome, the name given to a building crowned with a bronze dome reduced to nothing more than a skeleton of metal bars, my skin prickled realizing the intensity of heat needed to vaporize bronze. Not far from the a-dome, we visited a museum documenting the nuclear event and its fallout. I worried that photos of burnt and suffering people would be too disturbing. How do you, as a parent, explain and make sense of humanity's potential for cruelty? My kids weren't getting the unobtrusive history book lesson I'd had at school. This was in your face – no bell for dismissal education. I hoped it wouldn't haunt them.

The need to eliminate the production of nuclear weapons was the main message conveyed throughout the exhibits. Their mandate: Only the complete elimination of nuclear weapons can ensure there will never be another Hiroshima or Nagasaki. As we walked away from the museum, we stopped at the memorial where a flame burned and will continue to burn until all nuclear weapons are destroyed. Sadly we all agreed; that flame will likely burn for a very long time.

September 21

Another enjoyable morning train ride deposited us in Himeji. There we connected with a local family of friends of friends who kindly hosted us for a couple of days.

The main tourist attraction in Himeji was Himeji Castle, rated the most beautiful in all of Japan. For the tour, we had our own personal guide; a short but sturdy Japanese man in his mid-forties. He wore thick glasses and had that classic smart university professor kind of look. Exuding passion for his job, he was determined to teach us every historic detail about the castle. We listened half-heartedly to his facts until he started quizzing us on his delivered information, snapping us to attention. Telling us where to stand, where to take pictures, and how to carefully walk up stairs; the guy was obviously a control freak. Stairs, he barked: "can be weeeery dangerous." His intensity had us swapping "this guy is crazy" looks whenever he turned his head.

As we toured, he told many stories about the superior Japanese construction of the castle ending each one with the statement: "the Japanese were weeeery clever." When the tour was over, we had a great time mimicking and making fun of him, but truth be told, thanks to his intensity and the information he'd forced us to learn, we too were weeeery clever.

That evening, after a tasty home cooked meal, we received an unexpected visit from a neighbor bearing a shoebox full of handmade gifts, such as woven bracelets and little men made from knitted wool and beads, all made just for us. She'd heard Takashi had Canadian guests and wanted to welcome us to Japan.

The kindness of strangers will surprise you

September 22

The day had finally come for a good long run. Takashi, a marathon runner primed to go the distance, had us up early and out to the countryside. My legs burned as I gasped cool morning air and wondered just how far he intended to go. We eventually stopped at a Buddhist Temple where Takashi showed us how to pray. I diligently followed his instruction hoping Buddha would hear my clapping and chanting, and grant me the stamina to finish the run.

After enjoying Takashi's hospitality we traveled to a charming small town called Kameoka for sake tasting. When the gal dishing it out gave the kids a small taste, they grimaced, claiming it tasted like dirty socks. I certainly didn't agree. Hot, cold, sweet or dry, there was a lot to learn about sake.

On to Takayama, we settled into another small hotel room. Bunk beds stacked on each other like caskets made me anxious to get out for dinner. At an outdoor place, we ordered noodles covered in some kind of sauce. Teriyaki, oyster or soya sauce: who knew what it was? We always seemed to be eating something salty. My eyes were so puffy from salt-induced water retention, I was beginning to look Japanese.

September 23

Somehow, I managed a few hours of sleep even though claustrophobia had its hands around my neck all night long. Tired and frustrated, I lay in bed hating my fear; it was just so all consuming. Was this the way it was going to be for the rest of my life? Was there no cure? What if I could somehow get over it? There and then I decided to try.

In the morning we explored traditional old wooden buildings on bicycles. Focusing on the quaint ambiance of the town and trying to stay upright and alive on our rickety rented bikes wasn't easy. With skinny tires, loose handle bars, and one bike size for all, Makayla and I stretched for the pedals while the boys hit their knees on the handle bars.

It was the last day of validity for our Japanese rail passes, ending our exploration of Japan. Remembering how foreign this country had seemed the day we arrived made me realize how much we'd learned during our four week stay. We'd become travelers, comfortable in a foreign land.

In front of Himeji Castle

Hida Minzoka Mura folk village in Takayama

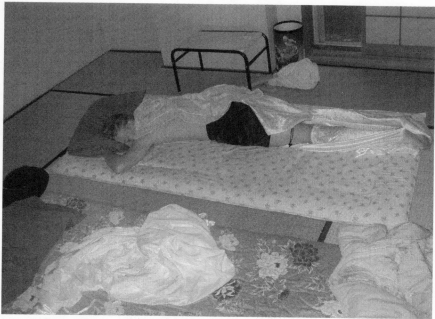

Sleeping on tatami mats

KOREA

September 24

Not wanting to miss our flight to Korea, I jumped out of bed and instantly started to pack. Admittedly I'm not the most punctual person. More times than not, I arrive fifteen minutes late for a social engagement. Within that buffer zone I feel comfortably late, but when there is something you can't be late for, like catching a flight, I stress about being on time. Ken, on the other hand, consistently runs late; his buffer zone has no fixed time value. Flying is like a game to him. How late can you be and still catch your flight? Getting to his seat against all odds is a win and Ken loves to win. Twelve years of playing professional football in the CFL (Canadian Football League) and winning two Grey Cup rings is proof of that. It bugged me that Ken, as a competitive and lucky guy, never seemed to lose. As a member of his team, I had to take part in strategies from his play book like: speeding and driving dangerously to airports, sprinting down terminal hallways and creatively negotiating to bypass closed airport gates.

We got mixed up while transferring trains on our way to the airport and ended up going the wrong direction. The badly timed mistake prompted a family debate. Should we spring for a taxi or retrace our steps on the train? The kids and I wanted the taxi and Ken, thinking the taxi expensive, wanted the train. It was three against one and thankfully a cab happened by at just the right moment.

The cab saved the day, getting us to the airport with just five minutes to spare. As we sat waiting for those few extra minutes to pass, Ken lamented about how we should have taken the train. Shaking our heads, we had to question the workings of a usually brilliant mind.

The flight included free flowing alcohol and a meal. The food, unidentifiable, was best left untouched; I couldn't say the same for the red wine. As I sipped, my excitement about Korea grew. We planned to meet up with Ken's old office manager, Nancy, who was living in Seoul and teaching English.

Upon our arrival, a small Korean girl with a pixie cut held a sign displaying our last name. Looking more like a young boy than a twenty-something year old girl, she spoke perfect English and introduced herself as Angela, a friend of Nancy's. The next thing we knew, we were running, with luggage in tow, weaving between cars on a busy three lane expressway trying to follow her. Twenty treacherous minutes later, Angela showed us a spacious studio apartment for rent in a high-rise apartment building.

The empty apartment, devoid of even toilet paper, required a trip down to the open air market to barter for supplies. Ken went to town getting good pricing on essential items, but didn't stop there. On he went, practically decorating the place. This was a surprise coming from a phobic non-shopper. In the end, I had to pull him away, saying: "enough already!"

Bartering is addictive

That night, we met Nancy and Angela for a traditional Korean Kalbi dinner. At a low table covered with small bowls filled with different colorful vegetables, we sat on the floor. Maybe we wouldn't lose our teeth to scurvy after all. After dinner, displaying similar mannerisms to our Japanese Himeji Castle Tour Guide, Angela ordered us to be ready and waiting for her by 8:00 a.m. sharp the next morning.

September 25

At precisely 8:00 a.m., Angela burst through our door. We followed her to the elevator doing up buttons and shoes and once again found ourselves on foot darting through morning rush hour traffic. When I commented on how modern Seoul appeared, Angela proudly explained how the city radically changed after winning the bid for Expo and the Olympics. In their haste to modernize though, the quality of construction often suffered. "People died in Korea," Angela matter-of-factly stated, "from collapsing, poorly-constructed bridges and buildings."

Looking around at the shiny new tile on the walls in the underground metro station, I suddenly felt the urge to get out!

There was no time to worry about potential disaster. It took all of our concentration to keep up with Angela, who once again darted out of sight.

By late morning, we ended up in Insadong, the old historic area of Seoul, and made our way through narrow, cobblestone streets to a quaint, traditional tea house. Climbing a steep, rickety flight of stairs and crouching through a low doorway, we entered a small, dimly-lit room. Once inside, a four foot tall, stooped, older Korean lady with a face like a prune directed us past walls of dark paneled wood to a low table. We kneeled down onto red embroidered satin cushions as the waitress passed out thick leather-bound menus. Angela told us about our choices, then took them away and ordered for us.

The tea, delicately placed in front of us, came in a big cup looking like a cereal bowl with a soup spoon in it. It was cold and sweet with a hint of cinnamon and cloves. What surprised us even more, were the live birds flying over our heads and Angela's orders to tent our hands over our cups to intercept incoming torpedoes of bird doo-doo.

September 26

Ken and I received an invitation from Nancy to visit her English class and talk about our trip. Arriving in the morning, Nancy reminded us to speak slow precise English and sent us into separate classrooms. There I stood in front of thirty, twenty-something-year-old Koreans, all eagerly focused on me. Taking a deep breath, I began. As I spoke all those eyes made me nervous, and those nerves made me talk faster and talking faster made me realize I wasn't being slow and precise. Trying to slow down, I concentrated on every syllable of every word and in the process forgot what I was talking about. Vacant looks confirmed their confusion. Stopping to gulp air, I began again, but my tongue refused to cooperate. My native English was suddenly foreign, even to me. Realizing I needed to simplify, I started dropping syllables and speaking broken English. Beads of sweat formed on my brow as the students cocked their heads like confused puppies. Having to look away, I caught a glimpse of Angela outside the classroom door motioning for me to leave and come with her. At that moment, I could have kissed our tour guide, even if she was like the Ever Ready Bunny, who just kept going and going. I'd happily follow her anywhere if it meant getting out of that classroom.

Back to following Angela, we spent a very interesting afternoon at the DMZ (demilitarized zone) between North and South Korea. It seemed strange, as we passed through numerous check stops, to see stern soldiers rigidly carrying huge loaded rifles. In Canada, Mounted Police wearing puffy black pants and funny hats rode in circles on horses holding nothing more than flapping flags.

The tour was informative. After talking to Angela and other Koreans on the bus, we got the feeling that Koreans living in Seoul were happy to feel protected by the United States, yet resented the presence of US troops on their soil. It was a real love hate relationship. To guard against the hate part we pinned Canadian flags all over our clothing in the hopes we wouldn't be mistaken for Americans.

Making a fashion statement can pay off

In the evening we joined a group of teachers for Duck Kalbi dinner and listened to a Canadian teacher talk about how he'd been dared to eat a live octopus. Apparently baby octopi are a Korean delicacy when dipped in hot sauce and eaten off a stick. Under pressure to accept his Popsicle, he heeded advice from his Korean friends to chew like a hyperactive rat. If he didn't get that octopus down fast, its tentacles could suck onto the back of his throat and suffocate him. Yum?!

September 27

It was time to explore the Korean countryside. Ken sat in our rental car ready to drive, but there was a problem. Nancy and her friend Sylvia, our guides for the day, lived in Seoul, but didn't drive in Seoul. They yelled for Ken to "TURN NOW!" oblivious to the four lane changes in bumper to bumper traffic required to do so. Making matters worse, once missing the turn, they had no idea how to backtrack.

Always uncomfortable with Ken's driving, I really started to worry when Angela babbled on about foreigners getting hauled off to jail after injuring Koreans in car accidents. Losing my husband to life imprisonment seemed like a real possibility.

I couldn't help but admire Ken's fearless and patient nature. He stayed calm, even after they led him on a wild goose chase, and not once did he tell me to stop reminding him not to kill anyone.

After a very long, tense hour we made our way through the smog to the countryside, finding clear air and blue sky. At our first stop, we visited a small historic town with colorful temples. The next stop was to be another town with more temples, but somehow we got off the main road and ended up on a stretch of pavement gradually narrowing to the size of a sidewalk and then disappearing into nothing more than a bumpy gravel path between two rice fields.

Questioning where we'd gone so wrong, we stopped and stepped out into the rice field. I was busy taking pictures of rice stocks, an unusual sight for a North American, when the farmer whose land we must have been on roared up on his motorcycle looking quite angry. Not impressed with our trespassing, he gruffly spoke Korean to Sylvia. She tried telling him we were lost, but he didn't seem to believe her. Maybe he thought we were agricultural spies or something.

After the conversation, Sylvia wanted to make a quick getaway. Clumsily packing ourselves back into the car, Sylvia was half in and half out of the car with the door still open when Ken, feeling pressured to go, turned the ignition key and forgot to engage the clutch. Lurching forward before the car stalled, our heads jerked and Sylvia fell to the ground. We all gasped, afraid she might be hurt, until she started to laugh. What a scene; Sylvia on all fours crawling around looking for dropped sunglasses as the rest of us joined in to howl along right with her. Not sure what to make of such a scene, the farmer let out a disgusted grunt, muttered something in Korean, revved his motor and sped off in a cloud of dust.

When we finally wiped away tears of laughter, visiting another somber temple seemed inappropriate. After all the frustration of trying to find the right road, we decided to relax, enjoy the sunshine, and go where the road led us.

A wrong turn can lead to the right place

September 28

    With our rental car not due back until the evening, we made our way out of the city once again. As we drove, Angela nonchalantly told us we'd be going for lunch on an island; to get there we'd drive through the ocean without a tunnel or a bridge. "Through the water" we questioned, but all she'd say was "you'll see." Fifteen minutes later, we turned onto a narrow paved road surrounded by wet, ocean floor mud. Angela explained. At low tide there was a road, at high tide the ocean claimed that road. Creeping along in bumper-to-bumper traffic made us ask "what happens if the tide comes in when you're stuck in traffic?" She thought for a moment and confessed that could be a problem.

    Once on the island, we sat outdoors at a wood picnic table topped with a small Hibachi type BBQ. Our waiter dropped off a huge bowl of shellfish and gave us instructions for how to roast them. When the shells popped open and we heard a soft screeching sound, they'd be ready to eat.

    Makayla freaked out. She thought the scream came from the little fish inside crying out as they fried alive. We couldn't convince her it was just the sound of steam escaping from the shells. She sadly mourned the death of every shellfish she popped in her mouth, reluctantly committing murder over and over again for their plump and succulent cooked flesh.

    When it was time to leave, we ended up in grid-locked traffic. Trapped between bumpers, there was nothing we could do but wait and watch the ocean rise.

If you can't get where you need to go,
breathe deeply and let it go

September 29

    We got to ride in Angela's car instead of chasing her on foot. I was relieved until she decided to talk to Ken. Turning his way to make eye contact, she brought the steering wheel along with her eyes. It was Ken's turn to be the Nervous Nelly bracing and yelling "look out!" as she swerved into oncoming traffic.

I sighed with relief when we finally arrived at Everland, Korea's equivalent to Disneyland. The kids couldn't get out of the car fast enough, partly to get away from Angela's driving, but mainly to start a fun day of rides. We'd be leaving them on their own and continuing with Angela to the Korean Folk Village.

Mattson and Makayla quickly disappeared into a swarm of black heads as I strained to keep them in sight. I started to fret, questioning my decision to leave them alone. What if today was the day the North Koreans decided to invade the South? Looking back longingly, we drove away.

I worried about the kids and half-heartedly listened to Angela ramble on about how Koreans dislike the Japanese. According to her, Koreans felt inferior to the Japanese. They desperately wanted to gain economic advantage and to achieve that goal were trying to become bilingual with English as a second language. She'd just finished her story, when a large green road sign overhead stated in bold white English printing, Korean Fork Village 5 km. Folk/Fork – they obviously weren't bilingual yet. At lunch, they didn't get it right either. One of our choices on the menu was steamed crap. Crap/crab, probably just a typo, but I wasn't about to take a chance on it.

In the late afternoon, my worst fears were realized. We were touring the Folk village when suddenly overhead, the sky filled with helicopters, hundreds of them, their propellers roaring and beating the air. Was it the invasion I'd worried about? "What's going on?" I screamed to Angela wide-eyed. "Military exercises," she yelled above the noise while nonchalantly continuing to stroll. She seemed convinced they'd do no more than fly. I, on the other hand, wanted to cry.

Just about right is far from right

Pork bun breakfast in Tokyo

Hiroshima a-bomb dome

September 30

What a wonderful morning. Ken went off to work, Angela was busy, and the kids slept in. Alone in our quiet kitchen, I felt decadent eating peanut butter and jam (unexpectedly found at the grocery store) washed down with a steaming cup of Nescafe coffee. What joy the simple pleasures of home brought.

We arrived at the Korean War Museum, a grand building built by the United States for retribution after the Korean War, the moment it opened. By noon, Ken, Makayla and I wanted to keep right on going, but Mattson started complaining about being hungry. He wanted lunch rather than just the snacks we'd brought along. Knowing Mattson was easy going and malleable, we put him off saying we'd leave in half an hour. When half an hour came and went, we gave him the old "ya, ya, in a minute" and let multitudes of minutes pass. Suddenly, Mattson dropped to the floor in front of our feet, sprawling out as if unconscious and refused to move. Shocked by his defiance, we stared down in disbelief at our Golden child. I say Golden not because we loved him more than Makayla, but because his nature was golden; he rarely gave us any trouble.

Ken, doubting the authenticity of his resolve, tried yanking him up by the arm, but the kid was dead weight and refused to budge. Sticking to his two-year-old tantrum antics, tourists had to step over him to pass.

Everyone has a breaking point

On the way out, we entered a long open air wing of the building covered with engraved plaques listing names of soldiers who'd died in the war. We passed thousands of names before making it out the door to stand before a huge statue depicting two brothers, one fighting for South Korea and the other for the North. Dressed in tattered combat gear, they looked to each other in anguish, reaching out, but not touching. The inscription below them read: "freedom is not free." All of us, even Mattson on his mission for lunch, stopped to solemnly take it in.

For our last evening in Korea, Nancy took us out for a wonderful dinner. How nice it had been to share laughs and adventures with good friends.

Next stop: Beijing, China.

Makayla enjoys seafood

Fork/folk Village

Mattson's breaking point

38

Bulgogie Dinner with Nancy and Sylvia

CHINA

October 1

Extreme turbulence and an out of control landing left us weak kneed. We sheepishly collected our luggage and met a driver sent by an old university friend living in Beijing.

On a tree lined three lane freeway, organized free flowing traffic led to an upscale hotel booked by our friend. We told him we were on a budget, but the hotel's opulent lobby made me realize budget means different things to different people. Our room felt like a mansion, yet surprisingly cost only $100.00 per night. We could afford it, but Ken thought something smaller would do. Not wanting the hassle of moving, a wink and a gesture towards our private bedroom changed his mind in a heartbeat.

Once settled, I was thrilled to run a hot bath. We'd had nothing but basic showers in Japan. Shower heads were mounted on the wall right beside the toilet; separate shower enclosures nonexistent. Forgetting to move the toilet paper outside the bathroom before showering made for a soggy mess. More than once, desperation had us begging a non-English speaking house keeper for a new roll. And let me say, it's hard to talk slowly when you have to go.

I soaked in my big comfortable tub until the water cooled, and sighed with pleasure as I wrapped myself in a big white fluffy towel. Getting dry with nothing but a swimmer's towel in Korea had been like wiping down a bus with a paper towel.

October 2

How exhilarating to wake up, knowing this was the day we'd visit the Great Wall of China.

The day was beautiful – clear and sunny, yet cool and crisp. Restless after a long drive scrunched in a small compact car, we turned the corner and there it was, looking like a majestic castle wall tracing the rise and fall of mountain peaks for as far as the eye could see.

Making our way to a part of the Great Wall crumbling from poor repair and rarely traveled by tourists, we had the place all to ourselves. To get up steep vertical steps you needed to have great lung capacity and no fear of heights. It was like climbing to heaven, and stopping on your way up to look down to China on your left and Mongolia on your right.

Makayla had a hard time at the beginning of our hike. With cherry red cheeks, after climbing our second set of challenging stairs, she cried out: "hey, when are we going to get to that wall we're having our picture taken at?" I felt badly, realizing she thought The Great Wall was nothing more than a place to stand for a quick photo. It came as a quite a shock when I told her we'd be hiking on the longest wall in the world for the whole day and sleeping on it that night. She stalled and looked at me in disbelief. A long processing moment passed before she sighed and resumed climbing to lead our way.

At sunset, before leaving the wall to find dinner in a small town, we stopped for a picture. Ken stretched out his long monkey arm as we snuggled together for his infamous, "take the picture while in the picture" shots. Still in our huddle, we pledged to travel together to see all the great wonders of the world.

With rented camping equipment in hand, we mounted the wall once again and laid sleeping bags onto hard stone. A canopy of stars, sparkling like spot lit sequins stitched to black velvet, engulfed us as we wriggled in. Overwhelmed by the beauty of it all, I turned to Ken to spill out my awe and instead burst out laughing. His 6'5" body extruded from his Chinese sleeping bag like our hard golf cases from the Japanese cab's trunk. Even a good hard tug barely brought the bag to his nipple line. I worried he might be cold on a chilly night, but then remembered, he wasn't generally bothered by such things.

At dawn, waking to the sound of loud Chinese conversation and footsteps marching past us, local photographers converged to set up tripods and shoot the sunrise. Ignoring chattering teeth and full bladders, we watched in amazement as the sun exploded over mountain peaks lighting never-ending turrets against a lavender and pink sky.

October 3

Ken and China had something in common; they were both cheap. His friends called him a grinder, but as the Chinese said about their designer knock offs, "same, same, cheap, cheap."

We set off to Christmas shop in cheap China, following our friend's advice to visit a high quality jewelry shop instead of kiosks in the general market where you could be ripped off. Trouble was, you had to pass through the general market to get to the recommended place. Aggressive shop keepers shouting promises for the very best deals hit Ken squarely in his soft spot. His pull toward their calls and my pull to bring him back locked us in a tug of war.

By the time we climbed our final flight of stairs, the noise and chaos from below drifted away. Before us stood a fancy store, with floor to ceiling glass walls adorned with poster sized images of famous shoppers like Hillary Clinton. Ken stood five feet away looking like a deer in headlights. Glancing longingly back to stairs leading to promised best deals, it appeared he might run when a bubbly young female clerk rushed to our side, greeted us and ushered us inside.

Charismatic and laughing at his corny jokes, Ken instantly bonded with our cute clerk. He lost his edge and happily shopped. Time passed, and not once did he complain about the mysterious back ailment which always seems to plague him when he spends time at the mall. The strange man I'd met when shopping for our apartment in Korea was back, and in a jewelry store no less. It was hard to exercise restraint and not take advantage of him, so I did, just a little. Hours later, with rings on my fingers and bells on my toes, well not really, but I did have a nice string of pearls and matching earrings in the pile of jewelry we'd picked out for family and friends, Ken closed what he thought was a darned good deal. Relieved to have our Christmas shopping done, we made a dash back to the hotel to pack and catch an overnight train to Xi'an.

The Chinese train's sleeping compartment had clean bunk beds and English movies playing from a small ceiling-mounted T.V. As the train reached full speed, we stretched out and relaxed until a particularly nasty smell grabbed our attention. Trying to hunt down its origin led to Mattson's shoes. His Teva-like travel sandals bought at

Costco, stunk. When I found those shoes at half the price they'd been at a fancy travel store, I went back and asked the clerk why her shoes, looking identical to those at Costco, cost so much more. She'd insisted it was due to a special odor reducing sole the Costco shoes didn't have. At the time I wasn't a believer, but holding my nose while tossing Mattson's over-ripe shoes into a plastic bag made me admit she was right. The Costco shoes looked good, but were of poor quality. I hoped the same wouldn't be the case for the $15.00 Rolex we purchased after I lost the tug of war on the way out of the market.

You get what you pay for

October 4

Caught in a cloudburst after getting off the train in Xi'an, we felt trapped in place by a mob of Chinese people hawking their wares. Having to plough our way through to the closest busy street we watched Ken wildly flail his arms trying to hail a cab. Twenty unhappy wet and dirty minutes later, a four foot nothing Chinese lady, old in a slightly petrified kind of way, came to our rescue. We gasped as she stepped into oncoming traffic holding her hand out like Superman ready to stop a speeding vehicle. Fortunately, she didn't have to prove her superhuman powers. A cab stopped inches from her outstretched hand. We thanked her profusely, and sped away.

At the Terra Cotta Warrior Museum we learned how over 6,000 life-sized clay men dressed in full armor were discovered by a farmer in the 1970s. He was drilling for water when he found them and immediately reported his discovery to the government. They thanked him by kicking him off his land with no compensation; a lifeless army still able to displace and ruin lives.

From the warriors, we caught a cab the "petrified lady" way, and I did my best duck imitation to get us to a Peking duck restaurant. Once there we mimicked patrons by rolling up greasy duck onto a small crepe and covering it with some kind of gravy. The flavor, uniquely strong and rich, initially tasted good but a few small rolls in we felt uncomfortably full.

That night, back at the hotel, my stomach gurgled and cramped as I finished reading the section in my travel book on Peking duck. The closing sentence strongly advised avoiding it at all cost. Apparently Peking ducks are force fed and injected with questionable substances to fatten them up before hitting the chopping block.

A good travel book is worth its weight in gold

October 5

In the morning we discovered the Muslim section of the city. Hordes of noisy people shopped in open air markets or squatted, eating food sold by a multitude of street vendors. We reacted to interchanging smells of roasting meat and concentrated urine. One minute we wanted to eat and the next minute we wanted to throw up.

Timidly, I started experimenting with my bartering skills. I worried my initial bid might be offensively low. Ken claimed I was missing the spirit of the whole thing, but to me those shop keepers looked dirt poor. I imagined them trudging home after a long hard day to a house full of hungry kids. If I didn't pay a good price, those kids would go hungry. Needless to say, my attitude wasn't conducive to scoring the best deal.

Now Ken, on the other hand, loved the challenge of "how low can you go." He was busy bartering on personalized stamps, one of those useless trinkets you take home for hard to buy for relatives, when I found him and interrupted his negotiations. We had a plane to catch back to Beijing, and I didn't want to be late. From there, it played out as it always did. The stamp guy was late, we got lost, the taxi driver, told to hurry, almost killed us, and The Mad Dash Moores raced down an airport hallway bursting through a gate about to close.

I collapsed into my seat red-faced and stressed, only to have Ken, all cool and calm, turn and purr "can you believe the deal I got on those stamps?"

Filter your words before letting them freely flow

October 6

Okay I'm not going to lie. I wanted a Starbucks coffee. I just didn't want to come right out and tell Ken that. Not being a coffee drinker, probably from some childhood tongue-scalding trauma, he never touched warm liquids, except soup (not sure how that computes) and consequently, didn't understand coffee addiction or why anyone would spend good money on overpriced designer coffee. We'd passed a Starbucks on the drive from the airport to the hotel. I was determined to find it on our morning run. When I did, I'd act all surprised and thrilled and Ken, being the nice guy he is, would support my visit.

Wouldn't you know? Within minutes of starting our run, we ran smack into a park. We always had a heck of a time finding parks in big cities, but there it was all big and leafy and beautiful. Looking the other way as we ran past, pretending not to see it, Ken grabbed my arm stopping me in my tracks. Disappointed to abort my coffee mission, I faked a smile and follow him in.

In the park, my fake enthusiasm became real. This park had it all, huge trees, fragrant flower gardens and a misty lake with locals doing tai chi along its bank. We ran and ran, eventually discovering an area with basic pulley and lever outdoor fitness machines. Local men dressed in business suits jumped on the equipment, worked up a sweat and then went on to work. Work clothes/work-out clothes, same, same.

After our run, we brought the kids back to the park to try the equipment. As we worked out, the locals on the machines around us couldn't seem to stop staring at us. With our matching, quick dry white t-shirts embossed with huge red maple leaves, we must have looked like Team Canada. On the bright side, all of their attention made us work out harder. We were, after all, representing our country.

On the way home, to my surprise (no, really!) we stumbled upon a Starbucks. The kids were as thrilled as I was. We rushed in while Ken opted to wait outside and pace.

October 7

No Starbucks this morning; Ken led the way for our morning run and headed the opposite direction.

Bikes and China; for some reason I imagined the two together like boats and Venice. How could a trip to China be complete without touring Beijing on two wheels? The concept was good, but the reality wasn't what we expected. Biking might have been the way to go thirty years ago, before the rise of the automobile, but in modern Beijing cars rule the road. There we were, on old, rickety bikes, darting in and out of traffic on three lane freeways trying to keep up with Ken, our fearless leader. Not smart. Mattson told us later he actually made contact with a bus as we veered across traffic trying to get to a quieter street.

Our little biking excursion turned out to be a life threatening ordeal. Throw in thick, chemical-laced exhaust making our eyes run, and burning coal fumes turning our throats to sandpaper, and we had a hellish outdoor experience. Still, we'd paid a daily rate for the bikes and a day we'd spend on them. Our leader wasn't one to turn back.

Eventually, we made our way to the Forbidden City and ran into a dense crowd heading toward the gate. Forced off our bikes, we tried bumping our way through and noticed people were stopping to stare at us. What was it about us that they found so interesting? Could it once again be the way we were dressed? We wore shorts and t-shirts. The Chinese wore down-filled coats. Maybe the Canadian winter really does turn your blood into antifreeze.

October 8

While preparing breakfast, I looked out the window through a curtain of oppressive smog all milky white and suffocating, like thick phlegm. Crawling back into bed to escape it was tempting, but I had kids to educate. We slugged through until noon, then walked to the park in crisp, cool, contaminated air, hoping to find tranquility.

The park had everything needed for the whole "Zen" thing; lily pads, still water, even the odd waft of incense floating by; but then someone would spit. Spitting was very popular in China. It always started the same way: a long, deep throaty rumble to collect mucus from the deepest lobe of every bronchiole. From there, imagine Darth Vader pointing up into the sky yelling "hawk, hawk." Multiple hawks eventually brought up a meaty wad. That wad, expelled with the speed of a fast ball, explosively splattered on pavement. Spitting definitely messed with my park Nirvana.

After the park, we made our way to the Summer Palace, taking an old, rickety hot and crowded Metro system. If I thought I'd made any progress in overcoming my claustrophobia, I was wrong.

After closing the palace down, a cab dropped us by a gorgeous river where we desperately tried to find a restaurant recommended by our travel book. We searched for almost an hour before someone told us it had closed a year ago.

Even the latest version of a travel book is out of date

October 9

The words "warning, warning, warning" spun around in my head like a flashing siren as Ken explained his plan for the day, the day we'd leave China – a dreaded travel day.

His plan: one last relaxing walk in the park, a quick stop to pick up clothes he was having made, catch a pre-ordered cab, make one pit stop at the post office to mail home our China purchases, then off to the airport to catch a plane with time to spare. I had a foreboding feeling the plan was flawed.

All went according to plan until Ken went into the post office to mail home our purchases. We sat in a cab waiting and waiting while the driver started to heavy sigh. The kids and I eventually joined in. Long painful minutes ticked by as the windows fogged up. Finally, I ran into the post office to see what was holding him up. Ken was nowhere in sight. We were in a communist country. Had they taken him away for shipping something illegal or exceeding some kind of limit? As I was about to panic, Ken flew through the door red faced with sweat running down his face. They'd made him repack our stuff in official Chinese packing material and then charged so much he had to run out and find a bank machine for cash to pay. Cheap China wasn't so cheap after all!

By the time we finished our post office pit stop, I pleaded to our driver "do what you have to do to get us to the airport." I'm not sure how people walking on sidewalks survived those things, but somehow, against all odds, we managed another win.

Thankfully, we flew Air Nippon. They plied me with so much tasty food and beautiful red wine that I loved everything and everybody, including my time-challenged husband and my kids who cheerfully told me the personal televisions on our flight ranked as their best experience in China.

October 10

After an overnight pit stop back at Kazuko's in Japan, we'd fly off to Australia, or so I thought. Feeling tense after two travel days in a row, everything went smoothly on our way to the airport until an announcement connected our flight number with a destination of Seoul, Korea. Korea wasn't where we wanted to go.

Booking our around-the-world tickets on Air Miles accumulated over fourteen long years, was no easy feat. Air Canada's regulations on what you could and couldn't do were vague and their ticket agents didn't seem to understand the program. After many long, frustrating phones calls patiently explaining itineraries we'd spent hours agonizing over, they'd tell us our route wouldn't work. The thing was, after telling us what wouldn't work, they weren't allowed to tell us what would. Instead, we had to play silly guessing games hoping we'd ask the right question and score a helpful answer. Worried we'd never figure it out, we had to call in a favor from a friend who worked in the industry. She worked out an itinerary so confusing it made our heads spin. Without her, I doubt we ever would have gotten off the ground.

The travel board confirmed our tickets were for Korea, but thankfully digging through a binder full of travel documents confirmed, after flying back to Korea and enduring a five hour layover, we'd eventually make our way to Australia. And so it went with an around-the-world ticket, one flight back before a flight forward.

Rigid rules compromise efficiency

Great Wall family selfie

Meditation in Beijing's Ritan Park

Ritan Park workout

Great Wall of China sleepover

AUSTRALIA
New South Wales

October 11

Sleep deprived after an all-night flight, I slugged through the Sydney Airport looking for a place to buy a map. Then it hit me. I was back in the land of the English; to find one, all I had to do was ask. The simplicity of it made me smile.

Ken's work destination, Adelaide, was over twenty three hours away. With no time to spare, we hopped in a rented car and hit the road.

Australia is really big

Our long drive presented a few challenges. Ken had to stay awake, drive on the unfamiliar opposite side of the road and avoid hitting kangaroos. Moving to the edge of my seat, I stayed on "high alert" until we arrived in Melbourne late that night.

Wanting the kids to appreciate aquamarine waves crashing against cliffs of layered sediment the next morning, I told them to stop playing their Game Boys and look out the window. Lifting their eyes for no more than a few seconds, they burped out a tonally flat "cool," before resuming play.

This word, "cool" was really starting to annoy me. It popped up daily in the kids' journal writing. They'd write about something they did or saw, anything really, from breakfast to a museum, and follow it up with, "it was really cool." I begged them to put more description and emotion into their writing, but more "really cools" followed. My plan to mold them into talented creative writers wasn't panning out as I'd hoped.

The afternoon slipped away with the falling sun. It was time for dinner. After picking up picnic food we drove to the beach, but a raging gale had blown in. About to give up and eat in the car, Mattson blindly stumbled upon a deep, cave-like crevasse sheltered from the wind. We comfortably enjoy our sandwiches while admiring the ocean.

Improvise and overcome

October 12

On our map, the scenic route looked direct, yet we zig-zagged and bounced off hairpin turns. Worrying he'd be late for work, Ken drove like Mario Andretti; well actually, maybe not. He drove fast, accelerating and hitting the brake giving us whiplash – probably not what Mario would do.

On our way into Adelaide, beautiful rolling hills carpeted with velvety lime green grass and vibrant purple wild flowers entertained. We got lost trying to find the hotel Ken's distributor booked for us, but four shiny stars made it all worthwhile. When we threw open the door to our suite, floor to vaulted ceiling windows looked down onto a spectacular park. I headed straight for the jetted marble bath tub. Traveling on a budget was certainly making me appreciate little luxuries I once took for granted

After a heavenly bath, I felt motivated to spend time on my hair and makeup, something I hadn't done in a long while. The hotel blow dryer (I'd left mine back in Calgary) felt foreign as I fought to straighten my natural curl. Losing circulation in my arm, I stopped. How I hated forcing my hair into the latest style. Right there and then I promised to set my curls free and let them fall where they would.

Personalize your style

I'd gotten so used to blonde disappearing eyelashes and pale unmade-up skin that I hardly recognized myself when I put on a little makeup. After a year of travel, would I walk back into my old life looking like some kind of hippie flower child? Would anyone even recognize me?

October 13

   With Ken off at work, I headed off alone for a morning run. It was perfect. I ran where I wanted, at the speed I wanted and for as long as I wanted. Don't get me wrong, I enjoyed running with Ken, but there were benefits when he was away. The search for a coffee shop began.

   Unable to find Starbucks, I settled for a quaint local place and discovered that Australians have their own unique coffee language. There were long blacks, flat whites, short blacks ... and on and on. What it all meant, I hadn't a clue.

   Hanging out and listening, I watched folks order and eventually figured out a Grande Americano was a double long black. With coffee in hand, I couldn't find the cream. Back at the pickup counter, the barista grabbed my coffee and topped it with swirls of whip cream making it look like a soft ice cream cone.

   So here's the deal in Australia; they don't have any kind of cream that pours like milk. For a girl used to customising with skim milk, 1%, 2%, whole milk, half and half or regular cream, not being able to control the amount of dairy fat in my coffee was a problem. When I asked the gal to take some of the whipped cream off, she decapitated my swirls into the sink with a thud and looked irritated when I asked for a little whole milk, but not too much, to try and concoct my own half and half. In the end, my first coffee in the land down under left me feeling a bit down under.

Control freaks get addicted to choice

   Later that night, back at the room, I was overcome with emotion when my sister called to announce the birth of her baby girl on the same day as our Mom's birthday. I'd missed the birth and the birthday. Hanging up the phone, I realized how much I missed my family.

October 14

After Ken left for work, I headed over to the coffee shop for another double long black. Funny how paying the extra price to go out for coffee made me feel like a drug addict sneaking out for a fix.

It was a bumpy morning. With only one of our two laptops working, the kids squabbled over who got the computer. Like a good drill sergeant I ordered them to switch off, but they always claimed that their very best friend, the one they hadn't heard from in ages, just came on-line. How could they sign off without writing at least a few lines to their very best friend? Giving in to their pleading left the next person frustrated. No doubt my kids were selfish, but popular, and I was a bit of a push over.

Computer frustration compounded with complaints from Makayla about missing dance. Feeling badly for her, I found a class, but on the way there we got lost and missed it. Makayla plummeted into a funk.

We slugged along, aimlessly wandering through downtown Adelaide until stumbling onto The South Australia Museum. The kids didn't want to go, but, getting tough, I ordered them in anyway. Once inside, we discovered fascinating exhibits on whales and dolphins, instantly escalating Makayla from miserable to ecstatic. Life was good again.

After the museum, Makayla decided she wanted to go to an evening dance class, but wanted a new dance leotard to wear. This decision came at 4:55 p.m. when stores closed at 5:00. Refusing to go without the leotard, she stomped into her bedroom, back at the hotel, and slammed the door. We were back on the dark side.

When I sat on her bed, she shuffled toward the wall as if I had the plague. I was, after all, the villain who'd taken her from her beloved dance classes in Calgary. I encouraged her to at least think about going to the evening dance class. She moved closer to the wall. I left.

Five minutes later, she emerged from her dark den ready to dance. We headed off holding hands and talking. Life was good again.

That evening, I decided we should try some authentic Australian food at a place recommended in our *Lonely Planet* guidebook. As soon as we opened the menu, I knew we were in trouble. Stupid expensive and a real tourist trap, our plan to eat dinner quickly changed to a shared appetizer before heading back to cook in our room. When the waiter, dressed in a starched black suit, promptly arrived at our table to recite a flowery description of the specials, his smile turned to a frown when we ordered one native Australian dinner, featuring ostrich steak and emu sausage, with three extra plates and water. Embarrassed, we slunk down in our seats, wishing we'd never come.

And so the day went, ups and downs, happy and sad, just another tippy travel day.

If you're not happy, wait a moment

October 15

Our days of luxury were over, but not before one last swim in the pool. In the change room, I caught a glimpse of myself in the mirror and couldn't help noticing a radiant glow to my skin. Back in Calgary, dryness sucked the life out of me and made the quest for a dewy complexion an expensive proposition. Thanks to Australia's humidity, I no longer lived in fear of forgetting my lip balm.

Humidity truly is the elixir of youth

After two and a half months of travel, things were finally coming together. The house was rented, online banking was set up, and our businesses were running smoothly. The Big Trip might not bring financial ruin after all. With a happy sigh, I immediately phoned my father to gloat.

October 16

Look out, trouble ahead. It was a travel day. We had to fly from Adelaide, Australia to Auckland, New Zealand with a layover in Sydney. Arriving at the gate with time to spare, I thought we'd outgrown our little time management problem until the flight was delayed and Ken let me know we didn't have much time to change terminals in Sydney.

Back on the ground, we flagged a taxi to get from the international to the domestic terminal, but when Ken's equipment wouldn't fit, it refused to take us. We had to wait for a van. I must have somehow transferred my nervous tension to Makayla. She started to fume about missing our flight, while Mattson aggressively insisted she calm down. His harsh words very effectively fanned her flame. Suddenly, there it was, playing out right before me – Makayla being me and Mattson being Ken; it wasn't a pretty reflection.

Who you are, your kids will be

Somehow we collected another win, but just barely.

A smooth and comfortable three hours later, after landing in Auckland, we walked through the baggage claim doors to a loud cheer from a huge mass of people congregated in the arrivals area. Turning to see who was behind us, there was no one worth the ruckus. It took a few minutes to realize the crowd was watching New Zealand's professional rugby team. The All Blacks game was televised on a large screen hanging over our exit door. It was our first taste of rugby and catching the energy of the crowd, we liked it.

Hanging out with Wally (my sister's father-in-law) in Adelaide

Adelaide Botanic Gardens

NEW ZEALAND
North Island

October 17

Indecisive about where to begin our tour of New Zealand, I settled in to read our *Lonely Planet* travel book while Ken got on the phone to find a rental car. Should we go north, south, east or west? I still hadn't decided when Ken suddenly stood up, puffed out his chest and cheerfully announced he'd found a steal of a deal on a rental car for only $20.00 a day.

I couldn't remember the last time I'd seen Ken quite so excited. The guy was practically doing a jig. This from Mr. Even-Tempered. He'd played twelve years of professional football in the CFL and after every game, be it a championship win or dismal loss, summed up his play with a tonally flat "it was okay." That okay covered the gamut from mediocre to amazing. To pin him down I had to bombard him with questions. Yet there he stood, blatantly effervescing over saving a few bucks on a rental car.

Ken bounded off to pick up the "deal of the century car," while I continued pondering how we should discover New Zealand. The hours passed and by early afternoon, when Ken still hadn't returned, worry set in. Convinced I'd be filing a missing persons report, he finally waltzed in explaining his long absence with a few wrong turns. Five hours of wrong turns seemed like more than a few, but that was Ken, the king of understatement.

It was time to find food, and fast. The visible huge Denny's sign seemed so close, but wrong exit ramps kept it, oh so far away. Finally inhaling a stack of syrup-covered pancakes, we unfolded the map and continued our indecision. In the end, a flip of a coin took us north, to the beaches of the Coromandel.

After a stomach turning afternoon on never ending winding roads a gorgeous sunset and calm ocean made it all worthwhile. The kids stretched out, doing cart wheels down the beach, while we sauntered along kicking up chilly ocean water close to shore.

When our stomachs reminded us it was dinner time we drove into town and found a cozy café. Ken raised his eyebrows at their prices, but all I had to do was reminded him of his "Deal of the Century Car." Just the thought if it made him smile and return to his menu.

October 18

Unable to find a regular hotel, we spent the night at a Caravan Park in a small trailer. When I say small, I mean small. An Austin Mini could pull the thing. Once in bed with the lights turned off, I felt squeezed between the camper's thin metal walls like cheese in a Panini.

In the morning, we had a strict time line to get to a geothermal area by the ocean called Hot Water Beach. If you arrived an hour before or after low tide, hot water bubbled up through the sand. Digging a hole to contain warm water created your own hot tub.

Ken cheerfully got us going, telling us to wear bathing suits under our clothes since there wouldn't be change rooms at the beach. I listened to his advice, but feeling tired, irritable and cold, couldn't get my head around near nakedness. Sure, we were going to a place called Hot Water Beach where they claimed the water was hot, but hot means different things to different people. Room temperature may be 20 Celsius for most, but I shiver in anything under 24 Celsius. Rationalizing, I figured hot water to the general population would likely be tepid for me. Probably best to exchange the bathing suit for a sweat suit.

By the time we made it to the beach, sun rays started warming the cold air and made the ocean sparkle. Starting to thaw, my sweat suit suddenly felt a bit excessive. We took over a hot tub from another family that was leaving and within minutes, Ken and the kids stripped down to swoon and sprawl out in hot water. I skeptically rolled up one pant leg and stuck in a toe. The water really was hot, even by Jennifer Moore standards.

There I stood with my sweats rolled up, soaking my feet and ankles, when I could have been enjoying a total body soak. Not happy with myself, I wished I would have pushed out of my comfort zone to put on my bathing suit. I promised myself the next time I would make the effort to participate.

Forgo comfort for fun

When we were well pruned, some of us more than others, we set off for Rotorua where Ken had a four day trade show. The drive on winding roads stirred up a headache as I swayed in my seat like Ray Charles at the piano. Mattson was having trouble as well and complained of nausea. Surprisingly, Makayla was oblivious to it all. She folded herself over at the waist with her head between her knees in airplane crash position and slept the day way. Ken – well, he happily steered his race car.

When you start smelling rotten eggs, you're getting close to Rotorua. Spending four days in a place smelling like a big juicy fart was going to be interesting.

October 19

Making sure my pony tail was just so, I took one last look in the mirror before running out the door. The night before, at a corporate dinner, I'd met a lovely gal. We just clicked, and after talking all night, we made a date to meet the next morning. Starved for girl talk, my excitement equaled that for any boy date.

My new girlfriend and I stopped for coffee after a jog around Rotorua Lake. Nibbling a fresh baked caramel scone and listening to her talk, I sat back, relaxed, and for what felt like the first time in my life, contentedly let time idle by.

Unproductive moments are not unnecessary moments

In the evening, we went to a Maori concert and Hangi (think Hawaiian Luau). The tour bus we boarded to get there was typical, but our driver/tour guide was not. Extremely entertaining and funny, he convinced us to pretend we'd been transported back to ancient Maori times. We weren't in a bus on the road; we were in a canoe on the ocean. Chanting and fake paddling at his command seemed a bit foolish, but for some strange reason, no one seemed to care.

Once at the village, our chief (voted in during the canoe/bus ride), presented a peace offering to a group of Maori actors dressed like traditional warriors. Back in the day the Maori weren't big on newcomers. Instead of an open-armed welcome, they chose to terrorize by jumping around pounding their chests, bugging out their eyes, and sticking their tongues out far enough to show their tonsils. No wonder the All Blacks, who opened every Rugby game with their version of a Hakka (the name given to the Maori welcoming act of jumping, pounding chests, and making faces) intimidated their opponents.

After a tasty meal we boarded our canoe/bus feeling like happy little warriors and soon found ourselves going around and around a traffic circle while our driver led us in a boisterous rendition of *"She'll Be Coming Round the Mountain When She Comes."* How he made a busload of supposedly sane people so uninhibited and silly, I'll never know.

A charismatic leader is powerfully influential

Back at the room, we sat in an outdoor spa soaking and rehashing the night. What fun it had been. Suddenly, taking a family photo with our faces decorated and distorted like the Maori warriors doing a Hakka seemed like a great idea (okay it was my idea). The kids mildly resisted, but my enthusiasm made refusing out of the question. When the timer went on the camera, tattooed with eye liner, we bugged out our eyes and stuck out our tongues in true Maori style. The incriminating photo was taken before anyone had a chance to realize its repercussions.

October 20

After raving to Ken about my wonderful run around the lake the day before, he decided to take a mid-morning work break and join me for some exercise. Experienced with the route, I led our way but didn't get far. Ken decided, without notice, to branch off to a narrow dirt path leading into the forest. Cutting me off, he called for me to follow. The way he always dragged me someplace obscure could be so irritating.

Shortly after our detour into the woods we ran, quite literally, into a swarm of unwelcoming sea birds. They must have had babies to protect because they defended their turf by diving at our heads like kamikaze fighter pilots, frantically squawking all the while. It was like a classic scene from the old horror movie, *The Birds*. Ken's head, a good foot and a half higher than mine, bore the brunt of their fury. What a sight. My fearless giant of a husband cowering and covering his head while frantically flapping his arms and running back from whence we'd come.

Expect the unexpected on the road less traveled

October 21

After dropping Ken and the kids at an internet café, I headed to the grocery store. It was my first time behind the wheel alone, and quite frankly, having to drive on the wrong side of the road had me a little nervous. Oops, is it wrong to assume our side is the right side?

The arrogance of North Americans is not a myth

Inside the car, the controls were opposite as well. Deep in concentration making sure I didn't turn into the wrong lane, I'd hit the wipers thinking they were the blinkers. When they released, making a loud scraping sound moving over a dry windshield, the unexpected noise scared me half to death. With every turn, even after picking up the kids and Ken, I made the same mistake, consistently reacting with a jump and gasp. The kids, mimicked my response and ridiculously ramped it up, while I kicked myself for providing more "make fun of Mom" material. On the bright side, I had ammunition to fight back. The tongue dangling family Maori Warrior picture on my computer could easily find its way to friends and family in Calgary; when I told them so, a golden silence fell upon us.

64

October 22

    We packed up in the early morning and headed to a town
where Ken scheduled what he thought would be a short, work related
meeting.
    Waiting in the car for him, the temperature rose until the rising
sun forced us out into the streets of downtown Hamilton, population
3,000. Browsing in gift shops, we soon learned the fickle nature of
time. When you need more, it can't be found. When you have too
much, it never ends.
    Ken's short meeting stretched into three painfully long hours,
leaving us loitering in the stores far beyond any clerk's comfort. When
he returned, he failed to articulate the three little words: "sorry I'm
late," which would have helped his popularity tremendously.
    Cranking up the air conditioning, we hopped back in the car
and drove to a home stay, beside beautiful Lake Taupo, with a family
of five. They had traveled the world and entertained us with stories
about their Servas home stays. I loved the one about their hosts in third
world Africa. Welcomed into a family's small dirt-floor hut, they
generously shared what little they had. How lucky we were to be part
of an organization allowing people of different cultures to come
together and be touched by such generosity.
    That evening the kids from our family and theirs bonded and
played soccer. Hearing their laughter was music to our ears.

October 23

    Ken, with permission to use our hosts' internet, skidded into
their computer chair still chewing his toast and turned robot-like.
Unblinking eyes and flying fingers tried to squeeze extra e-mails into
every minute. I on the other hand, sat alone (our hosts were at work
and Mattson and Makayla were still sleeping) sprawled out on a deck
lounge chair, sipping coffee and gazing down at a shimmering lake.
How I loved and appreciated the luxury of lingering over breakfast.
    In the early afternoon, we enticed Ken away from the
computer with activity, almost like throwing a dog a bone. Come on
Ken, we're going to go for a hike, come on now, there will be vertical

incline, it will be hard, come on now get off the computer, you're going to love it.

He came with his tail wagging to trudge up a small mountain. Our lungs threatened to explode with the climb but at the peak an amazing view of a huge volcanic mountain dwarfed by its crouching lake made it all worthwhile. Our gaze rested on the famous peak of Mordor from the movie, *The Lord of The Rings*. The trilogy was filmed in New Zealand, and Makayla was crazy for anything associated with it.

With time before dinner, we stopped for a walk around Lake Taupo and ran into a golf fundraiser. For a few dollars you could drive golf balls at a target out in the middle of the lake. Ken couldn't wait to support their charity.

Wanting the red sports car you could win if you hit the target, I jumped up and down like a peppy cheerleader as Ken settled into his golf stance, twitching and readjusting like someone with Parkinson's. Swinging and missing by a mile, I searched for more money while Ken sprayed balls everywhere but at the target. His lack of accuracy validated my suspicion he might be blind in one eye. He never could keep the car in one lane or get all of a person's head into a picture.

October 24

Pouring rain ruined our plans to spend the day mountain biking. My mood matched the weather – lousy. It was that dreaded time of the month when hormones turn you into someone you don't know or like. With nowhere to go, we lingered over breakfast, chatting with our Servas hosts, Neil and Raewyn. When I commented on their beautiful garden, obviously a passionate topic, they lit up like patio lanterns; Neil insisting right there and then, I take a tour of his garden.

Standing in the pouring rain, I endured a lengthy introduction to every bloom while my feet went numb and wet hair dripped water into my eyes. Evil hormones made me want to yell for him to stop, but somehow I managed to smile and shake hands with his last rhododendron before drying off and saying our goodbyes.

Along our drive to Wellington, we stumbled upon the Billy Black show. Billy was a talented guy who could shear sheep in the blink of an eye. Rubbing the clippings over a sheep's eyes made it lie down on its back with all four legs pointing to the sky. There it was – interesting trivia explaining where the old saying "he pulled the wool over my eyes" came from.

Travelers excel at Trivial Pursuit

Next on our agenda was a visit to the Waitomo Caves. We entered a spacious cavern filled with fascinating limestone formations. Amazed by it all, my claustrophobia was forgotten until we rounded the corner into a narrow dark cavern where small boats took us to see glow worms. Nothing like paddling through a pitch black small space filled with worms to get the old heart pumping.

As we skimmed across the water in silent darkness, worms hanging from the cave's ceiling glowed like stars in the night. With my head tipped back, my mouth dropped open in awe. Truly amazed, I forgot my fear, but only for a moment. Clamping my mouth shout, it occurred to me: if stars can fall from the sky, worms can fall from a cave's ceiling.

October 25

It was another windy, rainy day in Wellington. No wonder the place was nicknamed "windy Wellington."

The kids slept in, after our late arrival the night before, while Ken and I discussed what to do first: find breakfast or find an internet café. As always, my priority was my stomach. Ken, however, wanted to hit the internet café and then, once the grocery stores opened, buy a more affordable breakfast. In my unstable hormonal state, messing with my breakfast routine was a dangerous affair. Thankfully Ken quickly realized his mistake and gave in. We went for breakfast and I showed appreciation for his flexibility by ordering the cheapest thing on the menu.

There is a fine balance in the successful practice
of marital give and take

Hot Water Beach

Mimicking Maori warriors

68

NEW ZEALAND
South Island

In the late afternoon we caught a ferry to the South Island. Sitting at a large table, rocked to and fro by rough seas, many on board fell sea sick, but not my daughter. She found a way to sleep with her face pressed up against one of the ships porthole windows; her nose and cheek flattened against the glass as the churning ocean swirled around her head like water in a washing machine.

Back on land in Picton, a pizza joint instantly caught Makayla's attention. When a huge, steaming ham and pineapple pizza arrived she was the first to dig in, but before it got to her mouth, she dropped it like a hot potato and shrieked "onions!" Sure enough, there they were, curling and swirling all over the top of the cheese. Knowing Makayla despised onions, Ken quickly started picking them off, but his efforts were in vain. Makayla would have no part of it. Consumed by disappointment she refused to eat anything at all.

Refusing to make a bad situation better is childish

October 26

On my soap box during our morning jog, I preached to Ken about how lax our exercise program had become. As I babbled, our path took a turn and split; one branch leading up a steep hill and the other continuing straight and flat. After my rant, Ken turned toward the hill, while I stalled. Sure I'd just complained about increasing the intensity of our workouts, but like a smoker who wants to quit; I didn't mean right that instant. Come on, you had to at least finish your pack of cigarettes. Unfortunately Ken had never been a smoker. Cursing fate for that hill, I begrudgingly turned to follow. Ken effortlessly sprinted as I painfully struggled. At the peak, surrounded by breathtaking scenery, an unexpected feeling of exhilaration washed over me. It must have been an endorphin high; how else could I explain my sudden decision to run a marathon?

I'd never remotely considered marathon running before. After listening to stories from my hard core runner girlfriends about muscle cramps, throwing up and losing toe nails, I believed people who ran marathons were masochists. Keith and Lisa, Ken's brother and his wife, had just e-mailed us saying they wanted to meet in France to run the Paris marathon. My comment, after reading their message had been: "No way would I ever do that," and yet there I stood a few hours later pledging to be a masochist.

My mind raced as I considered the pros of committing to the race. We had time to train and it would be a great goal to keep us motivated and on a regular running program, something we weren't having much luck with. Why not go for it? At that moment, I felt I could accomplish anything. Ken, impressed with my ambition, agreed. We would run the Paris marathon with our relatives on April 4.

As we ran back down the hill my endorphins dissipated just as Ken's enthusiasm peaked. He rattled on about schedules and training programs while doubt eked out my euphoria. Nonetheless, we made the pledge; there was no turning back. We were both excited and in good moods until we started planning our day.

Ken wanted to move on and drive and I wanted to stay put and enjoy the sun. A debate began, as we aired our different points of view. With neither one of us wanting to compromise, our debate escalated into an argument. We were into it, going hard to get what we wanted until I remembered we weren't alone. Mattson and Makayla stood by, watching our every move. Realizing that, we switched into a more passive aggressive communication style; using nice words to try and get our own way. In the end we packed up and drove a short distance to a nearby hiking spot. I had to move, but Ken didn't get to do the long drive to the Abel Tasmin. Tit for tat, but not really, I had to say goodbye to the sun.

Resentful compromise isn't flexible compromise

At the end of the hike, we talked as a family about what we wanted to do while on the South Island. With input from everyone, we agreed to cut down on the time spent driving. It felt good to work things out, clear the air from our morning disagreement and discuss our future travel plans as a team.

"There is no I in teamwork" Michael Jordan

October 27

After a three hour scenic drive to Kaikoura, we drove through town and found a basement suite for rent in a residential area. Snow covered mountains lined the horizon, and only steps away an indigo blue ocean splashed. It was heavenly, and with our landlord's list of exciting things to do, Kaikoura seemed like a perfectly adventurous place.

We were especially intrigued by his suggestion to hike a path beside the ocean leading to a seal colony. Ken and the kids wanted to go right away, but we'd been warned to go only during low tide. At high tide, the ocean rose up and covered the path. Confused by the whole ocean tide thing, Ken and Mattson gave me a lesson on how the gravity of the moon determines the tides. They sounded like experts so I believed them when they insisted it was time for a seal hunt.

It was early evening when we picked our way along a narrow path squeezed between a steep cliff and the ocean. Trying to navigate irregular rocks slippery with moss and sea water, I kept an eye on the ocean. If the boys were wrong about low tide, the only escape would be up – way, way up a cliff only climbable by goats.

With our heads down studying the path, we almost tripped over a big fat seal. The search was over. About ten stinky, blubbery seals sprawled out on the rocks enjoying the warmth of the setting sun. The kids and Ken played chicken to see who could get the closest to them while I took pictures. I hardly noticed the sun setting until I looked up to see the tide rolling in.

We made it three quarters of the way back before the rising ocean blocked our path and left us trapped. Like it or not, we'd be going for a swim. Loving the adventure of not knowing how deep the water was Ken led the way. I was terrified we'd all drown.

In waist-high freezing water I wondered why I'd listened to the boys in the first place. It seemed I'd believe anything if it was delivered

72

convincingly. I was the one, after all, who believed my best friend when she told me pomegranates, a fruit I'd never seen before, were called Marsupials and came from Mars. Sure, I was only eleven years old at the time, but truth be told, my level of gullibility hadn't changed a whole lot over the years.

The water never did get over our heads, but with a rocky ocean floor and waves disrupting our balance, we did have to swim a good distance before finding dry land and safety.

Get real facts and stay safe

October 28

In the morning, happy to be alive, I took a little extra time appreciating my comfy bed. Good beds on our trip had been few and far between. Beds in Asia were too hard, and those in Australia were too soft, but New Zealand's beds were turning out to be just right. I could rate beds with one bum cheek bounce. And bounce I did, every time I entered a new hotel room.

With whale watching as our adventure for the day, a tour briefing began on land. To me, a briefing should be just that, brief, but our tour guide droned on about rules and regulations like an over-protective mother. I can summarize in one sentence what it took him thirty minutes to say. "Don't get out of your seat and go to the observation deck until you hear a whistle blow."

I was hoping his sermon was over, but he continued with a speech about sea sickness, telling graphic stories about how waves make people puke. According to him, seasickness was pretty much unavoidable. As he told us not to take the tour if we thought we'd get sick, it seemed to me that he wanted a day off.

Whale watching was exciting, but people watching, now there was the real fun. After our first whale sighting, I understood why our tour guide adamantly went on and on about the rules. The tourists on the boat (there must have been about 40 of us) were crazy. Trying to get from seats inside to the perfect viewing spot out on deck turned everyone into aggressive football players exploding off the line; unlike football players, though, no one worried about holding or rough play.

If you managed to push through the crowd and secure a small sliver of space with a clear view to the ocean, getting a good whale photo was still almost impossible. Well, at least it was for me. The thirty second automatic turn off on my camera admittedly made catching the flip of a tale before a dive harder than it needed to be. The kids suggested I change my camera settings, but hey, I'd just mastered e-mail. Messing with the settings on my new fancy Canon SLR had me totally intimidated.

In the end we managed a few good pictures and best of all, bid our guide goodbye with our lunch still in our stomachs.

October 29

With Ken off to work and heavy morning rain, the kids and I stayed indoors until it cleared in the early afternoon. A strenuous hike into town led to a cute little café where I let the kids order whatever they wanted for lunch. A new precedent had begun; when dad was away mom would pay.

That evening we snuggled up in blankets and watched the National Geographic channel. It was after eight when I remembered we hadn't eaten dinner and whipped up scrambled eggs and toast. The kids received their dinner with shocked confusion, staring at it as if it were dog poop. "But this is breakfast food!" Makayla complained while Mattson nodded in agreement. I had to assure them no harm would come from eating eggs after 10:00 a.m. but even so, they were reluctant to partake in such an unorthodox practice.

Doing what you normally do
doesn't have to be what you always do

October 30

It was a busy day for excursions. Makayla started at 5:30 a.m. with dolphin watching, then met her dad and brother to swim with the seals. Not wanting to endure cold water I kissed them goodbye and went back to bed. Trying to go back to sleep, the promise I'd made back at Hot Water Beach niggled at me like a dripping tap. I had, after all, vowed to push out of my comfort zone. Staying in bed didn't seem like much of a push – I'd definitely opted for the sideline.

Oct 31

Our drive to Christchurch put us in town right at dinner. Arriving in an unfamiliar city on an empty stomach with no place to stay always created a dilemma. Should you suffer through hunger while searching for a hotel with a family suite, checking in, driving to a grocery store, figuring out what to buy for dinner and finally cooking it, or just grab some fast food and be pleasantly full before finding a hotel? The kids and I opted for fast food, but Ken thought groceries were more cost effective. The thing was, when you're starving, even broccoli looks good. Hunger driven impulsive grocery shopping quickly filled our cart. Eating out probably would have been cheaper.

It was October 31. If we were back at home, the kids would be out trick or treating for Halloween candy. To ease their disappointment about missing out, I let them buy candy from the bulk food bins. The dentist in me squirmed, but giving the kids a little piece of their beloved tradition felt right.

Traditions bring home away from home

November 1

Over breakfast, we devised a detailed sightseeing schedule and were walking out the door to get to it when the phone rang. The sound of a ringing phone was so foreign we almost forget what to do. It took multiple rings before Ken picked up. The call was work related. They wanted Ken to report for duty in some town we'd never heard of by 8:00 a.m. the next morning. So much for sightseeing, we'd be taking a drive to tourist information.

To kill time while Ken figured things out, the kids and I wandered around downtown Christchurch and listened to Makayla swoon over every food joint we passed. Oh, she just loved the chicken nuggets from Kentucky Fried Chicken, and a ham and cheese Subway sub would really hit the spot, not to mention how heavenly a McFlurry

from McDonald's would be. You'd think the kid had a tape worm. It
went on and on, making me dizzy from shaking my head to say no.

Globalization scatters franchises like seeds in the wind

November 2

When Ken's work appointment got canceled, we set out for
our first long training run. Ninety minutes of perpetual movement
seemed like a terrifyingly long time. Thankfully New Zealand's
colorful rhododendrons, splashing hot pink, fire engine red and
tangerine orange around never ending lush gardens distracted us from
our complaining joints.

We met Avril, our home stay host. A sturdy thirty-something
gal with long hair wrapped in a bandanna, she looked like she was born
to ride a motorcycle. Standing in the doorway of her home, she said a
quick "hello," invited us in, and rushed out to work a night shift.

Avril's house had two large, lovely bedrooms and no heat.
New Zealand was beautiful, but with a biting wind that never seemed
to stop blowing and poorly heated homes, I was constantly freezing to
death. We Canadians may come from the land of snow and ice, but
with central heat, we live at room temperature.

November 3

Through my bedroom window, rays of sun beckoned. This was
one morning when I couldn't wait to get out for a run. When we got
back, Avril was home. We tried hard to make conversation, but every
topic pitched fell flat like the pancakes we all sat quietly eating.
Reserved and withdrawn, Avril wasn't anything like our other Servas
hosts. I couldn't figure out why she'd invited us in when nothing about
us seemed to interest her.

Our conversation turned practical as we planned our day.
When Avril's plans didn't include us, Ken insisted she let us take her
out for dinner. She declined, but Ken persisted. When she finally
agreed, I had to wonder if a forced gesture of good will was still a good
thing.

After breakfast, Ken and Avril left, leaving me and the kids to try and find our way to a movie. The newspaper sized map I unfolded while we were walking flapped and ripped in the wind. Giving up on it, I asked locals for help and made sure Mattson noticed how quickly we got where we needed to go.

Smart people ask for help

When it came time to meet Avril for dinner, Ken couldn't get away from work. I'd be the one left entertaining our reluctant dinner guest. She arrived and sat silently. Never comfortable with a lull in conversation, I started bombarding her with questions, a talent honed from years of deciphering Ken's "okays." I lobbed them out, one after another until the roast lamb arrived and I could replace words with food.

November 4

I settled into a chair across from Avril at breakfast prepared to resume my questioning, but to my surprise, she started to talk. A nice long balanced conversation began.

Time passed and when we finally pulled away from the table, she offered me a beautiful seashell I'd admired on her kitchen shelf. She was actually a very kind person who was just a bit shy.

Resist passing judgment on people you don't know

As nice as she was, I was ready to say our goodbyes and turn up the heat in the car.

In New Brighton we split up after checking into a hotel. Mattson and Ken went to the gym and Makayla and I headed to the attached leisure center.

The lazy river, good the first five times around, got old quickly. Convincing Makayla she felt the same way, I suggested passing the time swimming laps. When she wasn't enthused, I resorted to ice cream bribery. As we kicked, holding onto flutter boards, I figured the timing was right to pitch another lecture in my exercise and nutrition series. Training for the marathon put Ken and I back on a regular training program, and with his gymnastics, Mattson was staying fit, but Makayla was drifting. I worried that a dancer without dance who loved junk food might be a bad combination.

With long hours driving in the car, munching on chips, drinking pop and stopping for McDonald's ice cream helped pass time. Makayla was too young to understand that increasing calories and decreasing activity leads to weight gain. I didn't want to come on too strong, but standing by and watching her bulk up beyond a healthy weight didn't seem right either. It was a delicate subject.

We kicked and talked and in the end devised a plan to replace junk food with carrots, apples and water. Makayla agreed she should be more active and was willing to once again try running. As we left the pool, invigorated after our swim, our ice cream reward tasted great.

To make good choices, you have to know your options

November 5

Finally, a windless day: We dug down to the neglected area of our suitcases for shorts and headed to the beach for a run. No more false starts, this really would be the first day of our official family running program. Mattson and Ken began with a slow jog, quickly progressing to a competitive sprint while Makayla and I contemplated our start.

We decided on a walk-run program, but transitioning from walk to run was like prodding an old trail horse away from hay. I badly wanted to leave her and the drone of her complaining behind to break into the pace of my own stride but visions of mother and daughter joyfully jogging together kept me tossing out encouraging words. Truth be told, exercising Makayla was making me realize I needed to work a little harder exercising my own virtue of patience.

Leaving Makayla at the gym with the boys, I headed out to continue a run on my own. Settling into my pace, I soon found myself lost in thought. Travel as a foursome meant constant compromise. What would it be like to travel on your own, doing whatever you wanted, whenever you wanted?

While day dreaming, I took a wrong turn, and ran longer than I'd planned. Even when I finally found my way back to the gym, the pull of peaceful solitude tempted me to keep going. Forcing myself to stop, I gave my head a shake. Giving up your wants for your family's needs might feel like getting short changed at Christmas but the security of a family does bring – joy to your world, and peace to your earth.

November 6

With a warm hand on my toothbrush in our new homestay's centrally heated house, I stood in the bathroom thinking about the request our hosts made for us to make an authentic Canadian meal for dinner.

Exactly what was an authentic Canadian meal anyway? Our favorite dishes were either Italian or Asian. It's not like Canadians eat beaver burgers or maple leaf salads. At a loss, we finally settled on Fettuccini Alfredo – Italian made by Canadians, it would have to do.

After devouring freshly baked scones with real cream and strawberry preserves in a cozy café the kids and I arrived at the grocery store. I stood in the produce section trying to visualize the words on my recipe card back in Calgary. Doing brain gymnastics I stretched for ingredients memory pushed out of reach. When I got one, the kids ran for it.

Cooking in a foreign kitchen was a challenge but we managed to pull dinner together by the time our hosts arrived home. I held my breath in anxious anticipation as they took their first bite and didn't relax until they got up for seconds; their heaping plates proof of our success.

November 7

With Ken away overnight on business, I stretched out spread eagled and thought about the same old recurring dream which had woken me. In it, the story changed, but the premise always stayed the same; I was messing up. Sometimes I'd be back at the Keg where I used to be a cocktail waitress, trying to serve a full section of customers I'd forgotten about, or I might be at my dental office unable to extract a tooth, or the most popular, I was trying to write a university final exam for a class I'd never attended. How had these dreams found me in New Zealand?

Generally, I figured I was a pretty confident person, but my childhood piano teacher's motivational technique of telling me I'd get a big fat goose egg in competitions if I didn't work harder left its mark. Not wanting to fail, I did work harder and often found success; a healthy dose of fear seemingly served me well. No doubt the fear of failure as a dentist kept me tightly wound, but I figured once I left and got away for stress free travel, I'd become a new person – a light hearted, fun loving, fearless kind of person. The person I wanted to be. Yet, there I'd sat at dinner the night before, hoping and praying our hosts approved of my fettuccini, hoping it was perfect. God forbid if the pasta was overcooked, the sauce too salty or the garlic bread under toasted? Maybe the fear of failure wasn't so healthy after all.

November 8

Another early morning saw another hotel fading away in the rear view mirror. When planning the trip, I thought we'd settle into one place for at least a week at a time; how wrong I'd been. The reality of our trip was nothing like I'd dreamed.

Daydreaming about the future is a waste of time

We drove on a deserted highway trying to find a house we rented off the internet. Not finding it, Ken eventually broke down and phoned the contact number. Told to turn right at the round shaped tree, and left at a pile of rocks, he agonized over which tree looked more round. We eventually parked in front of an isolated farm house. When no one answered our knocks we pushed open an unlocked door hoping we weren't breaking and entering.

Mattson and Makayla, after being cooped up in the car all day, ran out into a large pasture as we unpacked. They weren't gone long. Screaming her way through the door of the house, a hysterical Makayla fell to the floor sobbing and screaming "I've been stabbed, I've been stabbed!" I dropped to her side in a panic and frantically searched for gushing blood, but found no puncture point. Between sobs Makayla panted out what happened. It took a while to figure out she'd touched an electric fence while trying to pet a sheep. The poor kid had been electrocuted.

Once we knew what was wrong and that she'd be okay, Mattson started teasing her, saying her hair was standing on end. She didn't find his humour funny and in fact, it was a good long time before she could look back and joke about electrocution.

November 9

Kiwi's, as New Zealanders are often called, don't hike, they tramp. Only a short ferry ride away, the Abel Tasman offered some of the best tramping in the world. We couldn't wait to go. In the morning Ken set off to find a ferry schedule, claiming he'd be right back. Right back, ya right, we knew all about that. Instead of rushing to get ready, we stayed in our pajamas and when he blew back in, expecting to find us ready and waiting, our peaceful morning came to a crashing halt.

In the car, in a rush to get to the ferry, our tires spit up loose gravel as we wound up a mountain like a garland being wrapped around a Christmas tree. Ken drove fast and passed on sharp turns leaving me pumping my imaginary brake. After somehow surviving, we parked at the beach just in time to see the ferry, a few hundred yards away, start to pull away from the dock. Undeterred, Ken burst from the car yelling for us to follow and sprinted down the beach, his unbuttoned shirt billowing behind him like Batman's cape. Kicking up sand with every long stride, he waved his arms and screamed for them to stop. We boarded that ferry, but when I looked at Ken through sweat infused stinging eyes, I didn't see a superhero.

The boat ride gave us time to cool down and enjoy a beautiful coastline covered with white sand. Dropped at Bark Bay, we tramped and tramped for the better part of the day. The experience was exhilarating for its cardiovascular challenge and for the ever changing, spectacular panoramic views of pristine, deserted beaches. I'll always remember trudging down our last stretch of beach, hand in hand, while the sun set, tired, but jubilant after finishing the tramp of a lifetime.

November 10

When we were ready to leave our farm house (we never did hear from the owners) we stuffed cash into an envelope, placed it on the kitchen table and walked out, leaving the door unlocked as it had been when we arrived.

Once again on a ferry back to the north island, I spread out sandwich ingredients and realized I'd forgotten to pick up plastic cutlery. Slicing meat off a whole chicken and cutting thin pieces of cheese for sandwiches was going to take some improvisation. Using my fingers to rip chicken from its carcass, I hungrily lapped up juice running down my arm until I got the feeling someone was watching me. Lifting my head, in mid lick, I looked up into the disapproving eyes of an older couple sitting across from us. Suddenly feeling quite uncouth, I paused for a moment and then thought what the heck, I'm doing the best I can – on with the ripping and licking.

Get out from under the judgment of others

November 11

At a home stay in Wellington, dense grey clouds enveloped the house forcing us to cancel our morning run. Guilt pinched me and for what must have been the hundredth time, I questioned why, oh why, we'd signed up for a stupid marathon. I so wanted to leave windy Wellington behind for the warmth of Australia, our next destination. Having to wait two more long, cold and miserable days seemed like forever.

The Te Papa Museum turned out to be a great place to spend a gloomy day. After closing the place down we drove Mattson to the gym. Ken wanted to stay and work out with Matt, leaving Makayla and I in the middle of nowhere with nothing to do. Suggesting a walk, I dragged her out to battle a fierce gale. Trudging along, shivering in silence, I tried engaging her in conversation. Every interlude fell flat until I admitted I was feeling a bit homesick and asked her what she missed the most from home. Hitting on the right topic, she started chattering a million miles a minute about friends, school, dance and our house. The house, she decided was boring and conservative, way too beige, as she put it. We simply had to redecorate. I suggested zeroing in on her bedroom. Off she went on a tangent about unique and wild decorating ideas. Instantaneously our bad weather was completely forgotten.

To cure what ails you, think about something else

November12

Too much knowledge can be a bad thing. At the Te Papa Museum, I'd learned New Zealand is located right on top of The Ring of Fire, a fault line circling the earth and responsible for earthquakes and volcanic activity. That knowledge had me dreaming all night long about earthquakes, tsunamis and spewing lava. I woke thinking the house was shaking, but then figured it was just a dream. Over breakfast our hosts let me know there had in fact been an earthquake in the night – one more reason to get out of New Zealand.

Feeling lazy, we decided to forgo any excursions and spend the day at the house. Ken needed time on the internet. We liked to give him a bad time for being cheap, but without his patience and dedication to organize and seek out deals online, our trip wouldn't work.

It was a good day to start a homeschooling project. We set to work to make a Christmas card to send back home. Our design, a globe topped with a Santa hat, was surrounded with flags from the countries we'd already visited. We did a good deal of flag research and when the job was done believed without a doubt that our Canadian Maple Leaf was by far the most beautiful flag in the world.

Travel elevates patriotism

For dinner that night we made Pavlova; basically a meringue topped with whipped cream and fresh fruit. I was so busy devouring it I didn't even notice if our hosts approved of our efforts. We lingered at the table after dinner enjoying conversation and then anxiously excused ourselves to pack for an early morning flight to Australia.

November 13

At 4:00 a.m., we wearily hauled our luggage out of the house into a torrential downpour and saw our pre-ordered cab backing out of the drive way. Ken turned superhero once again, splashing through puddles waving for the cab to stop, and – of course – it did.

We savored the novelty of boarding a flight all calm and on time and collected our bags in Sydney before catching another connection on to Cairns. When I hauled my bag off the luggage console, I instantly noticed a pungent fishy odor. The attendant tagging my bag for our next flight speculated something might have spilled on it during the flight. Eight more months of travel with a bag smelling like rotten sea food was concerning, but if we could get used to the smell of Mattson's sandals, we could get used to anything.

That night, seated at an outdoor restaurant in Cairns, not one hair on my head moved in the warm, still night air.

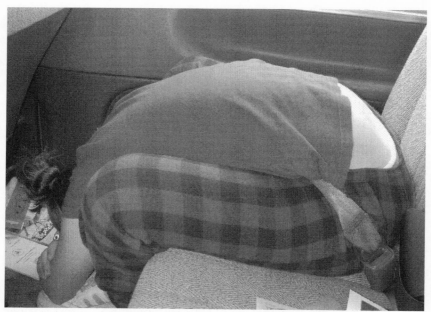

Makayla takes a nap

Kaikoura seal hunt

Mattson goes to gymnastics training

Morning run in Kaikoura

AUSTRALIA
East Coast

November 14

We left early for a run hoping to beat the heat, but the heat beat us. I was unprepared for sweat to gush from my pores like water from a watering hose. My sweat band couldn't contain it; a disposable diaper worn turban style wouldn't have worked. Blinded by sunscreen and trying to keep up with Ken, I once again questioned our decision to run a marathon. And to think I'd longed for Australia's hot sun.

Be careful what you wish for

Standing in the elevator, wet and exhausted after the run, the reek of body odor closed in on us. To my dismay, Ken wasn't the sole body responsible. The kids cringed and pointed us to the shower, but even after a cold one, the sweat continued to flow.

Learning to love your sweat is an acquired taste

The time had come to plan a snorkeling tour to the Great Barrier Reef. Different brochures offered different pricing. The one with champagne and a tropical lunch caught my eye. Imagining myself raising a chilled flute of bubbly to my lips, Ken passed me a brochure entitled Budget Snorkel Adventure. My vision burst like a bubble. We were in a familiar quandary. Do you go for it and spare no expense, or do you do the budget thing, hoping for a wonderful time without unnecessary extras? Is champagne unnecessary? It's easy to say "what the heck" when you're on a two week vacation, but when you're having once in a lifetime experiences on a daily basis for the better part of a year, the decisions get tougher. Still, I had to argue for the champagne. In a three against one vote, my brochure unfortunately hit the trash.

Meanwhile, Ken spent the day on the phone trying to chase down a rental car. Not finding one left him frustrated and in need of a break.

Some days, travel plans fell into place effortlessly, and other days, everything was a struggle. When things weren't coming together we'd learned that it was best to forget the planning. If you stop trying, the universe seemed to lead you where you needed to go.

Discover your third eye

Our biggest adventure for the day, turned out to be grocery shopping as a family. At home I shopped alone. Sharing shopping with Ken changed everything. Ken and I simply weren't on the same page. I wanted to get in and get out as quickly as possible. Grabbing popular, heavily advertised brands was easy and fast. Heck if those advertisers did a good job convincing me their products were the best, I believed them. Ken, on the other hand, didn't give a hoot about brand names. His mathematical mind analyzed the price per gram of every item, ensuring only those with the lowest prices made the cart. All that calculating took forever and left me frustrated. To calm down I'd have to escape to a different aisle for deep breathing. My panting and Ken's calculating left the kids alone to fill the cart with their favorite treats. By the time we sorted out what stayed and what went back on the shelf, grocery shopping took forever. So much for getting out in a hurry. No worries, Ken assured us, he'd just transfer what should have been done today to the to-do list for tomorrow.

November 15

Knowing what I'd face on day two of our Australian running program, I reluctantly tied up my shoes and prayed starting earlier would be cooler. It wasn't. Heat and searing sun brought my freckles together and made me, for the first time ever, brown. My mouth moved faster than my feet as I droned on about dying from heat exhaustion. "Just the other day you were freezing to death" Ken teased. What could I say? I had a narrow window of temperature tolerance.

At Hartley's Crocodile farm, we boarded a small boat for the crocodile feeding tour. Taking our seats, the captain sternly warned us to stay seated once we left the dock. "Stand and you could lose a limb," he boomed, making all of us slouch.

Once out in a swamp like lake, the Captain held a bloody chicken head tied to a stick over the water. Silence fell until, like a rocket, a canoe sized croc shot up with jaws wide. A thud, like an empty metal trap springing shut, left the stick headless.

I was glued to my seat, unblinking as the crocodile slithered past. Only the glass railing of the boat separated me from that croc. Just before slowly submerging back down into the depths of the murky water, his beady eyes locked on mine, making me quiver. Hey, I saw *Jaws*, the late 1970s shark-attack movie. Their boat hadn't protected them from the antics of a killer shark with a personal grudge.

On to the snake show (Hartley's wasn't all about crocs). A British commentator with coke bottle-thick glasses perched on a hooked nose passionately lectured about the Black Taipin, Australia's most deadly venomous snake. Totally engrossed in his topic and holding a wriggling coiling snake in his hand, he moved closer and closer to our front row perch. After he waved that hissing snake right under our noses it became very apparent that a hike or swim in Australia would never again be carefree.

November 16

The day had come to snorkel the famous Australian Great Barrier Reef.

Passing a long line of gleaming white ocean cruisers filling up with tourists sure to dine on lobster and champagne, we made our way to what looked like a tug boat. Hopping from the pier to a cramped deck shuffled us in with a ragged bunch of young back-packers.

The atmosphere was casual and our safety briefing, short. Basically, don't fall over board or plug the toilet. If either happened, we were to yell loudly and inform the crew. I didn't believe they would lift a toilet plunger, let alone jump over board to rescue us. Sprawled out in the sun, all young and hung over, they sipped coffee and laughed about the antics of last night's party.

Eventually we stopped at Hasting Reef, donned our wet suits, snorkels and masks and jumped in the ocean. For some reason, my snorkel let in more salt water than air, seriously dampening my experience. It's hard to relax and enjoy colorful fish when you're drinking the ocean. Between gulps, I managed to see a white-tipped reef shark, its tell-tale tail fin making me forget the consequences of breathing through my nose. Oh how salty ocean water burns. I was mighty happy to get out of the water when our guide called us in.

As we forged on to the next snorkel sight, I sure could have used a glass of champagne to warm me from the inside out. Not wanting to go back in the water, Ken suggested I ask for a different snorkel and when I did – voila – air, not water.

Good sport requires good gear

Back in Cairns, we relived the day's highlights over dinner and for the first time in my life, I got it. I understood why people jump into salty, cold, ocean water. Maybe I really could be the girl in the ocean rather than just beside it.

November 17

To add variety to our morning run, Ken suggested heading to the nearby golf course. Once there, we ran along a cart path bordered by fairway on one side and swamp on the other. The three feet of muddy bank between us and the murky water looked very similar to the terrain at Hartley's Crocodile Farm. Forgetting my hot run misery, I thought about how easy it would be for a crocodile to lurch up, grab me and drag me back down. Changing position with Ken, his eyes focused on the swamp as well. If he was crocodile paranoid we were truly in trouble. I turned to say "let's get out of here" just as Ken sprinted down the fairway leaving my words to hang in thick humid air. He never did go back and play that course.

Back at the hotel room, something stank and it wasn't just us. Ever since arriving in Australia, the pungent fishy smell coming from my luggage had intensified. The time had come to figure out its source.

Starting in on my bag like a bloodhound, I sniffed and searched, following the stench to an outer pocket. Reaching inside, my fingers oozed into something slimy and worthy of a scream. The bag hit the floor with a thud as I backed away shaking the guck from my hand. Ken took over the search, intently inspecting the slime pocket and pulled out a decomposing sand dollar. Holding it up for me to see, I met his accusing glare. It was my special sand dollar lovingly collected off a beach in New Zealand. I'd planned to carry it all the way home to my seashell collection in Calgary. How could a land locked prairie girl know that sand dollars have guts?

Leave what's on the beach at the beach

Later in the morning, we drove to Mossman Gorge, a national park about an hour away. The breathtaking gorge looked like someone pulled apart the earth, threw in some house-sized boulders and poured limeade all over them. Ken and the kids jumped in without hesitation. I held back. There were a few issues to be worked out: What if the water was freezing cold? How would I dry off without a towel? What would I do with my wet hair? I didn't work it all out before the rest of the family wanted to leave. How perfectly, comfortably, boring.

Change is hard

November 18

The time had come to say goodbye to Yorkeys Knob. Ken, finally found a rental car and went to pick it up. When he returned, he wore a sheepish look on his face and casually commented that the car wasn't much. Asking why, he mentioned something about the color and that it was an older model. "No worries mate," I chirped, in my best Aussie accent, "as long as it gets us from point A to point B, we'll be just fine"

The boys loaded the car, while I checked the room for anything forgotten. When I finished and made my way to the parking lot, there sat the ugliest of ugly cars. Yellow, in a bright canary kind of way, it was the trashy blonde trailer park version of a 1980s woody station wagon. So what if it was a bit unsightly; we'd only have it for a short time.

Radiating open mindedness, I seated myself on a scorching, dark brown seat, cringing as I noticed a mold-like growth on the roof where fabric should have been. How long was the drive to Brisbane, I wondered? Reaching for the door handle I pulled, taking only the handle as it sprang loose and hung by one last dangling screw. Okay, so it was gross and falling apart. As long as the engine worked, we'd still be okay.

Turning to Ken, I pleasantly asked him to turn on the air conditioning. The dark chocolate brown interior was sucking heat from the sun like a sponge. Not making eye contact, he looked down and mumbled that there was no air conditioning. So much for flexibility and no worries mate. There was no way in hell I'd drive anywhere in that repulsive poor excuse of a car. Cutting off my rant, Ken agreed the car was unacceptable. Arrangements had been made to exchange the car for another, due back that afternoon.

After killing time, we arrived back at the rental car agency. The owner, a real sleazy looking dude, nonchalantly told us he didn't in fact have another car as promised.

Determined to find something else, we stormed out the door and piled into Tweety Bird, our new nick name for the ugliest of ugly cars and quickly found a nice air-conditioned van.

Driving the bird back, we waited while Ken ran in to return the keys and get our deposit back. Over twenty minutes passed before Ken finally stomped back to the van, his face crimson with a big blue bulging temporal vein on the side of his forehead pulsing. That monster throbbing vein was a sure sign of Ken's anger. He paused and stuttered before spitting out "there…was a fight." My jaw dropped. I'd watched Ken play professional football for twelve years and not once did I see him fight. For a big aggressive athlete he'd always been extremely passive. Bombarding him with questions, I tried to piece together what had happened.

The problem began when the guy asked Ken to pay for the gas he'd used in Tweety. When Ken refused, "sleazy-used-car-guy" went into a tirade, throwing out curses and insults. Being called a "stupid Yankee" wasn't so bad, especially knowing you're a smart Canadian, but when the guy reached for a bat and started swinging, tempers flared. To protect himself, Ken had to grab the guy by the neck and push him up against the wall until his toes dangled.

Ken stared at the road in a trance as he drove. He needed constant prompting to continue his story. "What happened once you had him up against the wall" I questioned, afraid of what Ken might say. He swallowed hard, sighed and quietly went on: "I was so close to losing control. More than anything, I wanted to punch the guy's lights out, but I knew there would be trouble if I did, and a scum bag like that wasn't worth it." In the end, Ken let him turn a bit blue, demonstrating his superior strength, and when the bat dropped, he let him back down. From there he grabbed his deposit and walked out.

We all fell silent contemplating what could have happened. What if Ken had lost control and really hurt the guy? What if the guy had really hurt Ken? What if the guy had a gun?

Practicing anger management can be a life saver

November 19

After scoring a last minute deal to the Whitsunday Islands, we boarded a ferry to Long Island. Thirty gorgeous sun infused minutes later our feet touched down on talc-like sand embracing a turquoise ocean. It was paradise truly found.

There was, however, one problem in paradise. It was box jellyfish season. The jellyfish, small transparent little devils, or stingers as the Australians called them, were killers. They invaded Australia's beach waters every November and with their potent venom could kill a human with a single sting. We'd been advised to stay out of the ocean completely, but if you did go in, it was essential to wear a stinger suit (a light weight full length wet suit) to decrease your risk of getting stung. What about your exposed hands, feet and head I questioned, thinking maybe we should just steer clear of the water altogether. Trying to comfort me, Ken launched into a statistics lecture explaining how the minimal amount of skin exposed on our extremities left us with only a 5% chance of being stung. Even 5% seemed worrisome, but I reluctantly agreed to rent the suits and go for one short family snorkel.

We played the odds, enjoyed a plethora of fish in every shape, size and color and managed to survive, but I was certainly relieved to get out of the water. Ken however, decided shortly after returning our rented suits that he simply had to go back for another snorkel; a snorkel he wouldn't rent a stinger suit for. With surprise I growled "why won't you walk the few steps back to the shop for the $6.50 suit?" He flatly stated "no need to waste money, I won't be stung." Why should he be immune to a jellyfish sting? Weighing in at a beefy 245 lbs., according to his statistics lesson, his above average amount of skin made him more at risk.

Makayla started teasing him, asking why God made him so special and when she was done I took over, treating him like a child because he was acting like one. Not liking being made fun of, or being told what to do, he used the extra cost of the suit to bridge into a lecture on how hard it was keeping his extravagant family on a budget. Granted his budget quest truly was a challenge, but putting a lifesaving suit for $6.50 in the same category as extravagance seemed ridiculous.

As Ken's dreaded right temporal vein started to rise, I changed my approach. The kids needed their father and I needed my husband. Not able to come up with a good retort, he stormed off, leaving us to chuckle and shake our heads.

Fifteen minutes later, Ken joined us back at the pool. We all pretended nothing had happened and no one said a word about stinger suits or snorkeling, but the kids and I knew Ken's stinger suit incident wouldn't be forgotten. Over some meal in some country it would be Ken's turn to provide a laugh for the team. I couldn't have been happier to pass the baton.

November 20

We were on an exotic holiday, but unfortunately still needed to train. Faced with Cairns-type heat, we found a tree covered path leading up the side of a mountain. Okay, mountain was a bit of an exaggeration. Some might call it a big hill, but after running up its gradual, but steady incline for what seemed like forever, it became a mountain to me.

Loose, bowling-ball sized rocks scattered along the path made footing difficult. I was struggling and falling behind with my eyes glued to the ground. Not looking up, I didn't see a broken tree branch protruding out from the side of the hill at thigh level. Stumbling after impact, searing pain shot through my leg. I moaned for Ken to stop, but he only glanced back momentarily, before proceeding around a bend.

Hobbling along, I checked out a nasty blunt trauma with deep scrapes. Thankfully I hadn't broken anything. I'd be fine. Trying to run again, I wondered why Ken hadn't stopped and why he seemed to have no feeling. He was never unmotivated, hot or tired and never complained. Everything was so easy for him. His strength accentuated my weakness. Trying to suck it up and catch up was a struggle. The more I struggled, the madder I got about my unfeeling husband. Being mad at Ken must have released adrenalin. I made it to the top of my mountain and from there, quite literally, it was all downhill.

Back at the room, I dropped onto my bed sweating and exhausted. Even Ken showed signs of fatigue. When he noticed the nasty scrape and purple and blue welt covering my left quad, he was genuinely concerned. He hadn't realized I was injured when I called to him on the path. I had to confess, from the start of the run I'd been complaining about one thing or another. It was too hot, the path was too steep, blah, blah, blah. No wonder he tuned me out.

The rest of the day brought more physical activity as we tried to stay on Ken's schedule. When it came time for Club Crocodile's buffet dinner, we were more than ready to dig in. Using my injury for clout, I insisted on nixing tennis right after dinner to stay and linger over dessert. Over years of marriage to Ken, I'd learned there was a way to play the sympathy card, but to do it successfully you had to shove it in his face and mush it around a bit, otherwise he wouldn't notice you'd played it. I waved my swollen black and blue leg and our tennis game was abandoned.

After dinner the kids rushed back to the hotel room for T.V., leaving us alone to reminisce about past travel experiences. Still talking when they closed the restaurant, we took a cheese plate and night cap down to the deserted beach and snuggled on a cozy lounge chair to watch lights of moored sailboats twinkle in the bay.

Note to self: play the sympathy card more often.

November 21

Dragging my stiff, psychedelically bruised body out of bed, and dreading the run I promised myself after really enjoying the cheese section of the buffet, I reluctantly reached for my runners.

As always, getting out the door was the hardest part. Familiarity turned my mountain into the hill it really was. After our run, with the kids still sleeping, we headed to the beach to rent a catamaran. It was fully booked, but Ken begged and promised the lifeguard, if she squeezed us in, we'd be back in time for their next booking.

While a stiff breeze whisked us out to sea, I reclined, dangling a hand in the water (maybe a 1.5% chance of death by Box Jelly Fish sting) and discovered hidden shapes of animals in the fluffy clouds above. Ken was in control at the rudder, a regular Captain Cook, until the wind unexpectedly changed direction, causing the sail to swing across the catamaran and hit him in the head. Not quite Captain Cook after all, but certainly a guy with a good hard head. Shaking off the blow, he maintained an eye on the horizon with only the odd jerky paranoid glance back to the sail.

Heading out to sea was easy, getting back turned out to be a problem. The wind dialed down to a whisper, forcing us to slowly seesaw back and forth toward the shore. We were moving at a snail's pace while the rental gal stood on shore frantically waving us in. It wasn't like we weren't trying. All we could do was sheepishly shrug and feel terrible about messing up her schedule.

Don't make promises you can't keep

November 22

A 9:00 a.m. check-out time seemed so wrong. Half asleep, I stumbled to the bathroom and leaned on the bathroom sink until my eyes unglued. When they finally did, my reflection gave me a start. I'd gotten used to the natural look, but the unraveling of my unnatural was concerning. Chemical blonde highlights meant to start at the top of my head were now at eye level. A distinct halo-like line separated mousy brown on top and brassy blonde on the bottom. Even more disturbing, little grey hairs I'd never noticed before sprung out from my part line. My family pounded on the bathroom door but I wasn't leaving until every last one was plucked from my head.

Our ferry didn't head back to the mainland until the afternoon, giving us time to enjoy the resort. Ken hit the golf course, doing thirty-six holes in a row, quite an accomplishment considering you could fry an egg on the fairway. The kids and I headed for the pool. Parking myself comfortably under an umbrella, I worked on my daily trip journal. My new relationship with my lap top was still wrought with communication breakdowns. Hitting the key pad and hearing that miserable "boink" noise easily brought me to tears. As a poor speller, I'd never done much writing before, but with spell check and no one grading my work, I looked forward to capturing our days with words.

Back on the mainland, we hopped in the car and headed south, pulling into the small town of Rockhampton after dusk. With only two hotels in the whole place, the best we could do was a dump with no air conditioning. What a slap in the face after the Whitsundays.

We were moving our luggage in when a shrill scream made us stop. Makayla stood in the bathroom with her mouth still open pointing to a scurrying gecko running up the wall. Relieved that there was no real emergency, Ken and I laughed, thinking the gecko cute and explained to Makayla how mosquito-eating geckos were harmless and not to be feared. As Ken talked, my eyes drifted to two large, twitching antennae sticking out from the top of the shower curtain. Now it was my turn to scream. I ran out of the room while Makayla stayed in to give a play-by-play of Ken extracting a silver dollar-sized cockroach.

This was our first intimate experience with the cockroach and it left us feeling more than a bit "creeped out." Needing some air, I pulled open drapes to open a window exposing another unexpected scurrying gecko. Out came another scream and in came Ken. With a captive audience and nothing to kill, Ken broke into his favorite cockroach story. Back in the day, while playing college football in

Hawaii, he and some of his buddies bought an old beater car. Suspecting it might have a couple of cockroaches in it, he set off an extermination bomb and the next morning found four inches of disgusting dead cockroaches covering the seats and floor. Just the thought of it had the color crawling out of our faces.

Settling in to watch the rugby finals on television, everyone fidgeted and itched, until a close score distracted us. After the game, our bug phobia was pretty much forgotten until I got into bed to read and noticed movement out of the corner of my eye. A humungous cockroach sauntering across my pillow had me shooting out of bed. Suddenly, getting out of our cockroach infested hotel room and driving all night long seemed like a really good idea. The kids agreed, but Ken dragged us from the door where we stood in a fearful huddle, patiently explaining how true travelers put up with harmless cockroaches.

The next morning, very tired true travelers marked a Big Trip first – checking out before check-out time.

November 23

We were warmly welcomed at a home stay by Noel, Julianne and their eleven year old daughter, Megan. I hoped Megan and Makayla, being the same age, would become instant friends, but no matter how hard I tried pushing them together, they repelled like strong magnets.

On the trip, I'd noticed that both Mattson and Makayla seemed shy and withdrawn when it came to meeting new people. They weren't ones to initiate conversation and avoided eye contact. I made a note to add Steven *Covey's The Seven Habits of Highly Effective People* to their reading program.

For dinner that night, our hosts served what they called, a good old fashioned "Aussie Barby." It was similar to a Canadian barbeque minus everything but the meat. Good carnivores, those Australians. There were sausages (we'd call them Smokies), lamb chops and hamburger patties. Tasty meats left naked without buns, ketchup, mustard and barbeque sauce. Obviously Canadians and Australians weren't on the same culinary page. Their equivalent to our rich, creamy peanut butter was a black, tar-like substance called Vegemite – it's just my opinion, but it tasted like salty tar.

After dinner, we watched a video of Megan's Christmas dance production. I tried to concentrate on the group of sequin-covered dancers bouncing about in perpetual movement, but after ten minutes my eyes fell to half-mast. Our hosts gave us a play-by-play, excitedly pointing out upcoming moments not to be missed. I missed them. I did, however, realize something very important as I struggled through that video. They were us, we were them; sliced either way, we were both parents in love with our kids and everything they did. Their dance show could have easily been Mattson's gym meet or Makayla's dance competition.

Keep your home videos for yourself

November 24

Years ago, a dolphin became tangled and injured in a fishing net. A fisherman rescued the dolphin and nursed her back to health. When a bond formed between the two of them, she returned to his boat every morning to be hand fed. One day, to his delight, she swam up with a new baby in tow. The mother eventually died, but Mystic, the name the fisherman gave to the baby, still returns to Tin Can Bay for feeding every morning.

We arrived early at 6:45 a.m. and so did Mystic. Standing in waist deep water, Mystic fearlessly swam between us, touching our outstretched hands with his nose. We spent thirty minutes enjoying our very own personal wild dolphin experience and left just as a tour boat loaded with people arrived.

Getting up early for our dolphin encounter was worth the effort. Dealing with our ornery, tired kids for the rest of the day was another story.

Kids too early to rise can be your demise

November 25

While driving to Brisbane, the kids worked on their home schooling science project, asking questions all the while. Ken, the smart guy, answered most of them. He had, after all, been at the top of his class in high school. He'd even played on the "Reach for the Top" team (a televised, academic question and answer game show) until he got kicked off for choosing a basketball game over the show. All I remembered about High School was a perpetual broken heart from a string of unreciprocated crushes. It was hard to focus on your studies with such emotional drama going on all the time and likely the reason my response to most of the kids' questions was a clipped: "I don't think we took that at my school." By the time we arrived in Brisbane, it was obvious I'd learned little in high school and was lucky to be getting a second chance through the kids' home schooling.

At Brisbane's city limits, Ken did what he always did when we entered unknown territory; I was ordered to find a map in our *Lonely Planet* travel guide book. Finding one the size of a post it note, it showed only the city center. Rotating that book at every angle including upside down didn't help me figure out from which direction we were approaching. Meanwhile, Ken circled round-a-bouts waiting further instruction. After the third time around I felt like a kid spun round at a birthday party expected to pin the tail on the donkey. Giving up on me, Ken would grab the map to figure it out himself. At that point, I got comfortable and settled in for a good long city tour. On a positive note, it was a good way to get a feel for a place, even if Ken's tendency to merge into the oncoming lane while driving and map reading was a bit stressful. Personally, I thought we should just pull over at a gas station and get a proper map, but that never happened.

November 26

Waking early from a semi-trailer truck rumbling by, Ken managed to remain in a coma until I gave him a jab and asked if he'd heard the truck as well. Looking confused, his eyes fluttered as he agreed he must have. Since he was awake, heading to the South Bank for a run by the river seemed like a good idea.

After jogging past a sheer rock face scattered with climbers, Ken looked up while my gaze drifted forward to the museums and galleries directly ahead. Turning to each other we blurted out in unison "wouldn't it be great to" then lost our synchronization as Ken finished with "rock climb" and I with "go to the galleries."

Knowing we weren't on the same page, I tried some of Makayla's "get your own way" tactics, insisting we do something artsy. Sure enough, early that afternoon we sat as a family outside a gallery in warm sunlight diligently working on homemade Christmas decorations in a class found on-line. The hype for Christmas had begun.

November 27

Some days I felt I could run forever, some days, "not so much." Even though we ran by the ocean, it was a "not so much" kind of day. After forty-five minutes, I slumped into a seat on our home stay host's sunny deck feeling drained. Enjoying crunchy granola, fresh fruit and yogurt, we chatted about politics and travel and eventually settled on the subject of wine, something Max, our host was very passionate about. The next thing I knew, we were sipping vintage port from his well-stocked cellar at 10:30 in the morning. It wasn't going to be a "not so much" kind of day for long.

In the afternoon, fortified with more than just fiber and whole grain, we hit the beach in the town of Noosa Heads. This was truly the crème de la crème of beaches. Ken and the kids headed for the water while I carefully sculpted a body hugging lounge chair in the sand. Covering it with a towel and finding perfect support for my every curve, I closed my eyes and blissfully sighed until Ken's big head, like a storm cloud, blocked my sun. As I cooled down in his shadow he haughtily told me that the ocean without big waves was as boring as sitting in a bathtub. He wanted to leave immediately.

In my next life I'm marrying a soaker

Back at the house, dinner was served up with the best condiment of all; a robust red from Max's cellar substantially improving my opinion of the Australian "Barby."

November 28

With Ken off to work, we focused on home schooling then walked to the beach for boogie boarding. I analyzed the waves fearfully while the kids insisted they could teach me how. This from kids who'd only had one lesson from their dad, the very guy responsible for my introduction to the ocean. My "Ken" lesson came on our honeymoon in Hawaii. He marched me out into the water and held my hand until a huge wave crashed to shore and broke our bond. Knocked off my feet, that wave rolled me in sand like a sugar covered donut.

Mattson and Makayla were patient with me, even though I was a timid, slow learner. After multiple tries, miraculously, board, body and wave connected and, as the Beach Boys sing, I truly was "sitting on top of the world." I'd done it and after doing it, I was done.

It was dusk by the time we turned the corner onto our new home stay's street, on the island of Bribie. In the cul-de-sac, homes sparkled with hundreds of colorful Christmas lights. Our host Stan strung lights onto a tree while explaining that the residents of his street had entered a Christmas light decorating competition to be judged the next day. The timing of our arrival couldn't have been convenient, yet Stan and his family happily welcomed us. Our Servas hosts had all been comfortable letting guests fit into their schedules. It was such a contrast from the way I'd grown up. Life as we knew it stopped when company came over. My mom would scrub and polish, warning us kids she'd break our bloody necks if we messed up all her hard work. Admittedly her bark was worse than her bite – she couldn't hurt a flea, but those experiences made me an uptight hostess keen to please.

Entertaining doesn't have to be a human sacrifice

November 29

I'd be in big trouble if my mother saw the sunburns on my kids after their day boogie boarding. Trying to make myself feel better, I went on and on about how many times I'd reapplied their 45 SPF sunscreen while gently applying soothing aloe vera to their backs. Stan stood by listening to me and with conviction declared: "they burned badly because of the SPF in your sunscreen." According to him, I should have used tanning oil. At first I thought he was joking, but he was dead serious. Stan was a talker with strong opinions and views, often unorthodox, on many subjects. After a few hours of listening to his ramblings, I couldn't help wondering if he was a bit off.

It was a low day. The kids were miserable, I felt responsible for their misery and Stan was like a fly buzzing in my ear as he continued on with his out of the box opinions. Trying to stay politely engaged, I eventually needed a break. Driving to the mountains for a hike seemed like a good idea, but before getting out of the city, our rental car started acting up. Slipping out of gear and not responding to the gas pedal, Ken guided the car to the side of the road.

Giving the gear shift panel a good hard smack with his fist worked, but I doubted it would get us very far. Stalling and banging our way back to Stan's, Ken called the rental company expecting apologies and solutions but instead faced accusations and resistance. How dare he expect service on a Saturday! After a long conversation, their position was clear; nothing would be done unless the car completely died.

Being forced out onto the highway knowing your car would likely conk out somewhere in the middle of nowhere seemed ludicrous. There had to be a better solution. Passing the afternoon playing cards, I contemplated our options while disconnecting from Stan's perpetually moving mouth.

When evening finally came, Ken and I mixed a rum and eggnog (an exciting find at the grocery store) before joining Stan and his wife Diane outside in their Christmas wonderland. We listened to the hollow tone of life-sized plastic figurines dressed as carolers. They sang *Joy to the World* from concealed speakers while Stan talked about another weird and wacky idea. Being surrounded by all things

Christmas should have conjured up a warm and fuzzy Christmas glow, but like Stan, the eggnog seemed a bit off.

November 30

Getting up to go to a Sunday morning flea market at 5:30 a.m. made the kids groan, but taking the car for a drive in the hopes it would die while Stan followed behind us, seemed like a good idea.

When the car once again acted up on the way home Ken analyzed the situation. I could almost see the cogs of his brain turning. He was such a BEAKER. Beaker, pronounced boldly with slow enunciation on the first e to make it sound like BEEEEAKER, was Ken's nickname. It had been coined by his pro-football mates who figured putting his highly functioning brain in a beaker (the glass jars used in science experiments) and leaving it out on the football field would help the more mentally challenged players remember their plays. The Beaker thought hard for a few minutes, before proudly announcing he knew what was wrong with the car. It wasn't the transmission, it was the radiator. All we had to do was top it up with cool water and all would be well.

Our day wasn't a total bust. Back at our home stay, Stan's wife Diane surprised Mattson. She placed a homemade pumpkin pie in front him as Stan stepped up and affectionately draped his arm over her shoulders. It was a touching scene; one that made me feel badly for my irritation with him. I didn't have to agree with everything he said, but I did have to admit that he seemed to be a kind and loving man.

Charitably tolerate the idiosyncrasies of others

After filling up the radiator and saying goodbye, we began what I feared might be a disastrous trip to Brisbane. All went well until we approached the city limits. I was thinking my husband quite worthy of his Beaker nickname when the car stalled and my heart sank. We were close, but still so far from the city. On the downhill side of a large hill, Ken put the car in neutral. We coasted for two miles, before following an exit sign to a downhill ramp leading to a residential suburb. The car continue to crawl forward as we yelled "go baby go" and eventually drifted into the large parking lot of a shopping mall. When all momentum was lost we sat perfectly placed between the lines of a parking spot.

Believe in miracles

Ken left in the tow truck, forcing the kids and me to unload our belongings from the car into a shopping cart and wait for a taxi. When fifty minutes came and went, we doubted it would ever come. Standing in the dark beside our shopping cart of belongings, we felt like street people about to face a night on the pavement. Our cab did eventually pull up, but not before we felt a terrifying glimmer of the desperation of homelessness.

December 1

Mattson had developed a strange rash I didn't recognize. Initially, it looked like eczema, but steroid cream made it worse. Over the course of a week, it spread over the back of his legs, oozing and forming scabs. After online research, I came up with a diagnosis of impetigo, an infectious bacterial skin infection. Maybe he shouldn't have gone to gym all week?

Mattson hesitated before swallowing the pills I pulled out from our stash of antibiotics brought from home. After all, he reminded me, I wasn't a real doctor. I was only a dentist. As a dentist, I assured him I knew all about gums, and gums and skin were one and the same. Unfortunately his doubt ruined any chance for the placebo effect, if in fact I was wrong.

December 2

Having heard a great deal about Brisbane's amazing botanical gardens, we decided to go. I say we, but Mattson wasn't on board. Activities not involving roller coasters or food didn't excite him much and anything to do with photosynthesis made him shudder. His reaction probably stemmed from a bad childhood experience. At about age three he totally freaked out in the Zoo's desert terrain botanical gardens, thinking the "pricklies" (cacti) were out to get him.

He was so unhappy to be at the botanical gardens, he launched a mission to ensure his unhappiness didn't go unnoticed. Bugging his sister and moving like a tortoise through sand were just a couple of maneuvers in his assault. I suspected his sister's new status as official trip photographer added to his misery. She'd taken a shine to photography and enjoyed many accolades from us on her creative compositions. She joyfully buzzed around the gardens taking one picture after another. Praising Makayla seemed to intensify Mattson's quest to drive us all crazy. Only the exit sign made him stop.

Imbalanced sibling attention= unbalanced parents

December 3

En route to Manly, a suburb just outside of Brisbane, we stopped to buy tickets for theme parks. Visiting all three parks located on the Gold Coast didn't work with our budget. The kids squabbled about which park to visit, as a clerk strategically passed by and offered up a pamphlet on discounted packages. You could go to parks A and B on Saturday for price X or parks A, B, and C, on Wednesday and Friday for price Y, surprisingly less expensive. On it went, with enough variables that even the oversized Beaker brain required a pencil to calculate. In the end we walked out with tickets for multiple visits to all three parks. "What a deal!" Ken exclaimed, even though we spent way more than originally planned.

Realize the genius of marketing before your money is gone

We signed up as guests for a sailing regatta. Stepping aboard the sail boat, Makayla blurted out "this canoe doesn't look anything like the ones in Canada." Her comment blatantly confirmed our lack of sailing experience. The captain, slightly taken aback, decided a few pointers were in order before granting us crew status.

Our suddenly dead serious captain told us what to do when he yelled "tack." To turn the boat, we had to quickly shimmy from one side of the boat to the other, staying low to avoid being hit by a swinging boom. From there, the crew jumped in to tell us their sailing mishap stories featuring broken bones and unintentional trips overboard into shark-infested waters. So much for relaxing and watching the ocean pass by.

Setting off with our jovial crewmates, I tried looking casual and relaxed, but when the captain shouted "tack," my movements were that of a person fleeing for their life. I was so busy concentrating on staying low and not tripping on projectiles that I pushed and stepped all over my kids. My actions provoked a chorus of: "Mooooother, just chill!" And that was exactly what I tried to do as I adjusted crooked sunglasses slipping down my sweaty nose and geared up for the next tack.

Back on dry land, we poured out copious thanks to our crew and drove on to Surfers Paradise. When we finally arrived, every hotel was booked, forcing us to stay at a rundown small motel. Turning from the reception desk toward our room, the desk clerk chimed out: "Don't mind the Schoolies!" We wondered what a "Schoolie" was, but were too tired to ask.

December 4

After a long sleepless night listening to fun loving drunks singing at the top of their lungs, we passed back our keys. "Those damn Schoolies" our clerk whined. It was time to ask the question not asked the night before. "What is a Schoolie?" The answer, spat out with distain: "recently graduated high school students out to party during a weeklong post-graduation celebration."

An unsuccessful hotel search had us slugging our way back from whence we'd come. Surfers Paradise was literally swarming with Schoolies: a generic group of late teens all wearing baggy cargo shorts and wrinkled ratty t-shirts. They pressed cell phones to their ears and held boxed pizza in their hands. Ken and I had to be the only ones over twenty in the whole town.

If you're dropping in, find out who's going to be home

Ken left for work while I took the kids to the bus stop. They were off to the Wet and Wild water park; I was going Christmas shopping. As they stepped onto the bus and turned to say goodbye, worry pulled up and stood in my way. What if they drowned or didn't get off at the right bus stop? WHAT IF, WHAT IF, WHAT IF … I'd had enough of WHAT IFS. I was going shopping!

December 5

Rain pounding on the window woke me. It was supposed to be a run day, but the rain gave us an excuse to linger over breakfast. Our topic of conversation: Who's your favorite actor and why? On and on I went about Tom Cruise, unconcerned about the passage of time.

Time and idle chatter go together like cream and sugar

Ken and the kids set out for another day at the water park; two visits costing only slightly more than one, but Ken hadn't calculated in the implications of leaving me free for yet another day of Christmas shopping.

On my side of the family there was a tradition to go a bit overboard at Christmas. My mom started her Christmas shopping in August, determined to find absolutely perfect gifts and lots of them, for her precious family. By the time Christmas finally arrived, after a few cycles of buying, hiding, forgetting and buying again, we'd end up with a decadent mountain of artistically wrapped presents under our meticulously decorated real pine tree. Mimicking my childhood experience, I needed another day at the mall to find more perfect presents for my precious family.

Beginning to once again scour the mall, I stopped dead in my tracks and remembered – I wasn't my mother. Sure I loved my family, but I hated shopping. My sparsely filled closet of clothes, some dating back to high school, was proof of that. I couldn't possibly recreate the Christmases we had in Canada so why was I spending money on things my kids didn't need in order to grow a big pile of presents under a tree we wouldn't even have? Letting out a big sigh, I left the mall, happy to be me.

Alter tradition until it fits just right

Dec 6

Supposedly there was a drought in Queensland, but it never seemed to stop raining. To make matters worse, our nice warm rain from the day before turned cold, putting a serious damper on our plans for the day, but even a hurricane wouldn't have kept the kids from their amusement parks.

The girls headed to Sea World while the boys went to Dream Land. Makayla, completely dolphin crazy, wasn't bothered by the weather. We sat in the dolphin show's empty stands huddled together under plastic rain ponchos while she tried to take the perfect picture of dolphins all lined up in the air after a big jump. Clicking at just the right moment, with them evenly spaced at the height of their arc, was no easy feat. We trudged back to that show multiple times throughout the day until the camera batteries finally died. Even with all of those pictures, Makayla still wasn't satisfied she'd aced the shot.

Spending every moment of every day with my kids was exposing every nuance of their personalities. I was concerned to see Makayla's screaming perfectionist. Wanting to do something perfectly had always seemed like a good thing to me, but introspective time on the trip was leading me to believe otherwise. Grabbing and holding on to gratification was tough when good was never quite good enough. Makayla fumed while looking over the photos she'd taken, pointing out minute defects in each one. Suddenly a question popped into my head. If I could change and let go of the quest for perfection, would that change positively influence my daughter? They say daughters become their mothers. What better reason to get under the hood for my own personality overhaul.

At the end of the day, the boys picked us up, and down the Gold Coast we went – off to another home stay.

It seemed to take forever to get to Maclean. A full moon lit the sky and misty wisps of fog and pelting rain decreased visibility creating a spooky scene. We drove and drove until the road ended at the bank of a river, forcing us to stop. Engulfed in a thick soupy mist at

110

the river's edge, we weren't quite sure what to do. Suddenly the image of a man's face materialized through the opaque condensation on my window scaring me into my now notorious gasp and jump. Thin lips in a weathered older man's face mouthed "Roll down your window." Too stunned to respond, Ken gave me a jab. In came driving rain and harsh words. "Are you get'en on or what?" he hissed. "Get on to what?" I questioned, but he'd stomped away. Standing stooped like a scrawny hillbilly, he waved us towards the river. Like freshly scolded children, we drove onto a cement pad not much bigger than the car. Before pulling us across the river with a manual pulley system, the man drew a finger across his neck indicating we should cut our engine. On the other side, not sure what to do, Ken started driving off the plank, but hit the brakes when the guy jumped up and down motioning for us to stop. Moments passed as the sound of the churning river closed in. Looking to our hillbilly with trepidation, he raised a fist, and with a look of disgust waved us on.

We rang our host's doorbell two hours late. Thankfully Bob opened his door and flashed us a big, all teeth present smile.

December 7

I awoke to the smell of food cooking, but I couldn't match the aroma to anything breakfast. We collected the family from our mattresses strewn across the living room floor and shyly made our way into a sunny kitchen. Bob hovered over a steaming skillet frying yellow tomatoes and onions (poor Makayla, traumatized by the onion once again). He looked like a big strong construction worker, but in fact was a nurse in midwifery who loved to garden and turn wood into bowls. With great enthusiasm he flicked off the skillet to take us for a tour of his garden and work shop.

Passionate people are happy people

Getting back to cooked tomatoes, they went down smoothly until Bob started talking about human encounters with Australia's poisonous spiders and snakes; critters found in his very own backyard; the very yard we'd just walked through! We listened with amazement while he told us that his dad died from a brown snake bite. To top that off, people living across the street had just found that same kind of snake coiled around the base of their toilet. The hairs on the back of my neck sprung to attention. I searched the outdoor deck, where we sat, for creatures that slither and crawl. Bob assured me the risks of being bitten were minimal, but it seemed like a good time to say our goodbyes and get back on the road to Sydney.

December 8

I needed a sleep in after spending the night at the Formula One hotel. Appropriately named, their rooms weren't a whole lot bigger than a race car. I ended up on the top bunk studying a ceiling so low it practically tickled my nose. Blindly navigating our dark room in search of an over the counter sleep aid landed me on Mattson, asleep in the bottom bunk. He reacted to my foot by flinging an arm and hitting his sister in the head. They groaned as I jumped on Ken, asleep on the floor. From there, I stumbled into a dresser and stubbed my toe. By the time I crawled back up to bed, I was so beat up and exhausted I probably could have fallen asleep unaided.

At sixty dollars a night, including breakfast, Ken was in love with the Formula One. In fact, he started contemplating a franchise in Canada. I didn't share his enthusiasm. Canadians wouldn't settle for rooms smaller than a pick-up truck.

December 9

At a free show, we met a tall, lean guy about twenty-five years old. He sat on a bar stool in the centre of a stage decorated to look like the Australian outback and shared his life story. Raised by his mother, he never knew his father and didn't find out, until his late teens, that he was aboriginal. Embarking on a quest to find his roots, he united with his grandfather. In him, he found a mentor who taught him about aboriginal legends and music.

The didgeridoo he played looked like nothing more than a hollow log. It was five feet long and five inches round. Puffing up his cheeks and blowing into it produced a deep droning sound. While he played, his hand danced and depicted wild animals of the outback. Doing both must have been like patting your head and rubbing your belly at the same time, yet he effortlessly told wordless stories.

December 10

We'd worked it out the night before. It would be a Big Trip first. We were going to spend the whole day at the beach. Ken dropped us off on his way to work and there we sat, the only people on a gorgeous long stretch of white sand with nothing, not a single bush or tree, standing between us, a blazing sun, and the crashing ocean.

We didn't have beach supplies. I figured we were seasoned flexible travelers, able to forgo frills. Our needs were simple and besides, I had the essentials: a few books, hats and sunscreen. Admittedly, I wasn't an experienced sun goddess, but still, we were on Bondi beach, one of the most famous and beautiful beaches in the world.

Within minutes of our arrival, Makayla and Mattson plunked down in the sand and started fighting over the *Lord of the Rings* book I'd brought. Makayla was suddenly burning with desire for the one book I'd brought for her brother. From there it was all downhill. Mattson, whining that he was hot and that the sun was too bright for his eyes, refused to put on a hat. Sand on his skin bothered him and cooling off in the ocean was out of the question. Didn't I know that salt water made him itchy? Makayla carried on. She too was hot, but didn't want to strip down to her bathing suit. Why? She really couldn't say. She did however tell me in no uncertain terms that taking off her socks and letting her bare feet touch the sand made them dry and she really hated that. I looked at them in disbelief. How could this be happening? Kids were supposed to love the beach. My watch read 9:10 a.m.; we had 6 hours and 50 minutes before Ken returned, assuming he was on time.

It got hotter. By 10:00 a.m. it seemed we might melt into a puddle of goo with the *Lord of the Rings* book and our ball caps, the only nonorganic substances left to mark our existence. We had to abort the beach. Up a steep hill we dragged our miserable selves. Eventually finding a grassy park with trees, shade and an ocean view, it seemed perfect until Mattson complained he was cold.

By 10:30 a.m. we decided it was time for lunch. Unfortunately the restaurants didn't open until 11:00. We had to dust off our old Tokyo skill of killing time in a convenience store. The second the restaurant opened, we lingered over lunch, asking for water refills. When the place closed at 2:00 p.m., our waiter wearily bid us goodbye. I would expect, under his breath, he added "good riddance."

With only two hours until Ken might show up, we settled in back at the beach. I started to read. A chorus of morning complaints started up once again. That was it, I'd had it. They'd pushed me too far. Needing to be free of them, I stomped off down the beach. At a beach rental shop, desperation told me a few beach frills might be a good thing. With two boogie boards in hand, I ordered the kids out into the water.

Finally finding the peace to settle into my book, it was as if someone reset the clock two hours ahead. After spending the whole day trying to get my kids in the water, do you think I could get them out? And of course Ken was on time and parked illegally.

I laughed, when after frantically piling into the car, Ken asked enthusiastically how our day at the beach had been. I simply couldn't explain how heavenly Bondi Beach had gone so wrong.

The beach isn't for everyone

December 11

Over breakfast I chatted with our new home stay host, Jan. She was a talented painter. It seemed serendipitous how, over and over again, talented artists came into my life, encouraging me to get going with my own art.

December 12

What a morning! A kookaburra outside our window called out. It sounded like a witch's cackle escalating in volume and morphing into the likes of a wounded howler monkey. The addition of rumbling

114

thunder and rain pinging off the window ensured I was up for the day by 4:30 a.m.

The weather gave us an excuse for a lazy morning to visit with our hosts. There was even time to connect by phone with family back home. For once it wouldn't be the middle of the night when we called.

I always had trouble figuring out different time zones. Information online claimed the 24 hour time zone corresponds to medians of longitude. Each zone is 15 degrees apart and each time zone differs from its adjacent zone by one hour (earlier or later). That way, the time in each zone aligns with the local solar times of sunrise and sunset. Interesting information, but a bit too complicated for me. I'd stay with asking The Beaker.

At the Hunter Valley, we checked into a cozy, two bedroom villa. We paid for a single room with two double beds online, but when Ken politely asked for an upgrade, they moved us to a lovely two bedroom suite. I worried the clerk might be offended when he asked, but instead she smiled and pleasantly answered "certainly Mr. Moore, let me see what I can do for you."

When asking for upgrade,
you have everything to gain and nothing to lose

December 13

Trying to fit in a training run before our 10:30 a.m. winery tour was awful. The run, like the long rows of vines we ran beside, seemed to go on forever. I didn't want to follow those vines; I wanted to drink their fruit in wine.

When wine tasting time finally arrived the sampling began. I questioned starting before lunch, but hey, in my world, samples were like little bits of nothing, really too small for your body to even notice. Drinking a sample was like shaving off a sliver of cream pie with your finger. The pie after the shave didn't look noticeably smaller. After all, you took next to nothing. Extrapolating from there – how could multiple sips of nothing possibly do any harm? And so I set to work trying to learn the subtle nuances of wine, unaware that even miniscule fractions eventually add up to a pie.

Sensory alteration came after swirling maybe my sixth, seventh or eighth sample, little bits of nothing were hard to keep track of. I couldn't tell the difference between black pepper, cherry or cardboard; the time had come to head home to our neglected children.

By early evening my brain pounded as if wanting out from my skull; I had to pass on a family game of tennis. Desperately searching for aspirin, I obviously needed to change my philosophy on samples.

December 14

I awoke to a persistent headache and downed more aspirin. Ken felt no ill effect and enthusiastically planned another busy day.

Lazing about in the morning, we enjoyed our spacious upgraded quarters then jumped in the car and made a stop at the Blue Mountains on our way back to Sydney. Standing at a lookout point gazing down on a carpet of gum trees, we tried to see the blue haze our tour book claimed the trees gave off. All I saw was green. Thankfully a good long hike effectively cleared my head.

On the drive back, everyone but Ken wanted to rush back to Sydney to watch the last episode of Survivor. Frustration set in when we had to stop at every observation area we passed. Compelled to walk each site's full distance, Ken stopped and meditated over scenery, as if every step drastically changed the view.

We'd just left the mountains and settled into cruising speed on a multilane highway when the dreaded sound of a police siren came up on us from behind. Just what we needed, a speeding ticket and more delay. A burly police officer sauntered over and asked Ken how fast he thought he was going. When he sheepishly croaked: "about 110 kilometers," the officer shook his head and drawled "now that's a problem mate. You're not going fast enough to stay in the right overtaking lane." As the officer began to write us a ticket, Ken blurted out in disbelief: "you mean I was going too slow?"

Finally a stroke of luck. Feeling justified to drive at 130 kilometers an hour, we made it back to Sydney in no time flat.

December 15

One last night at the Formula One Hotel. Lying in my top bunk, I tried a new getting-to-sleep strategy and counted the beats of my pounding heart like sheep. Ninety-nine, the ceiling can't cover your mouth and nose like cellophane, ninety-eight, the ceiling won't collapse on you, ninety-seven, yes you can breathe, and on and on until back at zero I started all over again. Somewhere around my ninth countdown I must have fallen asleep. Opening my eyes to morning light was a surprise; I actually slept. It seemed I'd won one little battle in my war against fear.

Arriving early in the afternoon for our flight to Singapore, we made it on time and settled in to enjoy their wonderful service. Believing the flight was four hours long, I happily drank a combo of water and wine, following my new dehydration, rehydration plan, when the captain came over the P.A. system announcing an arrival time three hours later than I expected. Not on the seven hour bladder control program, I was in trouble. Airplane bathrooms were just so small. What if the door jammed, or the airplane crashed when I was in there? Obviously my war wasn't over yet. Such thoughts had me anchored to my seat with legs crossed, desperately trying to hold on until the plane landed. When it did, look out if you crossed my path as I darted to the bathroom.

Wine tasting

Car trouble

SINGAPORE

December 15

Why our cheap hotel was surprisingly luxurious became apparent during our evening stroll. Scantily clad ladies of the night loitered around every light post seductively calling out evening greetings to Ken.

On our run the next morning, street people stepped in for the hookers, reaching out hands for spare change. Red light districts weren't known to be safe, but Ken, a good old boy from small town Alberta, never worried about such things. I drank in his positive energy, throwing caution to the wind huddled under his shadow and followed along like a good little lemming.

After surviving the run and licking the remains of a pork bun from my lips, the efficient MRT Singapore subway system whisked us all downtown. We wandered along, window shopping and melting in excessive heat and humidity until Mattson came down with a severe bleeding nose. In a bathroom at a nearby food court he gushed blood into the sink while Ken searched for toilet paper or hand towels, anything with absorbency to help clean him up. Makayla and I looked as well, but none of us found anything useful. Poor Mattson was in a messy, paperless situation.

We were learning that Singapore is a rigidly controlled country. Petty crimes like stealing were punishable by limb removal, and fines were handed out for not flushing the toilet or chewing gum. They must have had a thing about paper products as well. In Singapore, any kind of orifice wiping was a problem.

Carry a little "just in case" tissue

We'd just gotten Mattson cleaned up when Makayla started complaining about terrible pain under her armpit. To make it feel better, she had to hold her hand up and out in front of her like a Third Reich soldier heiling Hitler. She parted couples holding hands on our way back to the hotel.

Impetigo is very contagious

BALI

December 16 - 27

Flying to Bali, we met up with my sister and her family for Christmas. We pulled ourselves away from the pool at the hotel a couple of times to sightsee, but when Mattson came down with a nasty case of dysentery and barfed all over the floor in some restaurant overlooking a volcano, we lost our stomachs for long hot drives around the island.

Having a break from trip planning was such a treat. Ken relaxed, not having to drive, and I relaxed, not having to watch him drive. We chilled and settled in to enjoy tasty Balinese food and the best perk of all: daily one hour massages for only $12.00 US.

Christmas, as we knew it, was a million miles away, but I was determined to recreate some of our Canadian traditions in Bali. While shopping in one of Kuta's department stores, we passed a Christmas display featuring a grouping of laminated paper Christmas trees about two to three feet high. They were adorable and the perfect size for our hotel room. I had to have one. My family thought my obsession foolish, but undeterred, I found a clerk and asked if they were for sale. She flashed a big bright Balinese smile and insisted I go ahead and take one for free. Feeling like a thief with that tree under my arm as I walked out of the store, I didn't care. I'd be bringing a little piece of Christmas back to our hotel room.

It took one second to put up our little plastic tree; unlike the tree toppling fiascos my dad endured trying to mount a towering, frozen, real pine tree. We were ready for popcorn garland and our homemade Brisbane ornaments in no time.

There is joy in simplicity

We had the tree – next came the treats. Making two of our favorite Christmas sweets was easier said than done. The Balinese grocery stores didn't have the ingredients I needed. Determined to improvise I asked at restaurants for missing ingredients and at an expatriate store found a stale fifteen dollar bag of mini colored marshmallows. The peanut butter balls and cornflake coconut almond squares I concocted were imposters and tasted nothing like those from home, but even so, they still helped us press into place another piece of our "how to bring Canadian Christmas to Bali" puzzle.

Christmas Eve, was a bit of a disappointment. The Hyatt's Christmas church ceremony was canceled, sending us back to my sister's Christmas Eve party. We didn't stay long. The kids sat forlorn and sullen in the living room while we mingled with their guests and my stomach started to gurgle and churn from Bali Belly (dysentery.) We'd ordered virgin Pina Coladas from room service for the kids, but a fancy creamy drink and my imposter treats couldn't compare to their Christmas traditions of singing carols around the piano, playing games and gorging on sweets that actually tasted good. As Ken and I politely socialized, it hit me. We'd forgotten the most important piece of the puzzle – making the night all about the kids.

Back at our hotel, Ken took Mattson and Makayla out by the pool to watch a movie on the computer while I went to bed. It was only 8:30 but I felt terrible. As I lay there feverish and cramping, home sickness washed over me. At forty-three years of age, this was my first Christmas Eve, ever, away from my parents. I desperately wanted my own bed and my mom and dad.

Thankfully, I felt better Christmas morning. We found a television station playing traditional English Christmas music and watched the kids look into stockings concocted from hotel towels. Starting to open gifts, Ken and I barely broke through the tape on newspaper wrapping when Mattson and Makayla, who'd done most of their shopping in Balinese markets, excitedly blurted out their bartering stories. Each one had a similar theme: how they'd used creative antics to get vendors down to crazy low prices. Their tales were Ken's best Christmas present. Nothing made him happier than knowing he was molding two chips off the old block.

Unknowingly, Makayla and I bought each other exactly the same dolphin shell necklace. I gushed with emotion as she did up my clasp and I did up hers. We hadn't been able to bring Christmas as we knew it to Bali, but we'd captured its spirit, creating beautiful memories we'd take home.

When you're with your family, home is where you are

Before we knew it, twelve days had passed. It was time to say goodbye. I was going to miss my sister, brother-in-law and their adorable children, not to mention our nice hotel with real feather pillows, and buffet breakfast. The time had come to close our bulging suitcases filled with Christmas loot and get back on the road.

Our next stop would be South East Asia: We had no plans and not a clue how we'd spend the next six weeks.

Visiting a temple in Bali

Christmas in Bali

Christmas Eve fancy drinks for Mattson and Makayla

Christmas morning in Bali

SINGAPORE AGAIN

December 28

    We arrived on time for our flight to Singapore. Travel days seemed to be getting easier, but not wanting to jinx it, I quickly pretended I hadn't noticed. Once on board, separated from Ken and the kids, I buckled my seat belt and immediately stuck my nose into a book. As I read, a lively conversation between two people a few rows up interrupted me. They'd obviously just met and were having a gay old time getting acquainted. Returning to my book, I had to admit that I rarely met people on planes. Come to think of it, I pretty much stuck to my tried and true friends no matter where I was. I was, after all, a busy girl who hated wasting precious time and wasn't idle chit chat with strangers you'd never see again just that? Wasn't it better to do something constructive like read a book? Thinking about it, my philosophy was a bit antisocial for a girl who considered herself a social extrovert. Maybe I wasn't quite the person I'd always thought I was.

    I sat and pondered my revelation. Both of the people I was listening to seemed so engaged and interested in what the other was saying. Maybe I needed to seize the moment and be the person I thought I was. After all, I had the time. Willing myself to start a conversation with the gal sitting beside me, I sucked in a deep breath and, turning a bit too aggressively, zealously blurted out: "How did you like Bali?" Slightly taken aback, she quickly recovered, broke into a big smile and launched into an interesting descriptive narrative. We spent the rest of the flight talking. We even exchanged e-mail addresses before landing. I'd made a friend, maybe only for the moment, but in that moment she'd left her mark on me. Listening to her Bali experience, which was quite different from mine, was like trying on a pair of sunglasses with lenses tinted a different color. Her experience, colored by a different view point, actually enhanced my Bali memories.

    In Singapore, we checked back into the same old hookerville hotel and started getting serious about our South East Asia travel plans. Where should we start? Should we travel by bus or plane? What countries should we visit? How far were the distances between countries? How much time should we spend in each place? The decisions were overwhelming. What we needed was a travel agent.

At a mall with multiple small travel agent shops, it took time to break free from paralyzing indecision to pick one. When we did, we stood in front of an agent, opening and closing our mouths like fish out of water. Condensing our unique needs into single syllables was impossible. We soon gave up.

Needing something to lift our spirits, a theater across the street drew us in. Watching the afternoon matinee of *Return of the King*, the last movie in the *Lord of the Rings* trilogy, was just the break we needed. Makayla couldn't have been more thrilled. She was so obsessed with the first two movies, she'd watched them over and over again on our laptop until she could recite each character's dialogue verbatim.

The movie was fantastic. No one could have loved it more than Makayla, yet tears trickled down her cheeks on our way home. For her, watching the last movie of the series brought the story to an end and that finality, like the death of a loved one, left her mourning a loss. Over the next day or so, she went through every stage of grief until we wished we could lose her.

December 29

In the morning Ken and I revisited a travel agent and learned about a special hopper airfare pass where you could book three to six flights at a reduced cost; savings increased the more you flew. The BEAKER moved to the edge of his seat, excited to calculate.

It was one of those days when everything is a struggle. You get lost and can't find your map. You have to go to the bathroom and by the time you find one, it's just a bit too late. After emptying what's left in your bladder, you realize you're thirsty, but no water can be found. Before long, it feels like you've been walking in the desert for days. Along with thirst comes hunger, stabbing your guts while you desperately search for an elusive restaurant. To make matters worse, not one of the multitudes of people you ask for help has the courtesy to speak your language.

Happy travelers don't need instant gratification

Dinner at the food court

More pork buns for breakfast

Ken makes a list

THAILAND

December 30

Outside the airport, there were no taxis to be found. We stood in a fish ball of tourists as loitering locals selling rides darted in at us like big tuna feeding. Sliding deeper into the ball, shouts for different fares left us confused. I told Ken we should pay whatever the nicest looking guy wanted us to pay to get out of there, but Ken wasn't intimidated. He patiently hunkered down to figure out what was going on. Our tourist ball was completely devoured when, in no uncertain terms, Ken announced what he would pay.

Beware of the insecurity of ignorance

December 31

Hotel rooms were hard to find. We checked out of an expensive room away from the tourist strip and finally found something in Karon Beach. It wasn't much. To sleep, we had to move two single beds together and sleep three sideways with one on the floor. No one complained. We were a block from the ocean on New Year's Eve in Phuket, Thailand.

The minute we checked in, Ken started phoning around to dive schools. He'd always dreamed we'd dive together as a family on our Big Trip. When we talked about it back in Calgary it seemed possible, but the reality of it scared me to death. It seemed to me that diving and claustrophobia went together like box jellyfish and unprotected skin. As I pulled Ken away from the phone, I insisted it wasn't time to worry about such things; it was time to party.

We set out for New Year's Eve in a Tuk Tuk (an open air vehicle with a motorcycle front and mini pickup truck back) and wildly swerved in and out of traffic, blinking away flying hair, on a twisting coastal road.

Our crazy ride had me thinking we'd be welcoming the New Year at heaven's gate, but somehow we managed to step back onto solid ground at Patong Beach. On the main strip, our senses reeled. From small electronic and souvenir shops lit with flashing lights, party music blared. One block down, closer to the ocean, seafood restaurants displayed their fresh catch, still dripping with sea water, in ice filled carts. Tourists passing by contemplated fresh fish for dinner. Some backed away from a 200 pound great white shark strung up and bleeding from where shark steaks had been cut away.

We walked for a while, taking it all in, until hunger encouraged us to find a restaurant. Attracted to candles flickering by the water, we scored the last table at a restaurant close to the shoreline. Excited with our view, we dug our bare feet into soft white sand (well everyone but Makayla – she certainly didn't want dry feet).

Gentle waves mixed with the soft hum of conversation while the sky filled with helium balloon torches. High above us, they glowed like candles on a centurion's birthday cake. We sat and laughed about some of our more colorful Big Trip moments until exploding fireworks marked the coming of the New Year. Raising our glasses to 2004, we kissed and hugged, ready for a new year of adventure.

Jan 1, 2004

With no planned activities for the day, we slept late. Considering our bizarre sleeping arrangement and the noise on the street all night long I was surprised I'd slept at all. Traveling was definitely having an effect on me. Back home, I needed my own bed, a feather pillow, silence and the right amount of darkness to fall asleep. Now, after just four months, I was sleeping sideways on a communal bed while firecrackers practically exploded in my face. If only the guy at the travel store, who teased me about being a high needs princess, could see me now.

Ken was back on his quest to find a dive school. Wanting no part of it, the kids and I went for dinner. We settled in at a casual place by the sea, ordered fruit shakes and waited for Ken. When he didn't show, we carried on and ate dinner. When he still didn't show, we were in trouble. I had no money and getting home involved a long walk on a pitch-black beach. Apologizing to the staff and promising to return and pay, I nervously grabbed the kid's hands and strutted out into an inky abyss.

Navigating the beach with no moon was tough. My heart pounded as I anticipated attacks and muggings with every step. When, quite literally, we ran into Ken, I immediately started in on him, but he had a good excuse for not showing up. There had been an accident outside the dive shop between a Tuk Tuk and a motorcycle. The injured driver wasn't wearing a helmet and sustained serious injuries. Ken sat with him for well over an hour doing what he could before a pickup truck, their version of an ambulance, finally arrived to carry him off.

Lend a helping hand whenever you can

After a long silence, Ken jubilantly announced that he'd booked our dive course. The kids cheered. I felt sick.

January 2

Down at the beach, we had pre-dive course homework to keep us busy. I tried to memorize every word in our instruction manual, hoping knowledge would edge out fear. So focused was I, that a big juicy drop of face sweat exploding on my page made me jump as if a bomb had gone off.

At dinner we couldn't wait to order fruit shakes. They were our new passion. Our unique concoctions were swapped and compared and when dinner arrived the passing around continued. Some would call it eating Asian style. We called it a competition.

Deciding to take a break from the beach we signed up for a tour to Phang Nga Bay. When the pick-up van arrived close to an hour late we had one more reason to love Thailand; they ran on Moore time. We picked up people until the van was full then continued picking up more. When it seemed we were running out of stagnant hot air, I was about to scream: "Let me out!" when we transferred to a larger bus. The rest of the tour, filled with caves, monkeys, temples, floating villages and amazing dagger like rock formations jutting from the sea, all provided great photo opportunities. I was madly snapping off shots when our Nikon digital, just back from its second repair, died.

Some things can't be fixed

January 4

The dreaded day had come. Dive school began.

We met our instructor, Paul, a burly English bloke in his late twenties, and spent the morning in the class room. All was well until he showed a video previewing the dive skills we'd do in the pool after lunch. I was one hour away from having to seal off my nose and mouth with a mask and regulator. Seized with fear, I paced back and forth while everyone left the room for lunch. Four words raced over and over again in my mind: I can't do this! I was in the middle of a panic-induced meltdown when Ken returned and quickly recognized my need for psychological counseling.

I wasn't in a good place. The thought of the kids seeing my fear, making me feel weak and helpless, was appalling, and I certainly didn't want to disappoint Ken and ruin his family dive dream. Ken, oh how I resented him at that moment; he was the one who'd pushed me into the class knowing full well I was claustrophobic. He should have known that when I said I wanted to dive I really didn't, but Ken was a wise man who knew me well. He offered up just the right therapy; telling me there was no doubt in his mind I could dive if I chose to, but the decision to push for it was mine. He would love me no matter what, even if I decided to quit.

How I hated the quit word. I was a lot of things, but I wasn't a quitter. No longer able to sulk under the premise that Ken was making me do it, I realized I really did want to dive for me and no one else. Joining the kids for lunch I pretended to be "normal me" while forcing lunch into a hostile stomach.

Standing at the edge of the pool, poured into my skin tight wet suit and trying to support a heavy oxygen tank on my back, I really did feel like I had the weight of the world on my shoulders. Sweat poured from my brow, making the cool water look inviting. I took the plunge and jumped in.

138

Once in the pool, we sat on the bottom and Paul began teaching us skills. He would demonstrate and we would mimic. He had removed, cleared and replaced his regulator and was pointing at me to do the same. My heart skipped a beat. Forcing my hand to my mouth, I removed the air source, paused, panicked and looked back up to the surface of the water. All I had to do was stand up and clean beautiful fresh air could be mine. If I stayed underwater and put the regulator back in my mouth it could be full of water, water I would inhale and choke on. I really wanted to stand up. I looked into the wide anticipating eyes of Paul motioning for me to put the regulator back into my mouth, I looked at my family's wide expectant eyes signaling me to put the regulator back into my mouth. I looked back up to the surface and to Paul who now forcefully gestured as if saying: "put the damn thing in your mouth!" Not wanting to make him mad, I stuck it in and desperately sucked for air.

I'm a pleaser

Paul shook my hand and I felt a split second of jubilation, but then we were on to the next skill.

The afternoon progressed. I received many handshakes and somehow survived the first day of our training.

At dinner that night, we laughed about the events of the day. I was teased about my lengthy freeze between regulator out and regulator in. Mattson got it for holding his breath, because holding your breath in deep water can make your lungs overinflate and pop like a balloon, and Makayla amused us when a button on her regulator got stuck, causing it to leak air and slither through the water like a snake with gas. Although Ken was an experienced diver and completed all his skills effortlessly, he got the biggest chuckle for constantly correcting Paul. BEAKER Ken seemed to think he knew a bit more than the dive master.

After dinner, reality set in. We had homework, an early morning and another day of challenges before us. When I laid my head on the pillow I was exhausted, but sleep didn't come.

January 5

The next morning, feeling tired and frustrated, I toyed with my breakfast while the rest of my family took advantage of a buffet.

Like the day before, I was nervous until I got in the water and focused on Paul. Once focused, I was like a panting puppy, watching his every move and waiting for my signal to do a trick. If I did it right, I received my treat, a congratulatory hand shake. Good performance let us finished early. We made our way to the beach for sunset.

As I laid on a lounge chair listening to the waves and watched the sun fall, exhaustion washed over me. We would leave behind the security of the pool and dive in the open-ocean in the morning. As apprehensive as I was, it didn't seem possible to muster the energy for another sleepless night.

Going to bed late, after finishing our homework, I refused to let one thought about the next day enter my head.

Practice mental discipline

January 6

It was time for our first open-water dive. The moment of truth had arrived. I figured if I could somehow force myself into the ocean, I'd either dive or die, and frankly I was so tired, the latter didn't seem like a bad option.

We bounced out to sea tossed to and fro on large swells. Wobbly sea legs carried me up a ladder leading to the top deck where I swayed hard into a seat. The cup of tea I carried emptied. With the amount of epinephrine flowing through my veins I probably didn't need the caffeine.

Less than an hour later, we anchored at our dive site. The time had come to take the plunge. All the divers, eight in total, merged on the lower level of the boat trying to get dressed in a beehive of activity. A rocking boat and one foot locked in my wet suit tipped me into the arms of my neighbor for a dance-floor dip. When he graciously plopped me back on my feet, the addition of fins and a heavy oxygen tank made me feel like I was walking in heels and a space suit. Doing the best I could, I stumbled to the back of the line of divers, hoping to delay my jump into the ocean. I didn't get far. A big guy repositioned his fin and stepping on mine, pinned me in place. I'd just broken free when Paul called my name to be the next person in the water. Hesitating, my heart suddenly a lifeless stone, I slowly turned to give him a limp smile.

On the launch platform, I held my regulator in my mouth, looked to the sky and wished I was anywhere in the world but on that boat. I thought about backing out, I could rip the regulator from my mouth and refuse to jump, but then I'd have to turn around and squeeze past the rest of the divers who'd think I was a real chicken. To sea it would have to be. Sucking in a deep breath, I hit the water. One small step for some; one humungous leap for me.

The first dive was a fun dive, no skills required. We followed a rope down to depth then started exploring. I had a vice grip on Ken's hand and sucked air like a vacuum cleaner. Amazing how your head can make something as simple as breathing difficult. I was fully occupied by it until Ken pulled my arm and pointed to a moray eel peeking out from behind a pebbly patch of peach coral. For the first time, I became aware of the underwater environment surrounding me.

During the dive, we saw a myriad of fish painted in flamboyant hues, a huge school of foot-long silvery fish and a beach ball-sized jellyfish. Through it all I felt like a scared kid on an amusement park ride, at first crying and screaming with her eyes shut tight and then sneaking a curious peak and realizing it wasn't so bad after all. Before I knew it, Paul was signalling us to the surface. I had survived my first open water dive.

Back on the boat, we all talked at the same time wanting to share our experiences. As it turned out, many of the fish we saw were dangerous. The wall of silvery fish was composed of many barracudas, and the big jellyfish inches below me was capable of inflicting a painful sting. No wonder Paul aggressively motioned me away. I'd been so worried about breathing under water that I hadn't even considered underwater perils.

In the afternoon, we had to repeat our pool skills in the ocean. I dreaded the mask removal task, the one skill I didn't think I could do. When it was my turn, I worried that air, trying to get to my lungs, would stick to my dry and fuzzy mouth like lint to Velcro. Forcing my eyes shut and slipping into a dark hole, I pulled my mask off and blindly fumbled. My mask didn't want to fit back on. It was as if it belonged to someone else. Finally getting it crookedly placed, I blew out through my nose to displace water and willed my eyes open. Managing a fearful squint; there was Paul's hand reaching out to me. It was time for another hand shake.

Thrilled, and overcome with relief, I gave Paul a big thumbs up, wanting him to know how happy I was. He stared at me with puzzled eyes and pointed to the surface. Confused, I gave him another more enthusiastic, bouncy, "thumbs up" and tried to smile at him with my eyes. Following his gaze to the surface one more time he seemed confused. Paul stared into my eyes for a few seconds then shrugged and turned to watch Mattson. It wasn't until we were back on the boat and the kids started teasing me, making the thumbs up sign in conjunction with a silly face that I remembered; when diving, thumbs up means you want to go up.

January 7

It was the last day of our dive course. I could see the finish line, but I wondered if getting there would be as painful as the last few miles of a marathon.

Rougher seas from the day before put us on high alert for green seasick people projectile vomiting. Even though I'd never been seasick, I popped a preventative pill. They say you can puke in your regulator, but I really didn't want to put that theory to the test.

When Paul gave me my PADI Open Water diver card it was one of the proudest moments of my life. Graduating from dental school and giving birth seemed trivial next to the mental anguish I'd suffered learning to breathe underwater.

Celebrating that night over dinner, I toasted Ken for putting up with my wrath and knowing how to support, yet push with just the right amount of pressure. Thanks to him (and me), we had a beautiful picture of the four of us diving with our thumbs up. Ken's dream wasn't just Ken's dream anymore. We all excitedly planned our next dive trip.

That night I slept like a baby.

January 8

After breakfast we sat around the table trying to decide what to do before our afternoon flight back to Bangkok. Ken opted for the beach but Makayla wasn't into it. A tedious argument began and ended when Ken, exasperated, stormed into the bathroom.

Tension filled the air until what sounded like a loud long juicy fart reverberated out from the bathroom. It rolled on and on and on. Makayla tried to sulk but had to crack a smile. The comic relief of noisy flatulence was too great.

The source of the superhuman fart turned out to be Ken transferring shampoo into a plastic bottle. When he popped his head out from the bathroom, wondering what was so funny, we couldn't stop laughing to explain.

Humor mitigates tension

January 9

No longer able to deny our need to buy a new digital camera, we headed downtown. Bangkok's horrible traffic left us trapped in a cab. Getting restless, Makayla blurted out "Wow, I guess Calgary isn't the biggest city in the world," once again confirming the educational benefit of travel.

In a four storey mall selling electronics, we ambitiously set out to find the very best camera for the very best price. Hours later, after meeting many camera makes and models, we still had no clue what brand would work best for us. We ended up buying from the only guy we could remotely understand.

January 10

After waking with an earache, I needed drugs fast. Upstaging my discomfort, Makayla moaned and pointed to impetigo creeping over her skin.

At the pharmacy we chatted with a helpful pharmacist. She explained that a prescription wasn't required in Thailand. Within ten minutes I walked out with dirt cheap antibiotics.

Health care doesn't have to be inefficient

We spend the afternoon at a huge outdoor market. When it closed we sat on the curb of a busy street, tired, hot and thirsty, and watched Ken try to flag down a cab. Not able to get one, it seemed we'd be walking home until a noise from above made us look up. We were right under the sky train. Giving thanks to the travel god we were starting to believe in, twenty air-conditioned minutes later we sat at the Lucky Star restaurant, home of icy fruit shakes and the best Tom Yum Goong soup ever.

January 11

We were supposed to run, but didn't. Our last run in Bangkok had been beyond difficult. A crowded street, extreme heat, humidity and pollution; it was enough to make you wish you weren't training for a marathon.

Off we went to the Grand Palace. Gold domes and shimmering walls of inset jewel toned glass called out to be photographed, but the workings of my new camera mystified me.

When intuition fails, let an instruction manual prevail

January 12

We were going stir crazy in Bangkok waiting for our Cambodia Visas to be processed. To kill time we signed up for a two day tour. It began predictably with a crowded tour bus and unexpected hidden costs. At the floating market, in your face vendors pushed their wares refusing to take no for an answer. Ken responded to their badgering with his usual polite "ah, no thank you." He said "ah, no thank you" over and over, each time with exactly the same tone and polite lilt to his voice. After about the millionth " ah, no thank you" the kids started teasing him cooing like a parrot, "ah, no thank you.....ah, no thank you."

The market was a bit cheesy, but at least there were plenty of good photo opportunities. After reading the camera manual I was ready to shoot. An elderly wrinkled Thai woman paddled toward me in a canoe filled with colorful produce. Raising the camera to click, the view finder faded to black.

Carry extra charged batteries

At our next stop, I was admiring an intricately carved wood elephant, when Makayla announced that her new impetigo antibiotic was making her feel sick. It seemed it would be "one of those days" until unexpectedly, the mood totally changed.

After drinking some water, Makayla felt better. We left the shop and transferred to a small air-conditioned van; our tour group whittled down to just five – our family and a clean cut Swiss fellow in his early thirties. After touring the Jeath Museum, beside the River Kwai, we walked out and couldn't find our van. Not sure what to do, we sat on a street curb until a Thai guy in his twenties approached and motioned for us to follow him to a train station a few blocks away. Wanting to know where the train would take us, the guy didn't speak English, and shoved his cell phone in my face. When I brought the phone to my ear, a soft spoken female voice, making a poor attempt at English, said to get off the train at a town with an impossible to remember Thai name.

Over two hours lapsed before the train came to its final stop. With no one to greet us, we sat discussing what one does when lost in rural Thailand when a guy approached and pointed to a pickup truck. He could have been a terrorist abductor for all we knew, but we hopped in anyway. We had a long bumpy ride before stopping at a weathered sign saying Elephant Camp.

Our driver led us through rain forest into a tarp covered open area with tables and chairs. While waiting for dinner, a guy introducing himself as Stone (ya like a rock) sat down. Looking like Jesus Christ, complete with a gauzy cream tunic, bearded face and long blonde dreadlocks, we soon got a handle on his antiestablishment "all you need is love" life philosophy. The guy, like Jesus, was a preacher.

It was late when, in the dark, we picked our way down a narrow path to a small houseboat tied to a rickety dock. Our beds were hard and short and Ken's feet hung over the edge, but the gentle rock of the boat hypnotically sent us off to sleep under mosquito nets.

January 13

Lit by the rising sun, a glass like river reflected the surrounding jungle. We sat in a small boat mesmerized as Mahouts (elephant trainers) rode elephants into the river, then scuttled around their bodies as if attached by suction cups to scrub them down with large brushes bubbling with foaming soap. Every once in a while, the Mahout shouted a command, and down his elephant would go, fully dunking them both for a rinse.

Breakfast woke up our taste buds with Thai spice, then once again we were on the move to float down the river on bamboo rafts. A guide welcomed our kids onto his raft and off they went. Ken and I, right behind them, stepped onto ours, but immediately sank. An alarmed guide shooed us off and looking up at Ken whistled "you big boy." Yelling to his mates to bring more bamboo, a group congregated around the raft weaving in extra poles. The raft was titanic size by the time we stayed afloat. A jubilant cheer went up as the workers bowed and stretched on tippy toes to enthusiastically pat Ken on the back. Standing taller than usual, Ken beamed with his "biggest tourist ever" fame.

After meeting back up with the kids we left the rafts and walked into the jungle heading in the direction our guides pointed as they waved goodbye. We hadn't gone far when two directional options presented themselves: continuing down to the river's edge, or crossing over the river on a narrow swinging rope bridge. The bridge seemed old and unsafe to me, but before I could protest, Frank and Ken crossed. It took a great deal of encouragement to get the kids and me to follow. Navigating over broken planks of wood exposing a surging river well over a hundred feet below made us take cautious baby steps while holding on to a swaying frayed rope for dear life. Surviving meant once again choosing the most obvious of obscure paths. Just when we thought we were so hopelessly lost even our travel god couldn't find us, we stepped into a clearing and found a truck waiting.

At lunch, to our surprise, we met back up with Stone. He felt like an old friend as he began another of his stories. He'd taken a trip to India to visit a friend living in nothing more than a huge tree. Not just any tree, Stone stressed, but a special spiritual tree. I wasn't sure what a spiritual tree was or how you lived in one, but suffice it to say, the tree was really big and his friend swung around in it and prayed a lot. Unfortunately, he was no monkey. Shortly before Stone arrived, he fell, broke his neck, and died. Stone was the first guy on the scene and soon found himself in jail, incriminated for murder. Desperately pleading his innocence, no one understood his English. It took weeks before an interpreter finally came to his rescue.

Our tour group expanded to six. After a few more war sites we made one last stop at a cave. It didn't look like much. We crawled in and out of its small caverns and were about to leave when Ken discovered a small opening with a ladder leading farther below ground. Following the ladder down seemed like the perfect adventure to end a perfectly adventurous day. Down they all went, with only the flash of a camera to momentarily light the pitch black hole. I, of course, stayed above ground to call for help if needed.

What stories they told upon their return. For Stone, their cave exploring had been a truly spiritual experience. His infectious enthusiasm had us all buzzing with appreciation for the wonders of life. A few more days with Stone and we just might have followed him back to India to live in his recently inherited special tree.

Amazing adventures happen when least expected

January 14

On our morning prowl for breakfast I discovered, tucked away at the end of Khao San Road, an American looking place called World Coffee. A Starbucks knock off, right down to the overstuffed chairs and chalk board menu, they offered lattes and frappuccinos at half the Starbucks price.

It all seemed too good to be true. World Coffee couldn't possibly be as good as my precious Starbucks. Knockoffs were everywhere in Bangkok. On the streets you could buy a $10.00 Louis Vuitton purse or pirated DVDs of newly released movies for a buck. The thing was, the purse was made from stiff vinyl and the movies missed strategic scenes from when the videographer slipped out for popcorn. Consequently, I doubted my knock-off coffee would taste like the real thing, but surprisingly it did. It was just right. How bittersweet to find World Coffee on our last day on Khao San Road.

Back at the hotel room the kids requested a lazy day to watch pirated DVDs on our laptop. Since we had to head back downtown to pick up our camera, we agreed. Once again, even though we'd bought a new camera, we tried to get the old one fixed. The third time wasn't a charm. The camera would only work on manual, the one setting I didn't know how to use. If there was a travel god out there helping us along our way, there had to be a technology god who really had it in for us.

A family dive

Shopping for produce

Boating through the floating market

Feeding elephants

Eating on Khao San Road

Grand Palace temple

Ken and Jen ride an elephant

An adventurous hike begins

Makayla makes a friend

Cave adventures with Stone

CAMBODIA

January 15

Our 5:15 a.m. wakeup call to catch a bus to Cambodia came at 5:45, yet we managed to sneak in a World Coffee despite Ken's warnings there wasn't time.

Boarding a luxury two level bus, we snapped up two long comfy couches in a small compartment on the bottom level. We gloated about our great seats until a guy opened a bathroom door we hadn't noticed and released noxious fumes.

Luxury, no matter how smelly, ended at the border. We had to leave the bus behind and walk into Cambodia. Two steps out of Thailand we entered a different world. Hot as molten lava with nothing green to block the sun's searing rays, it felt like a 360 degree stark grey backdrop had been pulled down behind us. Gusting dust stung and coated my sweaty body making my eyes water until real tears washed them clean. As we walked, filthy sad looking children ran our way. No older than seven or eight, with newborns slung on their backs, they swarmed and begged. Behind them came men with missing limbs. Overwhelmed by their desperate poverty, I looked away only to lock eyes with a human torso. With no arms or legs he sat propped up against a stone wall not far from where we stood. Feeling confined as they closed in, there was no escaping the distressing images my memory will forever hold.

We were herded like cattle into a crowded stifling hot one-room building to be processed through customs. Makayla, still having trouble digesting her impetigo antibiotic, grabbed my arm as we waited in line and desperately blurted out, "I'm going to be sick." Starting to retch, I rushed her outside catching what I could in my hands. There we stood – upset, covered in vomit and not sure what to do. Suddenly, a gentle tap on my shoulder made me turn. A wrinkled old local lady with kind eyes pressed a bottle of water and tissues into my hand. I tried communicating my thanks. At that moment I loved that women and wanted to give her all my money. As quickly as she came, she melted back into the crowd and was gone.

There are angels among us

Once through customs, we waited for transportation to Siem Reap. When an old beat up minibus finally arrived, tourists jostled to get on the bus shuffling us to the back of the line. By the time we boarded, we were one seat short.

Giving me a disgusted look the driver threw a small pillow on the floor behind the gear shift and pointed for me to sit. For comfort, I should have straddled the gear shift, but assuming Pap test position in a sundress didn't seem appropriate. Instead, trying to be a lady, I sat with my legs to the side for what turned out to be a very long, difficult journey.

The road, and I use the term loosely, was really just dirt marred with huge craters. Our driver swerved erratically to miss holes in the ground, or took them head on when oncoming motorcycles, ox pulled carts, herds of cows or bicycles were in his way. My head slammed up and down, and snapped to and fro as the bus threatened to break apart. Three head throbbing hours later we stopped to eat.

After dropping us off, our van drove away. We felt deserted until he eventually returned with a load of stranded passengers from a van that had broken down behind us. Immediately loading after they unloaded, our journey continued. I wondered what would become of those left behind and found out when our driver stopped to try and talk a farmer into going back for them. While they bartered, an Israeli couple on our bus boisterously complained about the delay. Going on and on, those sitting around them became irritated. Telling them to stop their belly aching, harsh words flew. An Israeli conflict was about to erupt when our driver, thankfully, returned.

Hardship breeds conflict

January 16

We were in Siem Reap, Cambodia; foreigners in an extremely foreign land.

After hiring an English-speaking driver, we drove to the centre of town and looked for breakfast. Buildings were small – mostly open air. Not in a tropical hotel, open-air-lobby kind of way. It was more of a bombed out kind of look. What structure there was, looked like it could crumble in a light breeze. Finding a secure place to eat took time.

During the short walk from the car to the restaurant we found ourselves once again surrounded by beggars missing limbs. I felt conspicuous in my big white body, complete with ten fingers and ten toes. There I was, all whole, suddenly feeling very rich and spoiled. I wanted to make a difference but there was no way to satisfy a never ending line of outstretched hands.

To be born Canadian is to be born lucky

Over breakfast we discussed Cambodian history. I'd started to read The Killing Fields, hoping it would shed some light on why the country had such a long history of death and destruction. Why did we see mutilated bodies and pulverized concrete everywhere we looked?

Our education began at the Cambodian Land Mine Museum. It was simple and basic, unlike the grand Korean War Museum, but just as unforgettable. A Cambodian guide, about twenty years old and barely tall enough to reach Ken's naval, took us through open air displays of field tanks, airplanes, guns and land mines. Knocking on a prosthesis replacing his right leg, he told us about his encounter with a landmine. Trudging over to a large poster board covered with sad pictures of maimed children, he pointed out that they had suffered the same fate. After the war, many lost limbs had been replaced with prostheses made from previously exploded long metal artillery shells. Using those shells was an inventive use for the wastes of war, but not a comfortable solution. Thankfully, Angelina Jolie realized the hardships of amputees when she came to Cambodia to shoot Tomb Raider. She started a program providing custom fabricated prosthesis. I didn't love her movie, but became an instant Jolie fan.

January 17

Bright light streaming through our window wasn't a good sign. We were supposed to be watching the sun rise over Angkor Wat, not just waking up. The wake-up call I'd ordered hadn't come.

Trust important details to those they are important to

Impatiently waiting for a cab and breakfast to go, my clenched jaw relaxed when coffee arrived in a plastic bag tied at the top around a straw. How could that kind of innovation not make you smile?

The drive to the temples was beautiful. For the first time we saw trees lining the road. Ancient and mammoth, their height made telephone poles look like toothpicks. Apparently most of Cambodia was once covered with those trees, but most had been hacked down and sold for ammunition money during the war.

By mid-afternoon we came upon our favorite temple. Featured in Angelina Jolie's "Tomb Raider," it had thick serpent-like tree roots scaling its moss covered walls. We couldn't take enough photos. Makayla was poised for yet another when, tripping on one of the temples doorways, she started to fall. Watching her from behind, the scene played out in slow motion. Horrified, I imagined our new camera smashing on the stone floor and screamed "noooooooo Maaaakaaaaylaaaaaa...the caaaaaameraaa." Acknowledging my cry, she lifted her camera carrying arm high before crumbling to the stone floor. I'm not proud to admit my first concern was for the camera. I just couldn't face any more technology grief. Thankfully it was intact with only a small scratch. Poor Makayla hadn't fared as well. Tears flowed as we examined nasty welts on her knees and hip. Luckily, showering her with accolades for saving the camera helped her recovery. Reveling in hero status, she accepted a helping hand up and limped off to resume her photography.

January 18

Over breakfast we moaned and complained about the return trip to Thailand. On the bright side, I wore shorts prepared for the straddle, if need be.

No doubt, Cambodia was a wild experience where the destination made up for the journey. What we learned and saw on Cambodia's marred soil wasn't comfortable; in the embrace of new knowledge, like hands on soft clay, we were changed.

Ignorance is bliss

Cambodia Landmine Museum

Makayla makes a Cambodian girlfriend

160

Angkor Wat

Water Pump in Cambodia

Angkor Wat

VIETNAM

January 19

So long Cambodia! Good Morning Vietnam!

An outbreak of Bird Flu in Asia had begun in Vietnam. My mom didn't want us to go. In an email, she attached an article from the Calgary Herald newspaper speculating that the virus causing the flu might mutate. Human to human spread rather than the current bird to human mode of transmission could cause a killer pandemic.

In a panic, I made Ken read her message. As always, he remained calm and pointed out key words like "could," "if," and "may" rather than "death" and "pandemic." He also reminded me about all the doom and gloom articles mom had cut out and left on our kitchen island during the lead up to our trip. If we'd taken them all seriously, we'd never have left our kitchen, let alone the continent. To avoid sleepless nights, I obviously had to stop reading sensationalized news articles, turn off my over-active imagination, and work harder on my mental discipline.

The minute we stepped off the plane in Vietnam, everyone wanted to be our friend. We responded cheerfully until realizing friendly interests often ended in a sales pitch.

Being friendly isn't always your best option

To get to our hotel, we had to cross six lanes of traffic on foot with our luggage. It seemed we'd never get across. Standing and watching mostly motorcycles and the odd car zoom by, we realized there would never be a lull in traffic. To cross, we had to do what the locals did. Walking slowly across the road, they let drivers steer around them.

Let me tell you, for someone taught to look both ways and not cross the street until the coast is clear, to step out into speeding traffic was terrifying. Half the way across, I had trust issues. Nervously stopping and starting while frantically looking around, I tried to do my own weaving. I almost got myself killed.

January 20

For some strange reason the beds in our hotel room had no covers. The time had come to pull out the travel sheets we'd brought along from Canada. Made from a silky fabric and configured like a marble bag with a draw string closing the top, crawling in and getting comfortable was like wiggling into a spandex body suit. Managing to free an arm for before bed reading, my book *And Then They Killed My Father* told the true story of a young girl who, separated from her family during Pol Pot's reign of terror in Cambodia, was forced into a re-education camp. I read until I couldn't keep my eyes open then spent the rest of the night tossing and turning through bad dreams. Unable to get away from Pol Pot's soldiers, my dream was in part real. My marble bag had me wrapped up as tightly as a mummy.

We spent the afternoon at the Vietnamese War Museum. Housed in a simple building, amateur displays featured black and white photos of war scenes. Below the pictures were typewriter typed recipe cards. The caption on one of the cards stated "An American soldier laughing at murdered Vietnamese" The look on the American's face looked to me like anguish and sorrow.

Interpretation weaves many truths

By the time we left, images of burned children and jars containing deformed fetuses helped us appreciate the horrific consequences of Napalm and Agent Orange.

January 21

One day in Saigon was enough. We decided to visit the beach resort town of Mui Ne. Since it was Chinese New Year, we thought it best to reserve our hotel room in advance.

Our room, with no air conditioning, looked like a third world hospital ward with five single cots lined up against stark concrete walls, but, like it or not, they had our money.

Walking the ocean shoreline in the afternoon, a stiff breeze churned water reflecting the grey sky, and garbage swirled in mini tornados. At the beginning of the trip we would have been disappointed, but third world acclimation had us stepping over what needed to be avoided while focusing on beautiful sea shells.

January 22

In the middle of the night, the skin on my arms burned, but the sensation fit in with my dream (the Pol Pot theme continued). It wasn't until the next morning, as I sat on the toilet and looked up to see a long narrow open air window a few inches from the ceiling, that I realized my arms were covered with mosquito bites.

After much debate over the side effects of prophylactic malaria medication, we decided not to take it. We instead diligently used repellant and protective clothing to avoid bites. Now, one stupid mistake put us at risk for disease.

Scratching myself raw, Ken tried explaining to the desk clerk why we had to leave. When the guy seemed confused, out came Ken's charades. Needing more clarification he grabbed my red mosquito bitten arm as a prop and thrust it in the guy's face. On and on Ken went, waving my arm about like a ventriloquist's puppet.

Eventually they shooed Ken and his plea for a refund away. Telling him they needed to talk to their manager they said to come back the next day. Ken optimistically agreed. I muttered under my breath, "ya right, as if we'll get our money back."

As it turned out, finding a nice room with air conditioning was easy.

Break free from confining reservations

January 23

We started our morning with purpose. With very few places accepting Visa and no cash, we needed a bank. Our run led to a hotel with a bank machine. Ken spent thirty minutes trying to get cash from plastic with no luck. We did, however, learn that five star hotels took Visa. We had no choice but to eat somewhere nice. I smiled while Ken continued to madly shake the bank machine.

My good mood ended abruptly when we resumed the second half of our run. It was hot, and my muscles had stiffened up after our stop. I so desperately wanted to be back at the room picking out my outfit for dinner. Thoughts of "should I wear runners or sandals?" and which of my three quick dry shirts has the most class were replaced with, I'm going to die before I have a chance to even dress for dinner.

The dream of successfully completing a marathon, something I'd started to believe in, once again slipped out of reach.

At the Sailing Club, on comfy lounge chairs by the beach, the misery of my run faded away. We used our plastic and lived the good life.

January 24

What a night! Late in the evening I got a terrible headache and by bedtime felt feverish and achy all over. Convinced I had some awful mosquito-borne disease, I lied in bed facing my ultimate demise. One minute you're sipping a cold one at the Sailing Club and the next, preparing to be carried off to some third world hospital. I worried and worried and then stopped. The truth was, I simply didn't have time for disease on our Big Trip. Popping two aspirin, it seemed appropriate to try a little of Ken's optimism, after all, it always seemed to work for him. He had gotten his money back from our first mosquito ridden hotel. With conviction, I told myself I was just a bit dehydrated.

In the morning I felt like a million bucks.

Trust the power of positive thinking

January 25

A late morning bus dropped us in Nha Trang. We settled in and then decided to visit a Vietnamese spa. Once there, no plush terry robes or white slippers awaited us. We received a towel the size of a tea towel and rubber slippers barely accommodating Ken's big toe. He had to shuffle along like a little Geisha girl just to keep them on.

At an outdoor tub just big enough for four people, therapeutic mud awaited us. I stepped in carefully, trying to limit mud to skin exposure, but the kids dragged me in for a full dunk. Letting mud ooze through your fingers and toes was an unfamiliar sensation. Like a rebellious kid getting dirty after being told to stay clean, wallowing felt satisfyingly naughty.

After a warm shower it was time for a massage. Mattson and I were in one room and Ken and Makayla in another. Two petite Vietnamese girls worked on Mattson's bulging gymnastic muscles. They swooned over his chiseled physique singing: "oh, big muscles, you want a girl friend?" I had to pop up and assure them in no uncertain terms, he certainly did not.

After being soaked, rubbed, stretched and walked on, we had to admit – a day at a Vietnamese spa was a good day. They know how to do "spa" right.

January 26

Starting the day early, we caught a full day snorkel boat tour to visit the islands around Nha Trang. On an overcrowded boat, cigarette smoke and black billowing exhaust drove us to an outside deck. We sat on an unanchored bench seat hoping Ken's weight wouldn't be the tipping point for the bench or the boat.

After snorkeling, we climbed a ladder to an outdoor upper deck to have lunch. Seated cross legged on the floor amongst our Asian boat mates, one gal in particular stood out. She wore black pants, a black leather jacket, a hat, wool gloves, sun glasses and a surgical mask over her mouth; good sun protection in 80 degree Fahrenheit heat.

Lunch was placed on the floor of the deck in multiple bowls. People circled the bowls and soon the click of chopsticks filled the air. Those sticks skipped from the main bowls to peoples' side dishes to their mouths and back to the main bowl for more. Talk about double dipping. Even the gal with the mask was in on it. We opted out of the whole spit swapping affair, taking nothing but a banana for our lunch. We watched them and they watched us. Two different races likely thinking the same thing – why are they eating like that?

January 27

It was Ken's birthday. Wanting to do something special, we decided to surprise him with a custom made birthday cake. "Mission Birthday Cake" began. In true James Bond style, we whispered and conspired whenever Ken turned his back. As it turned out, I could tell a pretty convincing white lie when necessary.

By dinner time, the kids were bursting with excited anticipation. At a lovely Italian restaurant our secret pre-ordered cake arrived along with a boisterous Vietnamese quartet of waiters belting out: "yappy earthway ew ou." A blaze of candles lit green icing neatly spelling out "Happy 43rd Birthday Dad." We ate decadently moist cake and left what we couldn't finish with the staff. They looked like they could use a few calories.

January 28

We checked into a lovely guest house in Hue after an early morning bus ride. French colonial in style (France occupied Vietnam in 1885) and beautifully ornate, it would have cost a fortune in Paris; we paid $15.00 per night.

The market, close to our hotel, had many tailor shops that made custom clothing. Off the rack clothes never fit Ken well. Exposed white socks worked for Michael Jackson, but on Ken Moore – not so much. It seemed like the perfect opportunity to get him clothes which fit. Dragging him into a shop to leaf through a GQ magazine and pick out a designer suit the tailor would copy had to be the closest he'd ever come to fashion.

Armani does make a man

January 29

I wanted time alone to shop, but couldn't get rid of my family. I had to explain to them – to shop you have to stop. Leading by example, I stopped dead in front of a beautiful painting. I simply had to have it. Making Ken barter for me, he established a price and went to pay. Daydreaming about the compliments I'd get on it at my next Calgary dinner party, I was surprised when Ken quickly returned to tell me there had been a miscommunication. He thought the price was in Dong (Vietnamese currency) when in fact it was in U.S. dollars. The difference almost doubled the price; still a bargain in my opinion but unaffordable in Ken's.

This was a crisis. I wanted my art. How dare he deny me? Why couldn't he for once coo "honey, I know you want that painting, and darling because I love you so much, the extra cost is of no concern – you shall have it." Oh how I wanted to scream and shout, but who wants their kids to witness an adult tantrum. Seething inside I walked away from Ken and my art. We would stay on our lousy budget, but someday I was coming back with my girlfriends and my Visa card.

January 30

After playing chicken with oncoming buses on steep cliffs through the mountains, I insisted we take an all night train rather than a bus to Hanoi. It took some convincing but Ken agreed. We hired two cyclo bicycles, something like riding in the front basket of a bicycle, and weaved in and out of traffic on our way to the train station. Trusting our drivers while speeding head on into chaotic traffic was like letting yourself fall backwards unguarded into a stranger's arms.

Stopping for dinner before our train, we settled in at our table and ordered four #8s, the dish recommended in our travel book. While waiting for our food the place quickly filled with tourists all dropping *Lonely Planet* books on their table and ordering #8s. What a slap in the face. You think you're a uniquely adventurous traveler only to find out you're just another Lonely Planet sheep, in a not so lonely world.

January 31

Confused by ringing bells in the middle of the night, Ken fumbled for the phone. A few minutes into his work related conversation, the phone went dead. Try as he might he couldn't reconnect.

The frustrations of being a world away from work were starting to mount. Biking through Te Duc's Tomb was just the distraction Ken needed. The grand palace reflected in a crumbling moat whisked us back to a different time.

In the early evening, we followed the crowd at the train station hoping they'd lead us where we needed to go. I could hear a train approaching and showed a guy in uniform our tickets. Motioning urgency, he pointed down the tracks. We walked briskly until his yelling sparked a sprint. The train whisked past and stopped ten feet in front of us. We were out of breath as we climbed the train's three steep steps. Ken, still on the ground, awkwardly lifted luggage for us to grab as the train once again started to move. Forced into a Hail Mary, he threw up the last bag then had to do a running jump onto a train already accelerating down the track.

Ken never misses a plane. Ken never misses a train

February 1

Pulling ourselves away from English television to attend the evening performance of the famous Vietnamese Water Puppets wasn't easy. The show was cute, but our best entertainment came from the lady behind us boisterously proclaiming "Isn't this the best show you've ever seen?!" followed by "those puppets are so wonderful!" followed by "oooh, can you believe how cute they are?!" followed by "I just can't believe how amazing this show is!" We thought the show was average at best. Maybe she was a "promotional plant." Whatever

170

the case, her over-the-top emotional joy couldn't help but make you smile.

Enthusiasm is infectious

February 2

It was a long run day. I didn't want to go, but what else was new. Convinced two hours would kill me, cool air brought renewed energy once again instilling hope we'd get the marathon done.

Famished after our run, we grabbed the kids and set out for lunch. At a somewhat western place we told the kids to order whatever they wanted. I was impressed when they settled on healthy fare and, forgoing pop, ordered water to drink.

Kids given an inch can be good rulers

February 3

It was breakfast time; the meal we'd come to dread. Not having any luck with toast (soggy) and jam (so sweet it made your teeth hurt) we decided to try scrambled eggs. A long time after ordering, an oxymoron of eggs arrived: burnt around the edges but raw at the yolk, with the whole mess swimming in a puddle of grease. Ken liked grease, but runny yolk was a deal breaker.

The kids and I chalked scrambled eggs up as yet another food best not ordered in Vietnam, but Ken really wanted his eggs. On he went, trying to explain to our non-English-speaking server just how the second attempt should go. When that didn't work he began his third rendition. He was into it when suddenly his gesturing hands deflated and fell to his side. He simply gave up. Ken, the king of persistence, brought down by an undercooked egg. It was a sad sight.

February 4

Our breakfast waiter approached the table with trepidation, but he didn't have to worry. On our last day in Vietnam, we finally knew what to do. Grabbing the menu and pointing to Pho, we held up four fingers. Vigorously nodding his head with approval, his face lit up in a big smile of relief.

When in doubt, eat what the locals eat

The time had come to leave Vietnam. We boarded our plane to Singapore happy to leave bird flu, malaria, and white rice behind.

172

Biking in Mui Ne

Ken and Mattson cooking

Cyclo in Hue

Cool weather in Hanoi

Sleeping car in overnight train

An unhappy lunch

SINAPORE AGAIN

February 5

A long morning phone call left Ken agitated. Slamming down the phone, he immediately rushed off to work. I'd always known our Big Trip might end early because of some unexpected crisis; for the first time, it seemed like a real possibility.

In the afternoon, the kids and I went out for groceries. We walked for twenty minutes in oppressive heat, not finding our way out of a complex with multiple apartment buildings. My soon to be twelve year old daughter, who overnight had become all seeing and all knowing, informed us in a huff, that she knew the way. Strutting with cocky confidence, we followed her in circles and arrived right back where we'd started. Beginning again, Mattson "the close walker" edged me off the sidewalk while nattering at his sister. When I joined in, barking for them to stop their bickering, the skies opened. From out of the blue, pounding cool rain struck. It was one of those moments when everything stops and you look to the heavens in awe. When our stalled moment continued, the sun broke through the clouds, we turned a corner and there was the store.

Memories hold tightest to the simplest of moments

February 6

Listening to Ken toss and turn all night long made for a restless night.

In the morning, during our run, he had time to vent. In a nutshell, he needed to be in Calgary and wanted to be there with every bone of his entrepreneurial body, but our trip, our once in a life time Big Trip, came first. He simply had to trust the people he'd left in control. We wouldn't be going home early.

Moving forward, we took the kids and our host's six year old twin boys to the zoo. Chasing those boys up one side of the zoo and back down the other was a deodorant vaporizing experience. If we'd ever questioned our decision to have only two children, we never would again.

February 7

Makayla was on my mind. I'd noticed such a change in her over the last few weeks. Moody and combative, she wasn't her usual cheery happy self. With her birthday approaching I figured it was just hormones and a bit of home sickness. Whatever the cause, she was disturbing my peace.

In the evening, we left the kids with pizza and a reminder to clean up. We proceeded on to an Indian restaurant. During dinner David, our Servas host, shared stories about the time he spent living in a Hindu temple in India. In a matter-of-fact tone he announced "I met God." Taken aback by such a statement, I paused to process his words before launching a barrage of questions. All he'd say was that he'd been in a deep meditative state and that the experience had been terrifying. Humans, he assured me, weren't built to meet God in person. A down to earth, seemingly sane guy, he had us at the edge of our seats as he went on to talk about Hindu spirituality. By the time we left, he'd made clear the importance of being at one with the universe. I was feeling peacefully connected until we walked back into the apartment and found the kitchen a mess and the kids watching T.V.

Mattson took one look at me and skedaddled into the kitchen grabbing dishes along the way. Makayla stayed glued to the set. When I marched over and gave her heck, she ran to her bedroom in tears. Shrugging to our hosts, I entered her bear den. A long emotional conversation unfolded. As it turned out, there were so many more issues than just unwashed dishes. The crux of it: Makayla felt we were being really hard on her. I had to admit twenty-four/seven did allow for a lot of parenting time and we did have high expectations. We both vented and eventually found enough harmony to attempt to carry on in the same universe.

February 8

We were making plans for the day when David suggested phoning the airline twenty-four hours in advance to pre book bulkhead seats for our long flight to Egypt the next day. Pulling out our itinerary, our flight date didn't jive with when we thought we were leaving. We didn't leave the next day, we left that afternoon. We'd almost made a very expensive mistake.

Don't guess. Check to avoid a mess

EGYPT

February 9-20

After restlessly enduring a seven hour red-eye flight to Egypt, we connected with Canadian friends living and working in Cairo. Tracee, Ric and their three kids lived in a beautifully appointed large apartment filled with the latest in technology. Their kids and ours, both sharing a love for video games, instantly befriended each other. They played *Dance Dance Revolution* and *Super Mario* for hours on end. During our stay, many peaceful nights saw the nine of us congregated in their living room, each plugged into some kind of electronic device; together, yet lost in our own little cyber worlds.

Tracee spoiled the kids and made them pancakes with their favorite Aunt Jemima syrup, and Ric stepped up to grill tender thick steaks imported from North America. Flavors from home comforted us like a warm blanket on a cold day. The best treat of all was the use of Tracee and Ric's driver to chauffeur us around Cairo. When he drove us to the Great Pyramids, he patiently waited while we mounted camels, wedged ourselves between two humps and galloped around their perimeter.

The construction of the pyramids was a good example of how advanced Egyptian society had once been, yet modern Cairo seemed disorganized and chaotic. Air pollution from burning garbage left the sky hazy and grey and terrible traffic had drivers at a standstill laying on their horns.

We drove past rows of unfinished buildings where spikes of rebar held up squatters' laundry. Obviously construction was delayed. When I questioned why, our driver explained, "taxes weren't collected until construction was completed, thus, construction was never completed." Somewhere along the line, it seemed they'd dropped the ball.

Our days passed quickly. Historically, there was so much to see. When we weren't touring, Tracee and Ric invited us into their inner circle of close friends. Some nights, it seemed we'd just fallen asleep when the 4:30 a.m. Muslim morning prayers, blaring out like a slowed down auctioneer's yodel, woke us. Burrowing our heads down into our pillows didn't block out the 5:30 a.m. and 6:30 a.m. calls to prayer.

We got comfortable and did some of the normal things settled people do. Makayla's impetigo was back, prompting the need for a doctor, and our hair needed cutting. At the hair salon, we faced the unique experience of follicle massage. A vibrating machine placed on the top of our heads effectively raised up a tingly full body case of goose bumps. Moving the machine from head to face tickled your nose and made your ears ring.

Our Cairo highlight came when Ric took us four wheeling in the Sahara Desert. Pulling off the main road, we headed straight out into rippling sand. Five minutes in, nothing but sand meeting sky surrounded us. Think about it. How often do you have nothing between you and the horizon? There were no buildings, no roads, no trees; nothing but sand. I'd never before experienced space like that. The feeling was surprisingly uncomfortable. It reminded me of when I was a kid lying in bed trying to get my head around the concept of infinity. It made my stomach hurt. It was midday in the desert and with the sun centered in the sky, getting oriented was impossible. South looked exactly like north, east and west. Without Ric's global positioning system, finding our way back would have been impossible.

We searched for Roman Ruins, speeding through the sand until our front tires unexpectedly hit wet sand and sank. Blurting out "holy shit, we're in trouble now," Ric hit the brakes. If the quick sand we were in managed to swallow all four tires, only a tow truck would be able to pull us out. Ric had a cell phone, but apparently it would take a day or two for someone to find us.

Imagining a cold night in a black car swallowed by open space left my mouth dry. Mattson and Ken headed out to push as Ric slammed the truck from reverse to drive, rocking us back and forth and coating the boys in spraying sand. When that didn't work, Makayla and I had to get out and help. It seemed we'd be spending the night, when one last superhuman push set us free.

You're stronger than you think

182

On the 15th of February we extracted ourselves from the comforts of Tracee and Ric's home to get back on the road. An all night train dropped us in Luxor. We immediately met a middle-aged Egyptian fellow named Ahmed. He seemed respectable, so we agreed to his good price on a room and when that panned out, dished out more cash for him to be our tour guide.

The day sped by as we explored ancient sites. By late afternoon, we strolled through a small village strongly resembling biblical Bethlehem. Ken generously pulled out his wallet when a group of teens approached to beg for money. After leafing through multiple bills, he had to apologise. With nothing smaller than a fifty he couldn't help them out. Our tour abruptly ended as Ahmed rushed us back to the car.

Smart and street smart are not the same thing

After dark, we ended the day at the Luxor temple where strobe lights forced our heads back and up to follow towering lit pillars. I knew the kids were impressed when they expanded their descriptive vocabulary from "cool" to "wow" and "sweet." I'm not sure I'd label that progress, but the variety was nice.

Ahmed followed us around the next day as well; pushing different tours all the while. He was starting to pressure us and it was irritating. I also didn't like his obvious infatuation with Makayla. He loved stroking her long dark hair while telling her how beautiful she was. He wasn't the only one noticing her. As of late, many sets of male eyes skipped over me and locked on Makayla. Talk about an uncomfortable double whammy. My head turning ability was gone and Makayla was looking like a teenager when she was still a young girl.

The time had come to part-company with Ahmed. We tried a warm hand shake and fond farewell, but unfortunately ended up having to swat him away like a wasp you're afraid might sting you.

After an incredible dive in the Red Sea, I started feeling queasy. Like a summer hail storm coming from out of nowhere, Pharoh's Revenge, clinically known as dysentery, pummeled me. That Pharoh took my guts, tied them in knots and squeezed me dry. It didn't seem possible to survive the all night bus trip we'd planned to take back to Cairo. To help me out, Ken wanted to rent a van. We soon found out tourists with private vehicles had to have a driver and travel in a convoy that would leave at 3:45 a.m.

When our driver fetched us from the hotel's lobby at 3:40 a.m. we were concerned we'd miss the convoy. As we followed him out, we were surprised to see a car, not a van. Ken asked where the van was but no answer came. When we stopped behind a bus and the driver started to move our luggage over, Ken went ballistic, shouting "Where's my van?" When the driver remained mute, Ken insisted he drive us back to the hotel.

The next morning, Ken woke us to catch a local bus to Cairo. By that time my cramps had subsided. It took Ken all night to piece together what had really happened to our van. Apparently, at the last minute it broke down. What we couldn't understand was why they hadn't just told us the truth. It wasn't until we were back in Cairo telling Ric and Tracee our story that Ric set us straight. Egyptians, he claimed, want foreigners to be happy and consequently refuse to speak of anything bad. They kept telling us the van was coming, even though they knew it wasn't, because they didn't want to disappoint us. After experiencing how angry that approach made Ken, I didn't hold out a lot of hope for peace in the Middle East.

The kids were sad to leave Cairo. They had so enjoyed their time with kids their own age, but ready or not, the time had come to camp our way through Europe.

Family camel ride around the pyramids

Nothing but open space in the Sahara desert

Technology togetherness

Felucca ride down the Nile

AMSTERDAM

February 20

Stepping outdoors after arriving at Amsterdam's airport felt like walking into a freezer. Thailand's hot air nicely transitioned to Vietnam's cool air, but like a stinging slap in the face, Holland's cold air shocked our systems. We were struck by how clean, organized and quiet Amsterdam was; gone were the familiar sounds of horns honking, motor bikes roaring, roosters crowing and Muslim prayers blaring. I sunk into supple leather seats in a shiny new taxi van marveling at how cautiously our driver, a rather senior fellow who looked a bit like my dad, drove.

The four of us sat in that immaculate van quietly taking in a country still in the embrace of winter. Naked trees and brown grass, familiar sights back in Calgary, felt comfortable until we remembered our small suitcases filled with summer clothes. Glancing over to Ken, I followed his gaze to a taxi meter already flashing double digits and increasing rapidly. With one Euro equal to $1.65 Canadian, the fare was going to hurt. Welcome to Europe, I sheepishly thought.

February 21

I slept well, but waking in the morning to the sound of forced air blasting from heating vents in a large sterile western hotel room felt strange. How could surroundings once so familiar suddenly feel so foreign?

Culture shock makes nothing fit like it used to

Wandering to the window, I cringed while watching chimney smoke curl and a flag whip in the wind. Shopping for a small RV camper suddenly seemed all wrong.

We decided the only way to financially survive five months in Europe was to buy and live in an RV. I'd never been a "rough it" kind of gal - quite the opposite really, but camping through Europe had perks. We could go where we wanted when we wanted, sleep in the same bed every night and do our own cooking. Back in Calgary it seemed doable, but I hadn't anticipated winter.

At a business that sold and bought back campers, we were ready to implement our camping plan. Our salesman, Renee, droned on and on about registration and insurance. We were starting to wonder if we were doing the right thing when Renee, sensing our trepidation, whisked us outside to look at campers.

I liked the brand new motor home as big as a bus but Ken quickly steered me towards something more in line with our budget. Touring the inside of a 1987 diesel Fiat camper with 200,000 km didn't take much more than five baby steps. I was still digesting the absence of toilet and shower in its paltry bathroom when Renee told us it would cost $10,500.00 Euros with a 65% buy back guarantee.

Ken seemed to like the camper and looked to me for my thoughts. I couldn't find words to comment let alone commit. This camper wasn't coming close to what I'd imagined our RV to be.

With the office closing for the day we left to think things over. As we stepped out into a fierce north wind Rene threw out one last piece of information. If we did in fact buy something, we should stay in Amsterdam for at least a week to be sure everything worked. He offered a warranty, but only if repairs were done in their shop. We knew one thing for sure – camper or no camper – we wouldn't be staying long.

February 22

It was Sunday. A three hour run day. After months of dealing with heat, we had to figure out what to wear in the cold. Forced to be innovative, long underwear became running pants, a sweat band was repositioned to earmuffs, and I wore, in layers, every shirt in my suitcase.

There was no problem finding an interesting place to run. We followed a dike (narrow channels of water running through Amsterdam in grids) into a huge park filled with locals kayaking in calm water. I wasn't keen on Amsterdam's weather, but their flat terrain was a runners dream. Time passed reasonably painlessly, or at least it did for me. Ken, who'd suffered many injuries during his CFL football career couldn't say the same. His arthritic knees revolted about two and a half hours in, allowing me, for the first time ever, to take the lead. For a split second I was the strong one, the front runner, and it felt so good. But then I realized the agony Ken must been in to stop. He never stopped. Reluctantly I left him at a park bench and carried on.

I finished the run, but finishing alone didn't feel quite right. Helping Ken up from the bench, he limped back to the hotel swearing he'd find a way to run our marathon even if he had to live on anti-inflammatories. Moved by his determination, right there and then, I promised myself I would stifle my complaining when we ran. Of sound and able body, I needed to be thankful for the privilege to run. I'd never fully appreciated, until that moment, just how lucky I was.

"If you don't have anything good to say, don't say anything at all"
-Thumper

In the afternoon we went to the Van Gough Museum and witnessed the progression of his art from dark realistic portraits to the bright impressionism, making him one of world's most famous artists. Even the kids were intrigued, giving me inspiration to continue jamming art history down their throat.

As we left the museum, hot dogs sold by a street vendor caught our eye. Drawn in by their aroma, enough to make even a vegetarian drool, we couldn't resist. Twenty-five Canadian dollars and three minutes later, we'd barely put a dent in our hunger. It was time to head to the grocery store. A friendly clerk educated us on Dutch cheese, handing out one sample of rich full flavored white cheese after another. There was an out-of-this-world amazing side to cheese I'd never experienced before.

After purchasing our favorite cheese and bread and wine, we were excited to indulge in a truly European dinner.

Life is too short to eat mild orange Cheddar

February 23

Helping Ken out of bed (he seized up overnight like a Tin Man in a typhoon) we prepared to check out from the last hotel we'd stay in for a long while. A decision had been made. The Fiat would be our home away from home for the next five months.

Hopping a tram, we headed to the inner city for a two night home stay with a gal named Shelagh. She lived in a small flat, and like all of our Servas hosts, was a unique and intriguing person. A widowed fifty year old with a bum leg, she told us how, ever since reading *Call of the Wild* as a teenager, she wanted to backpack through Alaska. Squirreling away money for years, she was set to go. If she could travel alone in the wilderness, I could certainly survive life in a camper, couldn't I?

February 24

After an enjoyable morning with Shelagh, we headed to an outdoor market hoping to buy a few things for the camper. As we shopped, sunny skies gave in to menacing clouds swirling like SOS pads drizzling dirty dish water. Not the lovely refreshing drizzle we'd become accustomed to in south east Asia, but freezing rain changing snow to slush. Giving up on shopping, we squeezed into the small lobby of a photography museum, dripping wet and shivering. The boys came up with a half price deal. They happily loitered in the gift shop while Makayla and I explored the museum. In the end, we achieved our main goal – thawing out.

Heading back to Shelagh's cozy apartment, we all worked together to whip up a tasty meal. Good food and good conversation helped us to forget the day's frustrations.

February 25

Snow on the day we picked up the camper didn't feel good, nor did Renee's long speech about the things that could go wrong once we owned it. On he went about engine trouble, accidents, theft and the dire consequences of running over someone. When he passed us a pen and a purchase agreement, I shot Ken the "this was your dumb idea" look and felt like I was signing my life away.

Renee must have drunk too much coffee while dragging on about the dangers of owning a camper because he hardly took a breath while explaining how the camper worked. Blazing from one thing to another, he lost me at the propane tank. Ken's head bobbed up and down with Renee's every word, so I mentally signed off, leaving him to it. Next thing I knew, we held the keys, and Renee was gone.

We'd made arrangements to meet Shelagh for dinner at her favorite pancake place down town. Pulling out and stalling to a symphony of horns, Ken wrestled with a temperamental stick shift. Driving a new camper in a new city, to a new place in rush hour traffic, had to be one of the bravest or stupidest things Ken had ever done.

Bracing for an accident and yelling at Ken to watch out for this and that, I tried to decipher an impossible tourist map. Narrow little one way streets rutted with cable car tracks made us question if such streets were even meant for cars. I anticipated colliding with a tram at every turn. When Ken started to wince, we gave up. Struggling our way back to Shelagh's, we arrived traumatized but in one piece. She forgave us and even gave us her handicapped parking pass to park on the street.

At a Chinese restaurant we gloomily watched snowflakes as big as silver dollars fall with enough momentum to form vertical white lines until Makayla broke our trance and suggested a movie.

It was just past midnight when the movie let out and we pushed into the unyielding glass doors of a closed subway station. In a sleeping residential community, getting a cab seemed as likely as finding grapes in the meat department. We trudged along, leaving footprints in pristine snowy powder, until finding a closed restaurant and banging on the door got us a phone and a cab.

By the time we squeezed through a camper door stiff from frozen hinges, we dreaded the night before us. Miserably shivering, we bumped into each other while trying to find lights and turn on the heater. As it turned out, Renee also lost Ken at the propane tank. He fiddled with buttons while we prayed, like we'd never prayed before, that he'd figure it out.

February 26

I woke in the middle of the night feeling like I was on fire. The camper was like an oven. Randomly pushing buttons on the heater until it turned off, I wearily crawled back into bed throwing off my covers. Sometime later, waking again and freezing to death, I tried to spark the heater back to life. And so the night went – off and on – boiling – freezing – and cursing.

Shelagh kindly invited us in for breakfast. Without that invitation and a warm shower to thaw my chilled weary bones, I don't know what I would have done, but nervous breakdown comes to mind. And so, with great sadness, we bid Shelagh and her heated apartment goodbye and trudged back to the camper to start our European adventure.

Mattson had gymnastic training lined up in Rotterdam, a Dutch city two hours from Amsterdam. Glorious warm sunshine streamed through the camper's windows during our drive, raising our spirits. Camping would be so much better once we got down south. We drove into Rotterdam on well-marked modern roads, thanks to the rebuilding of the city after World War II's carpet bombing, and found Mattson's gym – no fuss no muss. He was even on time.

When Mattson finished training, we whipped up dinner in the camper. It was fun cooking together in our new little kitchen. We were so comfortable we decided to spend the night right there in the gym parking lot. Why not? It was free and the gym bathroom was only a few steps away. Mattson would even get to gym on time two days in a row.

February 27

Obviously missing something strategically important about how to regulate the temperature of the propane heater, we spent another up and down night turning it on and off. Holland was too cold. We had to leave.

With Mattson off at gym and a long list of things to buy for the camper, we set out to find a store selling adapters. The prongs on our

North American chargers weren't lining up with the holes on our Dutch camper's plug-ins.

Don't leave home without a universal adaptor

The store wasn't supposed to be far away, but finding the right freeway exit through the process of elimination took time. We drove, stopped, searched and watched clerks shake their heads until it was time to pick up Mattson. Life without Game Boy was too terrible for Mattson to accept. We simply had to turn back and go to the mall we'd just passed.

To get to a huge above ground mall parking lot we drove down a narrow entry ramp and met a goal post like structure running an inch lower than the roof of our camper. Not being able to fit through wasn't convenient for a long line of cars stopped behind us. It was a good thing our Dutch license plates saved Canadian drivers a bad name.

If you don't succeed, try and try again. Finding a set of goal posts that appeared to sit higher, I got out to direct Ken. While I accessed the situation, the ruckus of horns and angry shouts from vehicles behind us left me ready to wave Ken under even if we lost our roof in the process. Ken's medical equipment mounted on our roof took a minor hit, but we made it through. With an adaptor and working Game Boys; our world once again turned.

The plan was to eat and then start our drive to Spain, but it wasn't meant to be. Halfway through the meal, as the camper cooled with the setting sun, we madly pushed buttons on the heater to no avail. Like it or not, we'd be heading back to Amsterdam, the land of snow and ice, to get the stupid thing fixed.

DRIVING FROM AMSTERDAM TO SPAIN

February 28

When Ken picked us up from an internet café, he cheerfully told us how a helpful mechanic took all afternoon to explain the workings of our camper. The heater could actually be set to a specific temperature instead of the all or nothing mode we'd been using. And the best revelation of all; our bed, pulled out to twice the size we'd been sleeping on (nothing more than an oversized single). How foolish we'd been. The thing was, we'd never camped before. As we drove out of Amsterdam, we had a fresh new start.

The day passed comfortably as the kids stretched out on their beds playing video games. We drove through Holland, Belgium and Luxemburg and finally stopped for the night in France.

Pouring myself a nice Bordeaux in a real wine glass, while fixing dinner, I cooked and hummed the only French song I knew "Alouette, gentile alouette. Alouette, je te plumerai."

February 29

Waking to acceleration and movement, but still surrounded by black night, it took a few seconds for me to realize Ken was driving. I laid in bed and considered rolling over and going back to sleep when a sharp turn dislodged a paperback from the shelf above. After flying through the air, the book connected with my head with enough momentum to hurt. Sinking deeper into my bed; another wild turn launched Tolstoy's *War and Peace*, the hard cover. I was – once and for all – awake.

It was painfully obvious the camper needed to be reorganized. Wanting to fold up my bed, I couldn't figure out the mechanism to convert the bed to a kitchen table. Questioning Ken on how to do it, he yelled back from the driver's seat "pull up hard." "Hard," I reconfirmed, receiving a nod from the back of his head. So pull hard I did, yanking and causing a grating sound as the table separated from its metal frame. It appeared I didn't have quite the right angle. Continuing my manipulation, a few screws dislodged before I figured out that a forward movement easily slid the table into place.

Grumbling under my breath about Ken's bad advice, I grabbed the handle of an overhead cupboard and heard a snap. Holding a plastic handle no longer attached to its cupboard, Ken cranked his head back questioning what I was doing. "Nothing dear" spat through gritted teeth seemed like the best response. When the kids poked their heads through their bed's privacy curtain, I confessed "I seem to be some kind of camper terminator." "Terminator what?" asked Ken, as he once again turned my way and brought the camper along for a sway.

Not able to make it all the way to Barcelona, we drove to a rest stop and called it a day. In the camper's small space, Ken and Mattson seemed like giants with skis for feet. After tripping over a congealed mass of bodies all evening long, I was ready to pare the guys down with a knife.

It seemed like a good time to reference a book I'd brought on the trip, called *Camping through Europe*. It offered advice about how to function in a confined space. Reading the book out loud, and speaking clearly and concisely with expression to hold the family's attention, I customized an example. I should say "Mattson I would like to move past you to go to the kitchen, could you please move so I can pass?" Looking up into the whites of rolling eyes it seemed we'd be staying with the push and shove.

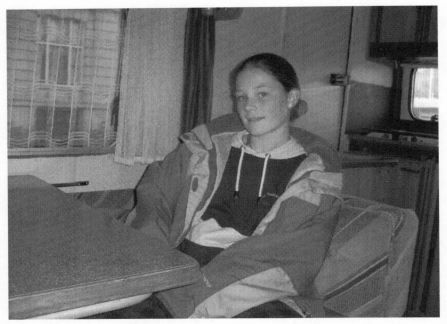

Makayla in the camper

Our home away from home

198

SPAIN

March 1

I met my first public shower with trepidation. Holding back in the camper, each wet-haired family member returning to the camper was interrogated "how was: water pressure, water temperature, water purity, water fragrance, water mineralization, water spray circumference, shower-size, shower cleanliness, shower availability..." Positive reports didn't boost my urge to get up and go. In the end it really wasn't that bad. Even so, I wondered; how long could I go without the daily shower I'd enjoyed back home?

Arriving in Spain in the early afternoon, it was cool, but we'd left the icy north wind behind. We stopped for groceries in Girona, discovering curtains of hanging sausages and smelly dried fish. Buying lunch would be our cultural experience for the day.

It was early evening by the time we pulled into a free parking area right beside the ocean. Once settled, Barcelona welcomed us for dinner with a reasonably priced four course meal at a set price. Included with the food was our choice of red wine or water. Imagine good red wine valued the same as water. I wanted to be Spanish.

March 2

Sitting by the ocean, I enjoyed a good book in lovely morning sun. It seemed our Big Trip was back on track, until Ken returned from the internet with a brochure showing the Hop On, Hop Off tour of Barcelona route. He figured he'd follow their map with the camper. It would be our own little free personal tour. We'd hop out and tour while Ken drove around the block. Sounded good in theory, but so did communism.

The problems started when Ken, also wanting to enjoy the tour, kept his eyes more off the road than on, and not knowing the lay of the land, unexpectedly found himself at our stop in the wrong lane. Unable to unload at the curb, he yelled "jump, jump," and like sky divers taking a risky plunge, we dropped into busy lanes of traffic.

Park Guell, designed by Gaudi, one of Barcelona's most famous architects, was located at the top of a steep hill. The camper was gutless on hills and lost speed struggling up the last hundred meters. As we disembarked, Ken crowed "take your time, I'll just go around the block a few times until you're back."

After taking our time in the park I hoped Ken wasn't getting bored waiting for us, but as it turned out, we were the ones left waiting.

Over a half an hour passed before I spotted him running up the hill with a distressed look on his face. "The camper's parked illegally," he hollered. Running back down, we hopped in, out of breath. At the same time, a man standing on the sidewalk motioned for Ken to back up. He wanted to open a small box like trailer parked inches from our hood. Obviously flustered, with sweat pouring from his brow, Ken's little forehead temporal stress vein throbbed. He turned the key flicking his wrist over and over again. When the camper didn't respond, I stared into surprisingly wild eyes, as he muttered "I think I blew the engine." For some strange reason, Ken was a mess. Meanwhile, the trailer guy kept waving for us to move. "The security code, I forgot the security code," Ken blurted out, punching in the numbers and trying again. This time the engine revved to a start. As the guy stepped up to knock on our window, Ken shoved the camper into reverse and waved him away. Hitting the gas, a crushing sound of impact, made him slam on the brake.

Now there were two people knocking on our window. Ken hadn't seen the Smart Car parked right behind him. Getting back in the car after checking out the damage, he dropped his head into his hands. I thought he might cry.

No one said a word as we waited for a damage report. When it finally came, we let out a sigh of relief. Only the hood of the smart car was dented. When Ken pushed on the hood, it popped back out as good as new. All was well, or so it seemed, until Ken started telling his story.

After dropping us off at the park, he'd looped around the block and ended up on a different steeper street. Halfway up, the camper started losing power. Needing to get off that street, he attempted to turn at the upcoming intersection, but unlike *The Little Engine That Could*, our chugging camper couldn't make it. Stopped at an awkward angle, inches away from parked cars at the front and back of him, gunning the gas pedal made the engine roar and cough out smoke. A shrill shriek of horns filled the air as Ken sat paralyzed by frustration. Getting out of his pickle without exploding the motor or hitting a car seemed impossible.

One foot on the brake and one on the gas, with the pedal to the metal, stopped him from rolling backwards and won him a smoky millimetre of forward movement. Multiple millimetres miraculously straightened him out. From there, he waited while a long line of cars backed down the hill onto a busy street and then did the same.

Our personalized tour ended at Gaudy's park. Even though the camper seemed to be running fine, Ken just stared into space at dinner that night. I left him alone, replacing his empty beer when needed.

March 3

Waking up to a beautiful warm morning, Ken and I left the kids sleeping and sauntered over to a huge open air flee market. Immediately losing Ken at the freshly fried potato chip booth, I carried on to marvel at what looked like 14th century relics. Admittedly my dating could be off. In Western Canada a foot pedaled Singer Sewing machine made in the 1930's was an antique. I wanted so many of those gorgeous old things, but decorating my house in Grand-Gothic-Cathedral style, would likely be a passing infatuation.

After visiting Monestir de Montserrat, just outside Barcelona, we carried on to Tarragona to search for a campground with showers. Two days without one wasn't going over well with Makayla. Combining happy with dirty wasn't something she could muster.

Trying to decipher a Dutch campground catalogue and Spanish road signs was as successful as finding a pin in a dark room. Totally frustrated, we listened to the kids and changed course to follow signs for an amusement park. With arrows popping up every few miles it seemed like a no brainer until an arrow placed right before a fork in the road left us confused. No trajectory lined it up with the three roads branching off the main. Randomly picking one, it wasn't our lucky day. We had to chase all three before finding the amusement park.

Joyously running to the ticket booth, we stood at the window reading a small sign stating PARK CLOSED FOR THE SEASON. The kids' faces fell in anguish. I felt their pain. What if I'd driven all over for a special bottle of wine anticipating how wonderful it would be, only to get home and realize I didn't have a corkscrew (actually that would never happen, but it's a good analogy). Denied fun when it was so close you could taste it brought such unhappiness.

Some quests can't be conquered

March 4

After camping in the amusement park's lot, we desperately needed a campground (not showering for three days makes your head itch). Giving up on Tarragona, we turned the camper toward Valencia.

Although apprehensive, we still drove right into the centre of Valencia without a map and looked for a place to park. Finding nothing but a loading zone, Ken and Makayla stayed with the camper while Mattson and I set off to find tourist information. Upon our return, Ken's red face and engorged t-vein (may as well give it a nick name) throbbed like an ominous beacon. Something was wrong. "We've been robbed," Ken blurted out.

He'd been sitting in the driver's seat waiting for us, when a guy banged on the back of the camper and pointed to the rear wheel. Getting out to check the tire, another guy threw open the unlocked passenger door, reached in over the passenger seat and grabbed Ken's wallet off the top of the console board. Makayla, in the back of the camper, witnessed the robbery and screamed out to her dad. The wallet guy was too far gone to catch, but Ken chased down and caught the guy who banged on the camper. Meanwhile, people on the scene phoned the police who arrived quickly and took Ken's kicking and cursing captive into custody. As the officers threw the bad guy into the back of their squad car, they ordered Ken to the police station, a few blocks away.

The thief took our credit cards and about 100.00 Euros in cash. Canceling the cards would be a hassle, but it could have been worse. Getting to the police station however, couldn't have been. In crushing traffic, we searched for a place to park and squeezed down roads barely wide enough for compact cars. Double parking illegally, while Ken went in to make a report, turned out to be our only option.

For the next two hours, every fifteen minutes, a different police officer banged on my window ordering me to move the camper. It simply wasn't possible. I mean come on, I hadn't driven a stick shift in years and wasn't about to renew my skills in a temperamental camper at rush hour in down town Valencia, Spain. Instead I performed a dramatic monologue, like a seasoned actress, calling on tears, if need be, to make them go away.

Ken finally returned with bad news. He had to go to court the next morning.

March 5

While Ken was at court, the rest of us went to the grocery store. A few hours later, he returned with his court report. Our thief would spend the grand total of three weekends in jail and was ordered to pay us restitution, yet no one asked where our money should be sent. All in all, Ken's tour of the Spanish judicial system had been a total waste of time. The kids and I, on the other hand, were having a great time discovering Carrefour, a mega store like we'd never seen before. They sold everything from food to Xboxes. There wasn't anything you couldn't buy there.

On a quiet residential street near a bus stop, we locked the camper and took a bus down town, heeding Renee's advice not to drive into city centers. Ken went to the internet café while the kids and I spent a pleasant afternoon exploring uniquely Spanish architecture. On the way home we cheerfully chatted about making tacos for dinner. Getting off the bus, we turned the corner and spotted the camper. Something wasn't right. I could see a window open. We hadn't left it that way.

A closer look revealed shattered glass and a shredded screen. Starting to shake, I opened the back door and gasped at cupboard doors ripped open; their contents spilling out like disemboweled guts. We'd hidden our electronics under the mattress of a neatly made bed, a bed ripped apart. Mattson looked to confirm what we already knew. Everything was gone.

Frozen in that moment, Makayla's crying brought me back to reality. Over and over again, in a rising crescendo of hysterics, she howled "I want to go home!" I crushed her to my chest, fighting back my own tears, and stroked her hair telling her everything would be okay. But it wasn't okay. A bad person in a foreign land had violated our space, touched our stuff and taken our special things.

Being robbed is a hurtful betrayal

By the time Ken got home, everything was cleaned up. His reaction to the fact we'd been robbed twice in less than twenty-four hours was practical and subdued. Immediately setting to work, he talked of insurance claims and police reports while trying to repair our damaged camper window. I watched his mouth move, not caring about the words. Like Makayla, I wanted to go home.

March 6

Precious photos – gone; a month of journal entries – gone; a laptop and Game Boys – gone. I felt sick. In the morning, pulling the covers over my head, I hoped to sleep our hardship away but Ken gave me a nudge reminding me it was a ninety minute training run day. He figured we should make the police station our destination. Numbly, with a body not plugged into its brain, I got ready.

It took about three-quarters of an hour to find the police station. We talked to a clerk who told us in broken English the station was closed and wouldn't open again until Monday. On those police station stairs, with fire in my eyes, I told Ken we wouldn't spend another day in Valencia. We were leaving even if we didn't get the police report our insurance company demanded. Our traumatized brains stalled until a police car driving past spurred Ken to jump out into traffic to flag it down. Despite his jumping jacks it sped on.

Ken was sure the police car saw us and would return. I was sure the car would never come back and wanted to resume our run. "Even if they do come back they won't speak English and help us" I snipped. Settling back into my frown, the police car pulled up in front of us. Thirty minutes later, after driving us to a different police station, we had all the forms we needed.

One positive outcome wasn't enough to improve my spirits. It was hot as we resumed our run. My body hurt, my head hurt and my heart hurt as stiff legs hit hard pavement and my brain clicked back on and revved into overdrive. The kids were back at the camper alone; what if someone broke in and kidnapped them? How would we replace our losses? Why hadn't I saved my journal and our pictures more regularly? Why, why, why?

The rest of the day was a blur. We shopped to replace stuff, then finally left the godforsaken city of Valencia to continue our journey south. That night as I lay in bed I knew I had to put the robberies behind me and move on. In the morning, I'd get up and put a smile back on my face, but at that moment, I was bluer than blue.

March 7

Enjoying breakfast in the sunshine was just the medicine we all needed to wash the blues away.

Thankfully, we still had Ken's laptop, as he'd taken it to the internet café with him. Trying to be positive, I sat down to rewrite my lost journal entries, but frustration set in as I stared at a blank computer screen. How was I ever going to rewrite what I'd lost and still keep up with my regular daily journaling? "One word at a time," a voice in my head whispered.

In the afternoon, ready to sightsee, we headed off to see a castle in Alacante. Perched high on a hill we stood in its massive courtyard looking down at the sparkling Mediterranean Ocean and imagined dueling Spanish knights shuffling up and down winding stone staircases, clashing swords held high.

It was 9:00 p.m. by the time we sat down for dinner. In Spain, you were only allowed to enter and leave your camp site at specific times. One minute late meant closed gates and no access to your campground until the next morning. Not sure when the gates closed, we gobbled down our food. Even on our Big Trip, we always seemed to be in a rush. Could it be our need to always fit in just one more thing – one last e-mail, one last castle, or one last picture?

Changing your location doesn't change who you are

Our luck seemed to be turning. We made it through the campground gates just before they closed and settled in for a game of cards before bed. Relaxed and cozy in the camper, it seemed appropriate to stop and give thanks. We made it through one whole day without being robbed.

March 8

It was another long run day – three and a half hours. A cool breeze and flat hard packed beach offered up the perfect setting, but even so – it hurt. Finishing a run like that suddenly made rewriting a few journal entries seem like no big deal.

Determined to get things done, the rest of the day passed doing school work, shopping for yet another elusive adapter (the nerve of every country to put their holes in a different place) and grocery shopping.

Our highlight of the day: McDonald's ice cream and empathetic e-mails from home soothed our "open oozing, poor us we've been robbed twice, wounds."

March 9

Greedy for warmth, we drove on.

At a camp site in Almeria, we sprawled out in the sun and marveled at the concept of European camping. Our camping spot was nothing more than a slab of concrete in a parking lot lined with campers. What a far cry from the rugged, back to nature, camping experience in Canada. With very few trees, and no bonfire pits or barbeques to roast meat or make s'mores, European camping was all about an affordable place to spend the night within walking distance to a bar, restaurant and bathroom.

We were doing a lot better in the camper. No longer practicing the "push and shove," we figured out it was easier to ask the closest person to get what you wanted rather than push for it yourself. The system did have one flaw – Makayla and Ken always seemed to be the ones asking. When Mattson complained that he felt like a personal slave, I had to proclaim "Welcome to my world." Two new nicknames were coined. I was Personal Slave One (PS1) and Mattson was Personal Slave Two (PS2).

Around 5:00 p.m. we drove into town and looked for a place to eat. When every door on a long street full of restaurants was locked, we sullenly accepted that the Spanish eat at Canadian bedtime.

Arriving back at the campground in time to see the gates close behind us, we fell into what was becoming our nightly routine – PS1 and PS2 grumpily passing out toothbrushes, toothpaste, brushes, books......

March 10

I woke in the middle of the night from a bizarre dream. Spanish men surrounding me yelled in my ear and stole my olives. How do the Spanish not suffer the consequences of late night eating? Once awake and unable to get back to sleep, I studied the ceiling and thought about how, in the last six months, apart from Bali and our time in Egypt with Tracee and Ric, we'd never stayed anywhere longer than three days. Day-to-day travel was wearing us down. What we needed was a holiday from our travel. I remembered an e-mail our good friends had sent telling us about inexpensive getaway packages available through their time share membership. A one week stay in a nice condo would be a dream come true. The comforting thought of it lulled me back to sleep. In the morning, after sharing my holiday thoughts with the family, we couldn't wait to get to an internet café to see what we could arrange.

When a condo in the Costa del Sol (South of Spain) was found, I smiled and dreamed of televisions and bath tubs. Ken worked out a jam packed sightseeing itinerary to be completed before we went.

The Alcazar, a famous castle in Almeria, had a huge cactus right outside its entry gate. It reminded me of the cacti lining the highway in the old Road Runner television cartoon series. We learned many historic details about that castle, but if anyone ever asks me about the place I'll have to stammer "hmmm…ah…well…I remember there was a big cartoon-cactus." My brain, already in holiday mode, wasn't capable of absorbing anything more.

March 11

Continuing on with Ken's long activity list, we drove to Granada to visit the Alhambra, a world renowned 12th century castle representing classic Islamic art and architecture. Upon arriving, a crowd of people stood waiting in front of locked gates that should have been open. We joined the line and heard from our fellow tourists that there had just been a terrorist attack in Madrid. Hundreds of innocent people were killed when a bomb exploded in the main train station.

A deadly terrorist attack in a place not all that far away from us hit hard. We'd visited sites of terrorism in Bali and Egypt, but ultimately believed it wouldn't touch us. Well – we felt touched. For the first time I was thankful for our little camper keeping us away from public transport. No longer would we feel guilty about driving into city centres. So what if we faced bad traffic or robbers; at least we wouldn't get blown to bits.

Once inside the palace, the beauty of concrete carved into lace and cathedral ceilings of rich dark wood took our minds off of the terrorism. With so much to see at the Alhambra, the day faded away with only one check mark on Ken's long list. Pressure was building as it always does before a holiday. At home, we'd be attending to details like canceling the newspaper, finishing work projects and packing. On The Big Trip it was getting through Ken's long list of activities. He wouldn't rest until we did.

Leaving Granada, we drove into the night arriving in Seville well after all campground gates were closed and locked. Having to free camp on the side of the road, I pulled out the dreaded Porta Potty, but with luxury right around the corner, no one complained.

208

March 12

Ken pulled out his pen and made one check mark after another. We ricocheted from churches with gold plated interiors, parks with entwined lovers and the Spanish Square's ceramic tile murals. Seville wasn't the kind of place to skip over.

At the end of the day, jubilantly throwing a completed sightseeing list away, we took a wrong turn on our way back to the camper. The sky opened for a torrential downpour as we hugged backpacks stuffed with computers and Game Boys (after our robberies we brought our valuables with us). We desperately needed a couple of umbrellas. I thought I'd come on the trip with everything we'd need: ear plugs, sink stoppers, clothes lines - everything but umbrellas. Isn't that the way it goes? Trying to remember all the elusive stuff, you forget the most obvious.

Back at the camper, wet, starving and tired, we worked together like a well-oiled machine to get dinner on the table. After sharing the work of doing dishes we capped off the night with a game of charades. Flailing about, making body language words in the confines of a camper, added a whole new hilarious dimension to the game.

March 13

The day had come to check into our condo, but not before stocking up at the local Carrefour. Grocery shopping was Mattson's favorite thing to do. He gladly spent hours in every area of the store but one. In Spain they had a large section filled with huge hunks of smoked pork, salted cod and fresh fish. The entangled smell of the threesome created a stench Mattson couldn't tolerate. One whiff made his mouth practically touch his nose. When he let out a steady stream of insults about how "super gross" it all was, I had to launch into an impromptu lesson on cultural sensitivity.

Be a respectful guest in someone else's home

March 14

When we entered our condo, I fell in love. Not usually attracted to such things, doing without in the camper made me starry-eyed for kitchen appliances. A big refrigerator, powerful microwave and sturdy oven – what more could a girl want? I lingered in the kitchen to broil, reheat, and chill. It gave me such pleasure.

After a morning of lounging, Ken decided an afternoon excursion was in order. Much to our disappointment, he didn't want to watch T.V. all day in pajamas. Off we went to Tivoli, an outdoor carnival a few towns down the road. The highway led through one congested town filled with generic high rise condos after another. Apparently the South of Spain is the retirement capital of Europe, attracting millions of grey haired people to its inexpensive sun and surf.

Tivoli turned out to be a small local flea market run by mostly Brits. The kids weren't impressed with ancient rides made for toddlers. All was not lost though, as I found a box of Act Two Microwave Kettle Corn and felt like I had won the lottery.

We watched T.V. that night. Every once in a while, I slipped away to the kitchen, overcome with the desire to open the fridge. I wasn't hungry; having that much cold food was just so novel. I'd run my finger tenderly over the oven, or pop another bag of kettle corn – ahhh, ecstasy!

March 15

On our morning run, we talked about how to make Makayla's upcoming birthday a big deal. She seemed to think a Big Trip birthday couldn't be fun and exciting. We were determined to prove her wrong.

Brainstorming on gift ideas, I drew a blank. No longer did I have my finger on the pulse of her taste in fashion, music or anything else, for that matter. It seemed as twelve approached, a new mother daughter trend was developing. Anything I liked she didn't. Just a month ago I'd been the centre of her universe; all seeing and all knowing. How had I taken such a huge fall from grace? There I stood confused and a bit melancholy in the clothing section of Carrefour, realizing my baby wasn't a baby anymore.

Trying to figure out what she'd like – it hit me. The shower, Makayla loved to shower. She was always asking to buy some kind of skin care product and had a real thing for the Dove brand name. Off I went to fill the cart with Dove shower gel, shampoo, moisturizing cream – anything that smelled nice with Dove packaging. Next came foods she always asked for that I didn't like to buy: Fruit Loops, Oreo cookies, and cavity-causing gummy bears, hit the cart. By the time we left, I could have bought two designer dresses for what I'd spent, but felt confident she'd love her gifts.

March 16

Captivating Ken with a big bag of potato chips strategically placed on the couch beside him; we watched the Discovery Channel until he licked the bag clean, ending his trance. He sprang from the couch insisting we explore the caves of Nerja. I was less than enthusiastic. We'd explored so many other caves. There was also the issue of entering miniscule-suffocating-dark spaces. Actually I was feeling a bit ho hum about travel in general. It was losing its effervescence and becoming flat in a "been there done that" kind of way. But with Ken's insistence, off we went. I entered those caves a lethargic dull girl, but by the time I exited Nerja's huge cavernous cave, I was once again full of fizz. Just when we thought we'd seen it all, we hadn't. Stalagmites and stalactites shaped like different animals left us amazed.

Driving home after our visit, I felt rejuvenated; my travel bug re-carbonated and bubbling.

Nature's wonders have no end

That night we ate authentic slow cooked paella by the ocean. Thanks to our Nerja cave experience, we planned the next part of our trip with the same euphoric excitement we'd had at its inception.

March 17

Homework, reading, relaxing, a couple home cooked meals and lots of good T.V. We finally had our "do nothing all day in your pajamas" day and loved every minute of it (even Ken).

March 18

It was my baby girl's twelfth birthday. After Makayla's bad bout of home sickness in Singapore, she'd made an effort to be more cheerful, and although we knew she was still missing home, especially around her birthday, she didn't complain. I admired the way she handled the challenges of our Big Trip and told her so in a little birthday poem.

~ *FOR MAKAYLA ON HER TWELFTH BIRTHDAY* ~

Around the world with your family you've had to go.
Giving up friends and dance, you weren't allowed to
say no.

We know that our travel can leave you homesick and
sad, especially when your brother teases you and makes
you mad.

But understand – together as a family we're making
memories that will only grow, more special as time
passes – right now you can't know.

Oh how we love the efforts you make, to record our long
journey with the pictures you happily take.

As days filled with ups and downs pass by,
you enthusiastically step up; giving whatever comes
your way a try

With only your father, mother and brother to stand up
and give you a hand, we wish you a HAPPY BIRTHDAY
in this foreign land.

Thank you for giving us this very special year,
I hope in the future you'll hold it dear.

Her birthday extravaganza began:

- Waking at 12:00 noon to a decedent chocolate meringue covered in whipped cream and lit with a birthday candle
- Serenaded by a somewhat off key rendition of happy birthday.
- Searching, finding and eating her first gift – fruit loops from a variety pack of her favorite cereals.
- A full body massage
- Searching for gifts (Dove shower products)
- Into the shower to become a Dove girl
- Profuse compliments on how good she looked and smelled
- Go-carting
- A stop at McDonald's for McFlurries (a step up from our usual cones)
- Lord of the Rings viewing at the condo
- More searching for gifts
- Dinner with her favorite home cooked Fettuccine Alfredo
- Phone calls with birthday greetings from home
- More searching for gifts
- A game of charades (we let her win)
- More searching for gifts
- Lots of before bed hugs and kisses

March 19

The time had come for the biggest challenge in our training program – the four hour run. How could running for that amount of time not be intimidating? I mean come on, you can roast a twenty pound turkey in four hours.

We ran along the ocean in the town of Fuengirola. I don't know if it was the ocean's ions or the spring in the wooden boardwalk, but time passed faster and my body hurt less than on our other long runs. Even Ken, juiced up on half a bottle of Advil, stayed by my side. But four hours was four hours, and when we were done we were physically done. What scared me, was knowing that at our pace, it would take at least another forty minutes to complete the marathon. As it was, we used the railing on a flight of stairs like a crutch to lift our dead-weight legs to our room.

March 20

Refreshed from our holiday, we were ready to get back on the road. I said sad goodbyes to each and every kitchen appliance and trudged back to the camper to find plastic bags, transferred from the condo to camper, covering every inch of floor space. Immediately wanting to organize, my need was canceled out by Ken's need to drive. Seconds after his foot hit the gas pedal everyone wanted something: Mattson, his book, Makayla, her brush and Ken, his map. The camper swerved around and around a traffic circle (Ken's way of getting his bearings) while I ping ponged about like James T Kirk on the *Star ship Enterprise's* bridge during enemy fire. Readjusting to life in the camper wasn't going to be easy.

A tightly controlled border at the Rock of Gibraltar left us in a long queue. While we waited, an interesting conversation broke out about why a British territory was situated in the middle of Spain. Ken talked about the significance of Gibraltar militarily and about the things we'd see during the day. Cleverly disguising a history lesson as idle chit chat, the kids bought his deception and put down their Game Boys.

History becomes real when it is seen and touched

Mattson in the Nerja Caves

Go carting for Makayla's birthday

Mattson and Makayla washing dishes in the camper

Gaudi's Park Guell in Barcelona

Parc De La Ciutadella in Barcelona

PORTUGAL

March 21

Standing outside the camper, inhaling blissfully warm air perfumed with jasmine and orange blossoms, we found ourselves in rural Portugal. Trees growing asparagus, walnuts, almonds, olives, and every kind of citrus fruit imaginable surrounded us. We picked and ate sweet oranges right off the branch and looked down at rotting fruit covering the ground. Delphina, our Servas host, explained how Portugal was a new member of the E.U. Forced to compete with other European countries, Portugal couldn't match their pricing. Frustrated farmers, unable to make a living, were forced to riot. The government responded by subsidizing the planting of trees even though the fruit those trees produced would never go to market. Ken couldn't believe the wastefulness of it all, and ever the entrepreneur, spent the rest of our hike conjuring up schemes on how to get rich harvesting Portugal's forgotten fruits.

March 22

In the morning, we sat on Delphina's sun soaked deck nibbling toast and olive oil and listened to her life story. Divorced with one independent twenty-three year old daughter, she became disillusioned with her Catholic faith and hectic unfulfilled life in Lisbon. Deciding it was time for change, a quest to find happiness began. She connected with a New Age, eastern based spiritual philosophy and found the courage to move to Portugal's beautiful Algarve by the sea. Like us, she was following her dream.

We sat together after breakfast under a clear blue sky, feeling very Bohemian as we discussed our mutual distaste for consumerism in a materialistic world. As time slipped by, the temperature rose – not a good thing on a training day. Reluctantly leaving Delphina behind, we continued our conversation on the run. Ending up lost in a maze of narrow winding dirt roads but still engrossed in our morning discussion, we ran way longer than we'd planned. Even so, we didn't care. It was one of those rare moments in life when the sun, moon and stars line up and after more than one wrong turn, you realize you've somehow stumbled upon your elusive road to happiness.

March 23

We sat in a camping spot under real trees munching chocolate granola and enjoying the "Morning Waddle" – a thoroughly entertaining stream of fresh from bed portly middle-age European men and women sauntering by on their way to the bathroom. Their bedroom attire included fuzzy slippers, flannel PJ's, boxer shorts and the odd head covered with curlers. Throw in beer bellies and tattoos and we were entertained by quite the show.

Makayla tore herself away to haul her bulging bag of birthday Dove products to the shower. A few minutes later she returned close to tears. Nothing, other than maybe onions on pizza, upset Makayla more than a shower glitch.

The shower was a push button type and to reach the button you had to stand under the shower head; a real problem when it took time for cold water to turn warm. A pressurized icy burst shot Makayla out of the shower like a cork from New Years' Eve champagne. Taking her under my arm, I assured her we'd find a way to overcome her problem. She looked doubtful. Twelve seemed to be the age when mothers lost their ability to save the day.

Grabbing a broom and taking her hand, we marched back to the showers. She stood with her arms crossed, while I used the handle to push the shower button from afar and let the water warm up. Rewarded with a quick hug and enthusiastic "thanks, mom," I still had the magic.

March 24

The camper was giving me a pain in the neck. I suspected it was because we never leveled it out at night before going to bed. The thing was, we just didn't know how, and even if we did, Ken likely wouldn't have bothered. A little angle on his bed didn't bother him – heck he could sleep standing up. I wasn't the only one finding life in the camper a pain in the neck. Mattson was having trouble with his sister's hair. Having to share a bed with her meant there was girl hair all over his pillow. It tickled his nose and made him sneeze. The hair bothered him so much he changed position, sleeping with his head by his sister's feet. Makayla found her brother's feet in her face a real pain in the neck, especially when he accidentally kicked her in the head during the night. Ken certainly thought we were all a pain in the neck with all of our bellyaching, leaving me to reiterate that the stupid camper was a real pain in the neck.

Needing some air, off Ken and I went doing running loops around our campground. At around loop ten (it was a small campground), a fellow Canadian greeted us. When he told us he and his wife spent every winter camping through Europe, I knew I had to pick this "King of Camping" guy's brain. Maybe he could unlock the secret of camping bliss still eluding us.

We accepted an invitation to his big sleek motor home and an hour later walked into opulent luxury. I felt as I did when walking into grossly expensive show homes; the type that make you turn green with envy. I glowed chartreuse, oohing and aahing as he showed off every awesome feature. It wouldn't be possible to get a pain in the neck in a place like theirs. It seemed the secret to blissful camping was spelled out in one word – MERCEDES. Thus, no bliss for us.

Later in the day, we drove into Lisbon to take Mattson to gym. After suffering the usual wrong turns, dead end streets, impassible tunnels, and outrageous traffic, we ended up at a standstill. Giving Ken instruction to pick us up, Mattson and I jumped out to walk the rest of the way.

I was standing at our pickup point when the street erupted into the epicentre for a major demonstration, complete with hundreds of angry ranting, sign carrying, face painted, marching people (likely farmers fighting for their harvest). They rolled in and washed over me like a tsunami. With them came swarms of shield-carrying police. There I stood locked in place in the middle of chaos, trying to look like a sympathizer for the cause or supporter for the police, depending on who glanced my way. As more and more people came, all I could think about was – where on earth did everyone park? Funny where the mind goes in stressful situations.

Finally spit out to be rescued by Ken, I ordered him to get us to the port-producing Douro Valley as quickly as possible. I desperately needed their fortified wine.

March 25

We spent the night free camping in an empty, quiet suburban parking lot. In the morning slamming car doors woke us. The lot, to our great surprise, had filled to capacity while we slept, locking our camper in place like tweens at a Brittany Spears concert.

Not sure where we were, Ken decided he should visit tourist information. It seemed like a "pie in the sky plan," but I was slowly starting to believe in Ken's special powers. Sure enough, he wasn't gone long before returning with maps and brochures.

With information in hand Ken buckled up prepared to drive, even though we were still trapped in place. I shook my head at his foolishness, but after a couple of minutes a fellow sauntered over, got in the car attached to our front bumper and drove away. From there Ken maneuvered his way out.

Positive intention will get you where you need to go

It was going to be one of those special days when the travel god shines down upon you. After a day of effortless touring we toasted gorgeous Portugal and its kind people with white port, generously poured by the owner of our campground. It was the perfect ending to a perfect day.

March 26

After a challenging (I hate hills) and exhilarating (downhill is okay) run filled with panoramic views of terraced vines lining the Douro Valley, we packed up and moved on. It was time to head north. The minute we crossed back into Spain, our camper as if remembering its assault on Spanish soil, started acting up.

Stopping at a few mechanical shops along our road, the language barrier seemed impossible to breach. Mechanics just shrugged and pointed us down the road. On we went, ending up on a bumpy gravel road making the camper Shimmy and the muffler rattle. It seemed appropriate to blurt out in my best Scotty accent "Captain, she's breaking up" (what can I say; I'm a hard core Trekkie). Appreciating the truth in my attempt for humor, Ken pulled over in a small town. The camper cooled while I scavenged for dinner. When a jar of pasta sauce with an expiry date of Dec 2000 wouldn't do, the kids happily accepted a bowl of cereal. They'd come a long way since the shocking 'eggs for dinner' affair in New Zealand.

After dinner we drove late into the night. Spain was obviously bad luck. We had to get to France as quickly as possible. Our marathon date of April 4th was quickly approaching.

March 27

Watching Ken make little boy "Dinky Toy" car noises for a dumbfounded mechanic gave us our first chuckle of the day. The mechanic didn't understand and then suddenly, he did. Sucking in his cheeks and nodding, he made his own car noises. Thrilled his message had been understood, Ken added one more "sick camper" vroom vroom for reinforcement. Those two men stood inches from each other revving their motors like kids trying to one up each other.

After time in the repair shop we drove off. We didn't get far. That "something isn't quite right" sound rang out. Back to the shop we went for another chorus of vroom, vrooms. When our mechanic drove with us to hear what we were hearing, wouldn't you know; the camper fell silent as a lamb. Minutes after setting our mechanic free, the camper returned to its noisy tricks. Down the road we shimmied, grinding our way to France.

Delphina's low roofed house

Visiting ruins

Douro Valley Vines

A countryside Portuguese Church

FRANCE

March 28

With a sigh of relief, we crossed the border into France. In Agen we met Maria, Andrea and their two teenagers. Just a year ago, Andrea, the dad, had been diagnosed with a very aggressive and debilitating form of Parkinson disease. Forced to leave a job he loved, tears of frustration ran down his cheeks as he stuttered and struggled to talk about the work he loved. I choked back my own tears when Maria, his wife, supportively squeezed his shoulder and told us how she'd been forced back to work full time to support the family. Caring for a disabled husband and driving two active teenagers about was a heavy load, but you wouldn't have known it by the smile on her face. I wondered how, with everything on her plate, she found the energy to welcome guests from another country into her home.

Maria was a gourmet cook. She took pride in introducing us to new and interesting French foods. Duck breast cooked rare and swimming in a puddle of blood had her daughter singing praises for dipping French bread into the sauce/blood. As she demonstrated, turning her bread blood red, Makayla's face turned snow white. Encouraged to give it a try, Makayla lifted her bread holding her hand like a rich lady forced to take a toilet brush to a dirty toilet.

I enthusiastically tried all of Maria's food until the ultimate French delicacy, foie gras, appeared. When passed to me on a communal plate, I stalled. The foie gras, rolled up like a jelly roll, had three layers: an outside quarter inch layer of snowy white duck fat, a brown red layer of smoked duck meat and a center of mushy mustard yellow duck liver pate. I told my hand to take a piece, but that outside layer of fat reminded me of the back fat on my cadaver in my university gross anatomy lab. Stifling a gag, I had to pass. Doing so set a welcomed precedent for the rest of the family.

March 29

In the morning, we packed into Maria's small compact car and drove. All circulation was lost when we finally pulled into an ancient monastery.

Prying ourselves out of the car we toured an amazing cathedral before entering an outdoor cloister. I instantly noticed a huge majestic evergreen tree in the middle of the garden like space. Gasping with excitement, I blurted out "that's the biggest, most beautiful tree I've ever seen. It looks like it could touch the moon." Admittedly it was an over dramatic statement, but that tree was really something. Makayla instantly reacted to my overblown comment, rolling her eyes and snipping "Calgary is full of trees like that." Not liking her tone and weary of her "you say black and I say white" thing, my cheeks flushed as I squared off in her face ready to argue tree size. Our tour came to a sudden halt as Maria and her daughter backed up behind us wondering why we'd stopped. Not wanting to hold them up, I let out a huge sigh and begrudgingly zipped my mouth leaving our argument unresolved. We moved on. A few minutes later, Makayla pointed to a run of the mill leafless deciduous tree and sarcastically commented "Look at that tree mom. It's as if it touches the moon."

For extended travel with daughters,
go before they're twelve

March 30

Once back on the road, I made the mistake of cheerfully saying to Ken "the camper sure is running well," Ten minutes later we stalled. The camper coasted to the side of the road and wouldn't start no matter how much Ken banged around. Shrugging and giving in to the reality of our situation, he set off to find the rest stop we'd passed a few kilometers back. Sensing we were in big trouble, I figured it was time for a drink. Setting up lawn chairs on the side of the hill beside the highway, the kids sipped pop while I indulged in a little red wine, a treat for both of us. While sipping I imagined the camper getting smashed to smithereens by a passing truck. Unfortunately it remained intact when Ken returned in a tow truck half an hour later.

It took about twenty minutes to find civilization. We drove through an industrial area in what appeared to be a small town and turned into a mechanic's shop. Our driver was obviously in a hurry. He haphazardly released the camper from his hoist half on and half off a curb.

With his head under the camper's hood, up popped his head out every few minutes to babble away in French. Ken had taken some French classes back in university but hadn't spoken a word in years. He did catch a few words though: "motor," "bad," and "wait until tomorrow."

Attempting to speak English, the driver eventually made us understand the mechanic wouldn't be back until the morning. With a shrug and sympathetic smirk, he jumped in his truck and was gone. Stunned by our situation, we stood staring at the camper slanting off the curb like the Leaning Tower of Pisa.

Not quite sure what to do, Mattson was the first to speak. His announcement of hunger prompted me to start dinner. The camper sat at such an angle I had to hold my pasta pot over the stove's element to keep it from sliding off.

Over dinner a plan unfolded. We needed to find out where we were and communicate with the people who'd sold us the camper. There was warranty on the motor, but only if it was fixed where we bought it. Ken figured we could have the camper towed from France to Amsterdam using our Canadian road side assistance insurance. It seemed like an awfully long way to me. Still if Ken thought it could be done, maybe it could.

Off we went, in surprisingly good moods, on an adventure of discovery. Five minutes later, after turning the corner off a desolate dark street, there stood a grocery store. At least we wouldn't starve to death. A bit further down the street at a pub we learned we were in Fontenay-le-Comte, a small place not big enough for an internet café – mission accomplished.

Cards slipped off the table during our evening game and when we crawled into bed, we fell into our bed mate – it was going to be one of "those" nights.

March 31

    I woke to the impressive sound of Ken speaking French. He could, in fact, string words together. He and two French mechanics standing at the front of the camper left me the privacy provided by a bay window at night. I got dressed under my covers before desperately running to the grocery store bathroom. Beginning my morning routine of washing and brushing (we were getting low on stored water in the camper) I hoped and prayed no one would come in. It wasn't my lucky day. When an early morning shopper pushed through the door, I was embarrassed to be caught brushing my teeth. Frothing foam exploded from my mouth like fireworks as I spat out a skittish "good morning." If I looked like some kind of vagrant it was only because – I was!

Bad luck will take you places you never thought you'd be

    Back at the camper, I munched my cereal while Ken popped in and out with reports. Yes, the engine was toast, and no he didn't know when it would be fixed or how much it would cost.

    Ken found himself with the difficult job of transmitting information from the French mechanic to Renee, the fellow we bought the camper from in Amsterdam. Back and forth he went from the grocery store where there was a pay phone, to the center of town to buy phone cards. Meanwhile the kids and I passed the day with exercise, school work and regular visits to the grocery store. It was the only place around to find a little fun. We'd read magazines or sample food and when that got boring, play creative games like "Who can find the most disgusting French food?" Between activities, we'd visit Ken at the payphone for an update.

    My ever positive husband was losing optimism we'd get through our minor glitch unscathed. Our towing allotment with AMA (our Canadian roadside insurance company) had been used up from our tow into town. The people in Amsterdam said they were working on ways to transport the camper back for repairs but kept stalling. Like it or not, we'd be spending another night in our Joker's Den.

    It seemed we'd be stuck in that small town walking back and forth to the grocery store forever. As Ken's positive energy waned, I started to panic. The marathon was four days away. After all our hard training we couldn't miss it. I was working myself into a tizzy when Ken stepped in to calm me down. He promised that no matter what happened with the camper, we'd somehow get to Paris.

April 1

Ken started camper fixing negotiations early, once again trudging back and forth between the grocery store and mechanic shop in the rain. Thankfully his French skills, driven by desperation, vastly improved; but even so, things got complicated when the French mechanic, let's call him Mr. France, claimed the rebuilt motor in the camper had failed because it wasn't done properly in the first place and Renee, Mr. Amsterdam, the guy responsible for the rebuilt motor, claimed Mr. France didn't know what he was talking about. Meanwhile, all attempts to transport the camper to Amsterdam failed. It would have to be fixed in France. Mr. Amsterdam agreed to pay for a portion of the repair, forcing Ken to be careful when throwing out blame. After all, technically the camper wasn't in Amsterdam making the warranty null and void. We could threaten to take Mr. Amsterdam to court for the faulty rebuilt engine, but things hadn't worked out very well for us in the Spanish judicial system. And truth be told, in the back of our minds we couldn't help wondering if Ken's little escapade on the steep street in Barcelona might have contributed to the ultimate implosion of our motor. There was smoke.

Meanwhile, Mr. France refused to install the new motor with warranty unless other old parts connecting to the motor were replaced. The price of the repair soared. Mr. Amsterdam felt Mr. France was taking advantage of the situation and over charging, leaving Ken, Mr. Canada, a nice polite boy hardly speaking their language and inept at their cultural nuances, trying to mediate an internationally complex situation.

Camper life as we knew it resumed. We adjusted to the lean of the camper with the help of anti-inflammatories; the kids caught up on school work while Ken and I fit in our last training runs.

As the day progressed, we learned the camper wouldn't be ready in time for the marathon. We would have to book public transport to Paris. Once that was worked out, we had twenty four hours to eat all the perishable food in the camper. Mattson set to work immediately.

April 2

The camper would stay, but we were getting out of Fontenay-le-Comte.

The kids and I worked on our journals while Ken went to sign approval papers for the repairs. After what seemed like forever, he trudged in looking somber and pale. Repair costs had increased $1000.00 overnight, forcing another phone call to Mr. Amsterdam to beg for more money.

When all was said and done, Mr. Amsterdam did contribute, but we were left with the majority of the costs. As we pulled our luggage to the bus station, Ken said he felt sick – sick about the cost of the repair and sick about dancing between people who didn't trust each other. Who knew who was right, wrong, good or bad? One thing we did know for sure; we were ultimately the ones left to pay.

I'd foreseen days ago how things would play out and dealt with my frustration. Ken, however, was blindsided by the ultimate result. Right to the end he believed some silver lining solution would come from out of nowhere. Absorbed in his thoughts he rewound and edited events from the last few days over and over in his mind searching for some way to a different outcome. I'd done the same thing after we'd been robbed. This time it was my turn to pat Ken on the back and remind him what was done was done, but no matter how hard I tried to comfort him, for the rest of the night he was bluer than blue.

After ten hours riding buses and trains we arrived in Paris. On the way I started my mental build up for the marathon with a good dose of the "WHAT IFS." WHAT IF the weather was really bad? WHAT IF I couldn't finish? Friends had told me horror stories about muscle cramping, diarrhea, and exhaustion, and I'd never forgotten footage of skeleton-like Olympic marathoners collapsing on the side of the road. What if all of those things happened to me?

232

April 3

Considering the way we were living, any hotel was heaven, but the Mercure in Paris was extra special. An all you could eat breakfast buffet included straight out from the oven, light and airy chocolate croissants. They were little pieces of heaven. I indulged guilt free. We were, after all, about to run a marathon.

Joyfully meeting up with Ken's brother Keith, his wife Lisa and her mother Marguerite, fresh off the plane from Canada, we bombarded them with questions about all we'd missed over the last eight months. They talked about our New Prime Minister, Stephen Harper and why the Flames came close, but ultimately didn't win the Stanley Cup final.

It wasn't easy prying the kids away from their care packages to go and see the Eiffel Tower, Arc de Triomphe and Champs Elysees. When it came time for lunch, the relatives headed for a quaint little French café while we looked for a McDonald's. They were two week vacationers, we were budget travelers. We'd pound the pavement together, but rarely share a meal.

That night we stayed with a Servas couple also running the marathon. Over dinner we discussed race strategy. Until that point mine had been – run, don't stop, don't die and finish. Thanks to our hosts, we learned there was so much more to think about: What was the best race day breakfast? How much should you eat during the race and how much should you drink? To drink, or not to drink? And if you did, where, when and how did one go to the bathroom?

April 4

Race strategizing replaced sleep. It seemed I'd just closed my eyes when I heard our hosts in the kitchen preparing breakfast. They had to be up earlier and promised to wake us up on the way out. Knowing I had a bit more time for sleep I rolled over and closed my eyes. When I opened them again, all I heard was rain pelting on the roof in a quiet house. Two realities hit like lightening; we'd slept in and it was miserable outside.

Shooting out of bed I grabbed my watch and realized it was 6:45 a.m. We had to leave the house by 7:00 to meet Keith and Lisa. I'd promised we wouldn't be late. We got lost on the way to the metro and then ended up at the wrong train track. By the time we found the right train, it felt like we'd already run a marathon. As the door clicked shut and we settled in beside runners with Paris marathon numbers pinned to their backs, my pounding heart slowed. We'd be late to meet Lisa and Keith but make it to the start line on time.

Standing under the Arc de Triomphe with thousands of other excited runners, the storm passed leaving behind a pleasant cool breeze and clouds lined with white light as the sun peeked through. After five months of training; suffering through sore muscles, extreme temperatures, pollution and self-doubt, the time had come to find out if we'd done enough. Were we strong enough, mentally and physically, to run a marathon?

After listening to marathon advice from our hosts, I'd worked out my strategy – run, don't stop, drink as little water as possible to avoid going to the bathroom, and eat chocolate whenever I felt like it.

The crowds in front of us began to move. We started into a slow jog moving like a large herd of cattle through the Arc de Triomphe before finding our own space as the crowd spread out along the Champs Elysees. And so our personal city tour of Paris began. The city, devoid of miserable automobiles and tourist buses, was all ours.

Time passed quickly as we marveled and pointed out one amazing site after another. By the time we passed the Place de la Concorde where Louis XIV and Marie Antoinette faced the guillotine, we'd reached the 5 km rest stop. It was tricky swerving between people slowing to grab water bottles and even trickier not stepping on the lids they threw after opening them. As careful as I was, while skirting past a slowing runner, my left foot came down on a bottle cap. My ankle gave way and twisted as my stomach sank. Sucking in a breath in the anticipation of pain; my foot came down and, to my surprise, still functioned. Out came a huge sigh of relief making me realize just how badly I wanted to accomplish my goal.

About an hour into the run, people started heading to the side of the road to pee. I'd seen a couple Porta Potties along our route, but with long line ups most runners headed behind parked cars – throwing modesty to the wind. I didn't want to give up minutes in line, but wasn't crazy about dropping my drawers in front of thirty-five hundred people. This dilemma successfully distracted me for the next thirty minutes.

I was feeling good, but starting to feel the urge. Passing a lush park with big trees and bushes, it seemed like my best option. Sprinting in, I hid behind a large Horse Chestnut tree enjoying what I thought was good privacy while squatting on overcooked spaghetti hamstrings. About to stand, the miserable business behind me, a noise made me turn to see four men, five feet behind me, relieving themselves into a low hedge. So much for being discreet. In a panic, I tried to get my shorts back up but rolled down panties stuck to my legs with the adhesive of sweat. With shorts and underwear refusing to budge, my wet noodle legs couldn't support me through the extra adjustment time. They gave out and sent my hands down to the ground and my butt up to the sky. Talk about a full moon. On the bright side, after fighting to get everything back in place, I lost no more than three minutes before jogging out of the park.

At around 2.5 hours my legs were tight but my body felt pretty good overall. The scenery continued to entertain and we were ahead of schedule. The most difficult stretch came between three and four hours. The muscle fibres of my quads and hamstrings felt like fraying over stretched rope, and the time between kilometers stretched out like a boring preacher's sermon.

The distance was starting to take its toll. Some runners hobbled in pain and one poor fellow retched at the side of the road. I felt numb. There was no severe pain, no urge to pass out or even throw up. Ken, right by my side, was also doing well. He would have bled out from a paper cut with all the anti-inflammatory in him, but it was getting him through. All of our training paid off. Close to the finish line, our competitive spirits kicked in. Sprinting to try and beat each other, Ken the true gentlemen, gave me the hundredths of a second and the win. We'd done it; we'd run a 4 hour and 23 minute marathon.

After crossing the finish line, I was high on accomplishment. It was a feeling like I'd never experienced before, although finishing our dive course had certainly been a sneak preview. I felt invincible, unstoppable, extraordinary and capable of anything. Any dream, any goal could be mine should I want it badly enough. I'd run my marathon and become a believer – a believer in me. That kind of euphoric faith made every single ounce of pain along the way so worth it.

Goals hard fought and won bring great reward

April 5

Marathon pain wasn't too bad right after the race, but overnight I stiffened up like Barbie before bendable joints. Inching my body to the edge of the bed and pushing unresponsive legs over the side, I stepped down yelping as pain shot through the ankle I'd rolled. How would I ever manage a day walking around the Louvre?

Oh the Louvre, an architectural wonder filled with breathtaking art, sculpture and so much more. The place was packed and runners easy to spot. We were the ones walking up the Louvre's grand staircases backwards, grimacing in pain with every step.

We hobbled past muscle ridden Greek and Roman marble men and through corridors lined with thirteenth and fourteenth century paintings to make our way to the famous Mona Lisa. A crowd held me on my tippy toes as I stretched to catch a glimpse of a cereal box sized painting obscured by tinted glass. After managing a mere peak at her famous half smile, a security guard waved me and my attached mass of humanity on.

We'd promised to meet up with Ken's family for lunch. It seemed like an easy thing to do in the morning as we held up our maps to pick a spot. But we didn't know the Louvre was like a maze with randomly placed staircases almost always leading somewhere you didn't want to go. When the time came to meet, we felt like game pieces on a snakes and ladders board. Thinking the finish line close, down a staircase we'd go to find no end in sight.

After finishing what felt like our second marathon, we begged forgiveness for keeping the family waiting again! To the food court, attached to the Louvre, we went. I was starving and wanted something big and filling even though menu items were highly priced. Ken was obviously put off. He wasn't one to come right out and tell us what we shouldn't do, but instead led by example. Stepping up he loudly ordered a side of rice while looking back to be sure his effort to economize hadn't gone unnoticed. One lousy side of rice and nothing more, for a monster of a man who'd just run a marathon. The kids and I could only roll our eyes and ordered what we wanted.

April 6

I woke a couple of times in the night to check my watch. Excited about leaving my family behind to spend the day sightseeing with my sister-in-law and her mom, I didn't want to be late. What a wonderful day it would be. There'd be no dragging Mattson off a museum floor, Makayla whining about visiting another art gallery or McDonald's prepackaged salads for lunch. My day would be spent with "two week vacationers" who enjoyed culture and could afford things like morning cappuccinos and afternoon cafés – perks I'd enjoy right along with them.

After starting the morning ON TIME we strolled down stylish St. Germain Street admiring eloquent boutiques until pounding rain forced us into a quaint café buzzing with the lunch business crowd. I salivated just holding the leather menu until glancing over to the gal at the table across from us about to stick her fork in a mound of what looked like raw hamburger topped with an uncooked egg. Happily shoveling it in, I wondered why she wasn't worried about hamburger disease or salmonella. Shuddering and praying for her kidneys, there'd be no meat in my lunch.

April 7

When trip planning, there are always special places you can't wait to see. During history class, back in grade nine, I'd daydreamed about life in the Palace of Versailles and vowed to one day see it for myself. Even though the weather was miserable, overcast and cold with a penetrating wind, I sat on the edge of my bus seat waiting with anxious anticipation to discover Versailles. Finally, there it was; not a fairy-tale castle with turrets kissing the clouds, but instead, a rambling rectangular structure encased in drab brick resembling a parliament building.

We entered into a blur of flowery gold moldings, huge crystal chandeliers, cathedral ceilings painted with murals, tapestries, and curvaceous furniture covered in shimmering brocade. Trying to take it all in was like standing in an electronics store surrounded by televisions all blaring on different channels. Individually any one could captivate and hold your attention for a good long time, but all together the overstimulation was overwhelming. Room after room of opulence dulled our senses as we jostled with our fellow tourists for prime viewing position. Don't get me wrong, the Palace of Versailles was a spectacle, but as was so often the case, not quite like my dreams.

A bar set by dreams is hard for reality to reach

April 8

After building chocolate croissant towers and devouring them without leaving a crumb, we waddled off to sightsee. Climbing three long flights of stairs, we stood under the massive cement arches of Sacre Coeur savoring a spectacular panoramic view. From there, as if descending from heaven to hell, down we went into a seedy area of Paris to find the Moulin Rouge made famous in Hollywood's movie of the same name starring Nicole Kidman. We were making our way to the opera house when, like switching off a light, the kids went dark and were done. Disappointed to call it a day, Ken serendipitously found a multiple museum pass on the ground and sent me off with a kiss.

There I stood alone on the street, thrilled to be on a date with myself in the most romantic city in the world. Like all good dates, I started with a nice dinner then headed off in search of masterpieces. When the galleries closed at nine o'clock, my heart burned with passion for Paris and oh so many artists.

Excited to get back to the family to tell them all about my night, I arrived at the metro station and found it unexpectedly barricaded shut. Refusing to let a minor glitch ruin my perfect night, my love affair with Paris continued on a long walk home. An hour and a half later my feet burned right along with my passionate heart. Happily bursting through the door of our hotel room, I met three frowning faces all demanding to know where I'd been for so long.

Didn't I know my family would be worried sick? Surprised by Ken's concern, I was unfazed. It was good for him to have a taste of the unfamiliar burden of waiting and worrying.

April 9

Ken was off to retrieve the camper leaving the kids and me with a day in Paris. We were a glum bunch. On top of knowing we'd have to give up warm chocolate croissants and head back to the hardships of the camper, Mattson was getting a cold and the ankle I'd rolled was killing me. Standing out on the rainy streets after checkout time, we didn't feel like doing much of anything.

A short walk landed us at the Centre Pompidou. We could have passed our day watching entertaining buskers but it started to pour rain. Finding shelter in the Modern Art Gallery, I happily plopped down on a bench. Having spent hours in the museum the night before I instructed the kids to go and explore without me. A short twenty minutes later they returned summing up three extensive floors of world famous art with their favorite statement: "it was really cool." I sent them back to take another look, insisting on a more complex summary. Returning five minutes later, they boldly stated their favorite painting was the yellow one with red in it and could they please go to McDonald's for ice cream? Oh how their lack of art appreciation brought me down.

After dinner, we headed back to our old hotel to wait for Ken who'd promised he'd be back with the camper at 10:00 p.m. When 1:30 a.m. came and went, we got a room. Falling into bed exhausted, Mattson looked on the bright side. His dad might be dead or in a hospital somewhere but at least we'd have one last breakfast buffet with chocolate croissants.

Always look on the bright side of life

April 10

Opening my eyes at three in the morning with Ken's face inches from mine gave me a start. Wanting to hug him for being alive and blast him for making us worry, I began my questions.

He'd made his way to Fontenay-le-Comte, hitchhiking when train and bus schedules didn't coordinate and arrived just in time to see our mechanic walk off the job for lunch. For the next couple of hours all he could do was wait and wonder how much raw meat and wine one could consume. When the mechanic finally sauntered back into the shop with glassy eyes rubbing a distended belly, a hungry and slightly tense Ken couldn't wait to pay up and put the whole miserable camper repair business behind him. Handing over his Visa card, he phoned us to say he'd be on time.

He was just about out the door when they called him back. Our Visa card was declined. Unable to connect with Visa by phone, Ken began a quest to find bank machines and get cash. Taking his limit from three, all surprisingly hard to find, still left him short. Flash forward another hour to Ken standing in a phone booth banging his head against the glass after what seemed like his hundredth unsuccessful phone call to Visa. As he tried one last time, he puzzled over his next move as the phone rang. Deep in concentration he hardly noticed when a human voice said "hello, hello." Our Visa had been red flagged and blocked after multiple transactions in three different cities on the same day. When Ken confirmed it hadn't been stolen, they politely apologized and lifted the block.

Visa, like your mother, needs to know where you are

By the time he paid up, he was four hours late. Bidding the mechanic goodbye there was one last question to ask; "would the sporadic problem we'd had starting the camper be gone?" The mechanic assured Ken all was well, but sadly it was not. After his first stop for gas, the camper wouldn't start. Thirty minutes passed before it sputtered back to life. From there, Ken drove straight to Paris, afraid to stop.

In the morning, chocolate croissants made us all feel better. We were back together and, although worried about what adventures might be around the corner, ready to move on.

April 11

Ken's family had moved on to Bonne, France. With the camper running well, we stopped to call and give them our arrival time. After hanging up, the camper wouldn't start. There could only be one explanation. We'd suspected it all along, but now knew without a doubt; the camper was possessed and out to drive us mad. Every time we had something on the line, like a specific place we had to be, it acted up.

Not a believer? After the camper didn't start, Ken set off in search of a phone to inform those waiting of our delay and on the way stumbled upon a mechanic. Dragging him back to diagnose our problem, the camper turned over perfectly. I rest my case.

After totally disrupting everyone's morning with our tardiness, we eventually connected with the relatives. Luckily, Keith and Lisa were in very good moods after staying in a beautiful castle the night before. They not only accepted yet another of our profuse apologies, but insisted on treating us for Easter dinner at their castle hotel that evening.

How quickly Easter had come. I'd planned to stage an Easter egg hunt for the kids in the camper, but when Lisa offered up their room I was thrilled. What a memorable experience they'd have searching for chocolate eggs in a true French castle. While playing Easter Bunny hiding candy in their romantically medieval, yet luxurious room, I couldn't help daydreaming about being the princess in the castle rather than the pauper in the camper.

Ushered to an opulent Versailles like grand dining room that evening, we enjoyed multiple courses of fine French food and free flowing wine. Chatting with other guests from all over the world ensured, thanks to our generous relatives, an Easter we'd always treasure.

April 12

Free-flowing champagne and red wine seemed like fun until the next morning. Under its influence, I was going to one day live in Paris and speak fluent French. By morning light, my dry reptilian tongue barely articulated English. What was I thinking? I was, after all, the girl my French teacher proclaimed to have the worst French accent she'd ever heard.

Thankfully, an early morning walk in crisp cool air served up a picture perfect French countryside and cleared my head.

It was time to say goodbye to our relatives and begin yet another quest to get the camper fixed. It was mid-day, making mechanics hard to find. When we did luck out, the camper started perfectly every time. Giving up, we carried on down the road determined to overcome never ending French lunch breaks and the antics of our possessed camper. No pile of evil nuts and bolts was going to push us over the edge.

Arriving in Lyon, a dreamy French city where colorful heritage buildings coiled around a reflective shimmering river, we began our search for mechanical help with two strikes against us. It was Sunday, and it was between 12:00 and 2:00. By dinner all we'd accomplished was finding the hospital where Ken would work the next day. Unable to find a parking spot, we tried to squeeze into one that was a bit too small. Making the camper fit required putting our back end up and over the curb. With Ken "just running in," it shouldn't have been a problem, but the camper didn't start when he returned. Once again we'd be spending the night off kilter.

Popping Advil and running my fingers through greasy hair, I got down on my knees to pull out the Porta Potty. Lifting a fist to the sky I vowed, in grand Scarlet O'Hara style, as God was my witness – once the trip was over, I'd never camp again.

April 13

From time to time, when Ken went to work and needed his medical equipment, he climbed up onto the camper's roof where it was stored to fetch it. When he did, the kids and I sat inside watching the

242

shape of his foot prints through thin buckling metal. We worried – like a can opener, he'd open up an accidental sun roof and crash down on us. Looking up, we kept our heads out from under his feet by swaying like wheat in the wind.

Ken came down a good while later with golf cases in hand and entered a surprisingly still intact camper. We'd already gone to bed and were half asleep when he followed us to bed. I slept well until around 3:00 a.m. when, in need of the Porta Potty, I ran smack into Ken's medical cases blocking the bathroom door. I wasn't impressed. A middle of the night wresting match to move them wasn't my idea of fun. For retribution, after muscling my way into the bathroom and making my way back to bed, I couldn't resist creating a teeter totter effect by stepping on a spot at the bottom of the bed causing the pillow end to spring up. Ejected into a sitting position, Ken looked startled and dazed. "Sorry honey," I icily quipped "just coming back to bed after moving the golf cases."

With Ken gone all day, I stepped in as Mattson's spotter for gymnastics training. He flipped up into a handstand outside the camper on the sidewalk, while pedestrians passed by on their way to work. At the start of the trip, Mattson was embarrassed to train in weird public places. He'd look around to see who was watching and fall out of his handstand. It took time for him to understand if he wanted to retain his gymnastics skills, he had to keep his mind on the task at hand.

A disciplined mind finds focus
even when the world turns upside down

Ken returned around 2:30, dropped us at the mall and resumed his "camper fixing" quest. We didn't see him again until 5:00 that night. Meeting us at the grocery store, he wearily reported another futile day spent watching mechanics shake their heads in confusion as the camper started on a dime. We put groceries away and took our seats to drive to a campground, but the camper wouldn't start. It was 7:00 p.m. and the gates to the campground closed at 8:00. We had a time line and the camper knew it.

With disappointment becoming the norm, we shrugged it off and settled in to play bridge (Ken was teaching us) and free camp in the parking lot. Just after 8:00, once the campground gates were securely locked the camper easily revved to a start. The motor noise sounded like a sinister mwah, ha, ha, ha.

April 14

Ken had rendered himself black and blue banging on our camper trying to get it to go. Not one to give up easily, and able to use tools like any highly intelligent primate, he grabbed our broom and used the handle to bang away under the hood until the camper started. After ignition and a speedy drive to a campground, we headed straight for the showers. Whoever said "cleanliness is next to Godliness" was wise. Dirt brought out the evil ugly in us while soap and water, like a good Sunday morning preacher, turned us back into the good people we wanted to be.

April 15

~ A TYPICAL EUROPEAN BIG TRIP DAY ~

7:00 a.m. - Ken leaves for work and I lay out tour plans for the day (no need for an alarm clock with Ken around)

8:00 a.m. - force kids out of bed for a breakfast tour briefing (received with the same enthusiasm as any school day)

9:00 a.m. - explore a couple of churches (good photo opportunities for Makayla)

10:00 a.m. - walk up a big hill to ruins of a Roman Amphitheater (exercise requirement for the day satisfied)

11:00 a.m. - take the tram back down and visit St.-Jean Cathedral (greatly grand and gothic)

11:30 a.m. - walk to the Musee Gadagne featuring wooden puppets (so cute, yet no pictures allowed)

12:30 p.m. - visit an English book store to restock reading material

1:30 p.m. - McDonald's lunch break

2:00 p.m. - walk to the Musee Historique des Tissus a textile Museum (highlight –gorgeous silk gowns from the 17th century)

3:00 p.m. - Musee des Arts Decoratifs a museum of Design (highlight – Ideas for Makayla's bedroom makeover)

4:00 p.m. - McDonald's ice cream break (taken like a daily vitamin)

4:15 p.m. - one hour internet time (the fastest hour ever)

5:15 p.m. - one hour waiting for Ken (the longest hour ever)

6:15 p.m. - Chinese food dinner (not same, same like China)

7:15 p.m. - arrive back to the camper after a day as busy as any back home.

April 16

Our "camper fixing" saga continued. Another mechanic waved Ken away saying he was too busy. Once he was gone the camper sputtered and refused to start. Ken banging away with his broom brought the mechanic back out. Feeling sorry for him, he took a look. The camper hadn't anticipated an act of human kindness. Finally our exorcist was found.

Getting up in the morning to drive to the mechanic for camper repairs felt like Christmas morning until we found out it would take most of the day. Once again we'd be waiting for mechanics, waiting for parts and waiting for mechanics to finish lunch and put in parts. I tried settling into my book, but suddenly felt like a caged animal. I had to get out. Grabbing the kids, we walked to a nearby mall and immediately lost Mattson at an electronics store. From there, for some strange reason, I had a compulsion to shop.

Makayla didn't like the tacky red shoes I fell in love with or any of the other funky shirts and dresses I simply had to have. Sensing I wasn't her normal mother (I never wear red) she dragged me out of the store to a petting zoo in the middle of the mall. I sat on a bench and stared at those penned up goats and chickens empathizing with their captive plight until my eyes glazed over. Thinking the camper had finally succeeded in knocking me off my block, Makayla once again tugged my arm, pulling me into a hardware store where we looked at paint colors for her bedroom makeover. Still lost in a fog, only her choice of candy cane red with midnight black trim snapped me back to reality. Somewhat myself again, it was my turn to pull her out of the store. Grabbing Mattson, we headed back to the camper.

By the time we returned, the repairs were completed and Ken was ready to go. Voluntarily, I entered my pen with a meek smile.

April 17

For the first time in a very long time we were glitch free – computers, cameras, campers, and even our metal health had been restored to working order.

A working life has working technology

We had no worries until arriving in Avignon, an ancient walled city bathed in the kind of luminous light the impressionist painters loved. On a winding road into the city, every turn sent an awful smell through the camper. We usually associated noxious odors with Mattson. He had trouble digesting European cheese. When he aggressively denied responsibility we pin pointed the smell to the waste water holding tank. Unsure how to deal with the problem, we called on Mr. Clean and poured a gallon of bleach into the tank thus introducing chlorinated pool stench to the reek of garbage dump. The time had come for an outdoor family workout in clean fresh air.

In the afternoon we followed a medieval bridge over a moat and passed through high stone gates into town. Exploring a complicated mesh of narrow streets led us past outdoor cafés and patisseries displaying decadent sweets. The fun began on the way home. After leaving Ken at the internet café we headed out into pouring rain with no umbrella (still!). It wasn't long before we felt like lab rats trapped in a soggy maze. We laughed and skipped through puddles (okay I embellish a bit) for a good hour before finding our way back to the camper. The instant we got back, wagers flew on how long it would take Ken to get home. He burst through the door at 11:30 p.m., soaked to the bone. He admitted only a few wrong turns. We knew the internet café closed at 10:00.

April 18

While lazing over breakfast, I recalled that French towns often have Sunday morning markets. Instantly motivated to find one, Mattson happily accompanied me for a walk into town. Matt somehow seemed taller than the day before. During our time away my special boy was quickly becoming a man. While Ken was at work, Mattson stepped in to be the voice of reason when we were lost or frustrated. I stood in awe of his easygoing nature and ability to make the best of any situation. Like his father, he remained ever even. He never complained, unless he was deprived of food. Despite his shy nature, he found a way, when walking into a foreign gym, to hold his head high even though he freakishly towered over all the other gymnasts. As I strolled beside him, I felt so proud. He might stink up the camper, but he punctuated my happiness.

In the afternoon we explored the old Palace of the Popes. I poured over religious works of art from the 12th century while Ken and the kids waited outside playing a slingshot game hitting rocks with elastics.

On the way home, after walking past too many tempting chalk boards advertising three course meals in flowery culinary lingo, we decided to stop for dinner. It was time to celebrate. Ken's company officially signed a deal for worldwide distribution with a large international company.

April 19

Ken started driving while the rest of us still slept. He couldn't wait to get to a golf course offering an affordable daily rate for unlimited rounds. Jerking to a stop in front of the club house, he licked his chops, mumbled a distracted "see ya later," meaning "much, much later" and headed out to get his money's worth.

I pulled myself out of bed and surveyed the parking lot. It was nicer than most. We were in the country, surrounded by trees and mountains and best of all, close to the clubhouse bathroom. It was going to be a good day. Unlimited hitting for Ken – unlimited flushing for us.

April 20

Ken and Mattson headed out early for gymnastics, leaving Makayla and me to work out in a playground by our campsite. We'd long given up on Makayla's running program, and instead settled in on skipping. She exercised without complaint as long as I did it with her. Strangely, the more I tripped and stumbled through my five sets of 125 skips the happier she seemed to be. And believe me, I gave her great cause for happiness. Her joy, although somewhat disturbing (is it normal for a daughter to be so thrilled about showing up her mother?) was worth the sacrifice of my pride.

In the afternoon we packed up and drove along the South Coast of France to Marseille. As we walked through the old port area just off the city centre, I noticed a very different atmosphere from the other French towns and cities we'd visited. I didn't feel like I was stepping back in time. Marseille was a big step forward into a busy,

248

dirty, graffiti covered modern city. Tightening our money belts, we didn't stay long.

April 21

At an internet café we madly typed, and tried to squeeze as many emails as possible into a paid hour. The French computer keyboards had q's where our letter a's were usually located. In our haste, we sent out misspelled emails like

"hi mom and dqd, hqving hqppy times in France, too bqd you're freezing your butts off in Calgary, hq, hq,hq!"

Our friends and family must have thought – "have another glass of wine."

Planning to drive to St. Tropez in the late afternoon, we were delayed by the ocean. Sun and sand called for us to pull over and soak up some rays. Late afternoon sun worship was one of my favorite things. What could be better than warm rays, drained of their burning power, on your face? Add a good glass of French red wine and I turned into a cement block – immovable. Ken happily joined me. Surprisingly, he too could "just be" as long as a computer was attached to his sun and sea. The kids had a bit of trouble with the concept and complained about being hungry until I decided to try something new. In nice mother words, I suggested they make their own damned dinner. To my great surprise, they were excited to comply. What a revelation, if I gave them a chance, they actually wanted to do things for themselves. For the next hour Ken and I enjoyed the sun while answering cooking questions called out from the camper's window. When they finally called us in for dinner the table was attractively set with paper towel place mats, a vase of fresh cut weeds and fajitas that were done to a turn.

Step back and give your kids room to grow up

Comfortable and content after dinner, we decided to spend the night right where we were; St. Tropez wasn't going anywhere.

April 22

On to St. Tropez – what a place to play! Big boats, rich babes, would-be Picasso painters along the sidewalks and gelato, billowing gelato, decadently displayed at every corner. I could have easily spent the day gawking at the rich and famous like a big eyed goldfish, but no – my family had other plans. After one quick circumnavigation of the harbour, barely long enough to savor the last luscious lick of a gelato-filled cone, I was dragged off to The Garden of Eden adventure centre, a half an hour drive from St. Tropez. Unfortunately living vicariously through sun bronzed beautiful people wasn't enough adventure for the rest of my family; they wanted mountain climbing and flying fox zip lines, making me, not for the first or last time, curse democracy.

When we arrived at the adventure centre, I decided not to go. Apparently I made the right decision because three hours later when everyone returned, the kids excitedly shared their escapades ending every story with "you would have hated it mom." I probably would have, but didn't like being thought of as such a wimp.

Hungry adventurers needed food. Whipping up pasta in red sauce right there in our deserted parking lot, we ate while appreciating the beauty of towering fragrant pine trees and the pinks and purples of a spectacular sunset.

April 23

Distracted by a competitive game of bridge (we were catching on), we spent the night in the Adventure Centre parking lot and headed to a campground in the morning. Finding laundry machines made us happy; no amount of hand scrubbing could remove the grey from our clothes. The washing machine worked well, but the dryer gulped down endless euros, emitting puffs of air not capable of blowing out a candle. Forced to air dry, there were no trees to string a clothes line to. Getting creative, we hung everything to dry: pants on open camper doors, tank tops off windshield wipers and undies out of sight inside the camper on anything that stuck out. By midday, evaporating moisture turned the camper into a wet sauna. We had to let our underwear out. My A cup bra, flapping off our antenna, must have left full figured European ladies passing by puzzled. They'd likely never seen anything so small.

April 24

On to Nice and Monaco, beautiful cities to tour if you could find a parking spot. Signs banned campers on every potential slab of pavement, sending Mattson into a fury after our third loop around the core. "This is discrimination," he cried "our camper isn't good enough for their high class city." And so our boy learned the cruel ways of the world.

Eventually we squeezed into a loading zone, leaving Ken with the camper while we explored the Promenade des Anglais, a busy paved walking path between the beach and grand hotels. Beside the path, a gorgeous blue ocean collided with a beach of small pebbly rocks. Scads of topless male and FEMALE sun worshippers lined the beach. Certainly Mattson was mesmerized, and it wasn't from the color of the water. Ladies of all ages, very few young and beautiful, came in every shape and size (I'm not talking weight and height) and exposed what they would have been arrested for in Canada.

Some things are best left to the imagination

Our next stop offered a bird's eye view of drop dead gorgeous Villa Franca. When we win the lottery, that's where we will live.

Interesting how Monaco, a small little enclave ruled by the Grimaldi family since 1297, managed to remain independent from France and Italy. Could it have something to do with the wealth collected in the Monte Carlo Casino, a neutral little place to win big? We hoped the casino could win us our new address sooner than later.

Parking problems forced us down into an underground lot where the camper just barely ducked under the height restriction bar. I felt a bit guilty leaving the kids locked in the camper while we went out to gamble, but they were thrilled with Kraft Dinner and a movie.

That night, the closest we came to wealth was walking past a row of exotic sports cars parked outside the casino on our way out the door. Still it had been fun playing the odds and dreaming "WHAT IF."

Eiffel Tower with Keith, Lisa and Marguerite

Inside the Palace of Versailles

Our Paris Marathon begins

The Louvre in Paris

Our camper implodes

The kids cook

Drying laundry

Ken trying to get the camper to start

Mattson at the Eden Adventure

Street art in St. Tropez

258

Mattson's sidewalk work out

Avignon outdoor work out

Outside Versailles Palace

NORTHERN ITALY

April 25

We cruised down the highway on a bright Sunday morning enjoying coastal views of the Italian Riviera in a camper no longer smelling like garbage. Finally able to dump our dirty water from the holding tank, we learned that food debris rinsed down the sink ferments quite nicely in warm water.

The beautiful simplicity of quaint farming communities nestled between ocean and sky nicely erased the images of yachts and casinos.

Cruising into Milan, the streets were devoid of cars. In fact the city showed no signs of life. Easily parking and walking to the central Duomo (main church) we soon discovered why. Every living soul in Milan had to be either in the huge park beside the Duomo or strolling on the streets around it. How delightful to discover a place where Sunday was still a day of rest.

Thankfully gelato scoopers were still hard at it. We drooled while staring at long tubs impressively displaying overflowing flavors like rippling pale yellow lemon or Bacio, the color of milk chocolate, cresting up into thick meringue-like peaks. A multitude of unfamiliar flavors left us full of questions. When we finally made up our minds, Mattson inhaled his cone and professed excitedly "I think I'm going to really like Italy." Enjoying our third lick, we had to agree.

Good travel is all about the food

April 26

A noisy disco not far from our camper made it hard to sleep. At discos in the late 70's, one song melded into another making it hard to get away from the geek you were stuck dancing with. With that kind of continuity the music might have turned to white noise conducive to sleep, but no, Italian disco started and stopped, sending me into an all-night tossing and turning hustle. Finally giving up and getting out of bed, I made my way to the shower where any grudge I had with the campground's noise dissipated under steaming hot pressurized water. I'd do the hustle every night for that kind of good, hard, hot shower.

Things kept getting better. Ken received an unexpected call giving him the day off, and, after discovering Garda Land, Italy's version of Disneyland, we decided to surprise the kids with an amusement park day. They would get a day away from their school work, but would have to work together and strategize for the best use of their time and money.

Life skills aren't learned in school books

Waving goodbye, we snuck away for a little of our own amusement (constant family time did have limitations).

April 27

We searched for a campground just outside of Genova where Ken had a trade show. On a narrow highway twisting up the side of a mountain, I worried about the steep incline we were on. I wasn't the only one. Perspiration streamed down Ken's long forehead, forming swimming pools in ears that should have been pinned back (I know, a bit of a slam, but I married him for those ears. I loved his confidence despite them). Driving higher and higher, we realized we missed our turn at an altitude where oxygenated air thinned. Doing a U-turn with no guard rail to prevent falling off a sheer cliff made Ken's foot trembled on the gas pedal. I closed my eyes to say a prayer, while the kids, oblivious to the dangers of our situation, nattered on about the where, when, and how of dinner. Fortunately, after what must have been a divinely guided turn, we resumed our planning.

Finally arriving at a campground looking like it might slide down off its steep mountain perch, Ken dropped us off. Our plan to head down to town for groceries was going to get physical. We skipped down stone stairs carved into the side of a mountain, looking at a puddle like ocean taking forever to zoom in. When it finally did, the thought of climbing back up made us cringe.

262

Hoping for gelato fortification, we were out of luck. The place was – blinds pulled down, doors locked tight – closed for the afternoon. How does that work in a competitive global economy?

April 28

After seeing Ken off to work in the morning I began my first duty of the day – laundry. Lunging up three flights of outdoor stairs, two at a time, I bounced up to where I thought the washing machines should be and noticed my legs instantly burned from our climb the day before. Unable to find the machines, I skipped down six flights to enquire at the reception. The clerk, kindly pointed me back up to a room beside the showers, but first I had to buy a token costing 4 Euros 50, to operate the machines.

After getting money at the camper, three flights down and three flights up, my 50 Euro bill couldn't be broken at the reception. Heading down for something smaller, I eventually ended up back at the laundry room shaking and kicking a locked laundry room door. Down six flights to the reception, the clerk apologized and called to have the door unlocked. Back up six flights using the railing and my arms for forward momentum, the door was unlocked but sadly, the token they'd given me was actually a Euro. Back down six flights, the gal who mistakenly gave me the Euro instead of a token apologized profusely. I tried to appear cheerful while panting out "no worries," but in truth, I was good and worried I might die before making it back up those stairs again.

After successfully loading the washer and walking down three flights to wait for it to finish, I stumbled back up for our clean laundry. Looking through the glass door, our clothes didn't move. The only sign of life, like a fish long out of water, was the odd flip. Waiting for the cycle to end, odd sporadic movements like a last gasp for life ensured it wouldn't be done any time soon. Back down to the camper I went, returning on the half hour to find our clothes still flopping. Something wasn't right.

The maintenance guy took a look and after a few more gruelling encounters with the six flights, the glorious little red light came on, setting our clothes free. I'd just hung them to dry and fallen exhausted into a lawn chair when the kids appeared, questioning with hands on hips what was for lunch. Our cupboards were bare and the only place to find groceries was in town, way down at the bottom of our mountain. If we didn't hurry, they sternly reminded me, the town would be closed for siesta.

That night, sitting around the table at the pizzeria, Ken effervesced about the beautiful model hired by his distribution company to lay half-dressed on his leg positioning medical equipment. With elbows on the table and my head in my hands, I was drifting off when he asked how my day had been. What could I say? All I'd done was one load of laundry and bought a few groceries.

April 29

Three flights of stairs between me and the bathroom seemed daunting. It was going to be a day when you'd give your back teeth to have a bathroom down the hall.

Pouring rain kept us in the camper until early afternoon when we caught a bus into Genova. In typical old city style, our path split and merged making map reading impossible as we tried to find an aquarium.

We walked and walked in pouring rain laughing at the stupidity of still not owning an umbrella. Truth be told though, giving yourself up to the rain felt kind of nice. You knew you'd end up a mess, but it was liberating not to care. When the aquarium closed, we grabbed a cab to meet Ken back at the convention centre. Puddles formed under our feet as Ken excitedly introduced us to the gorgeous, scantily clad Italian model he'd told us about the night before. Saying a stiff "hello" I wiped wet matted hair from my unmade up face and sized her up. This stunning girl would have been so easy to jealously condemn, but there was no denying her charm and intelligence. Ken and the kids locked big teddy bear eyes on her while I desperately searched for just one lousy little flaw.

The trick to liking beautiful people, is liking yourself

April 30

After cursing, praying to God and humming a few rounds of "Rain, rain, go away," it continued to pour. With a heavy sigh, I prepared for the three flights. On the bright side, we'd be leaving our made-for-mountain-goats campground with toned calves. There had to be a flat dry place somewhere in Italy and I intended to find it, but before we left, Ken had to "just run in" (translation – I won't be back for a least half a day) to pick up his medical equipment at the convention centre.

When half a day came and went, I started pacing, making myself dizzy with three steps up and down our kitchen galley. The kids not noticing my agitation played their Game Boys. Maybe I needed a little Super Mario in my life. Giving it some thought, I concluded, no, what I really needed was to have it out with my husband who'd left me waiting one time too many. Out into the rain I stomped to find him. When I did, he sat hunched over a computer in a partially disassembled trade show booth. Not wanting to let loose on him with some of his work mates around, I gruffly suggested he follow me back to the camper. His head remained in line with the computer screen as he insisted he'd come after sending one last e-mail (translation – I'm not coming anytime soon).

Totally frustrated, I trudged back through the rain, past the camper, and out into city streets. Wandering aimlessly, eventually I found a book store and leafed through books for well over an hour hoping Ken would return and worry I'd run off for good. When I finally extracted myself to arrive back at the camper, the kids hadn't noticed I'd left and Ken still wasn't back. Thankfully warm sunshine on my way home and a good book under my arm changed my hostile state of mind like a good marriage councillor.

Next stop – Austria, for a seven day vacation from the camper.

Sunday in the park in Milano

Church in Milano

AUSTRIA

May 1

After a night in a truck stop we enjoyed chocolate granola by the gas pumps. It wasn't our first truck stop picnic. Cereal and the odor of gas were starting to go together like peas and carrots. One whiff of petrol had me drooling like Pavlov's dog.

Our day passed enjoying lush green mountains capped with snow-covered peaks. It was a scene right out of the Sound of Music. I could almost see Maria (Julie Andrews) twirling up the slopes belting out *"the hills are alive."*

We checked into our condo at 4:00 p.m. sharp, flopped onto pillow top mattresses and sighed in ecstasy. A whole week of modern convenience and an indoor pool had us jumping for joy.

May 2

A middle of the night jaunt to the bathroom landed me in the hall rather than the bathroom. Sleep sealed eyes concealed my mistake until an entry door swooshed on its way to close and lock. Realizing the situation I was in, my eyes popped open and I grabbed the door a split second before it closed. How embarrassing would walking to the lobby in my little nightie have been?

It was midday by the time we broke away to visit the Liechtensteinklamm Gorge. With such a long name, we expected great things, but upon arrival the gates were closed and locked; the place not yet opened for the season. The kids and I happily anticipated more T.V. while Ken struggled with the concept of closed. We looked on in disbelief as he unsuccessfully tried to shake the gate open, wriggle under the gate, or as a last resort, climb over sharp spikes after scaling the gate.

Entrepreneurs are persistent

That night, after a swim in the pool, we walked through a shower/sauna room door. The first one in, I was the one to discover two people, NOT of the same sex, showering stark naked in a big room lined with shower heads. Stopping dead in my tracks, the family rear-ended me as I did an about face and pushed them out the door. Safe behind the closed door, I studied the signage and sure enough, there was a caricature of a male and a female. Even more surprising was a picture of a bathing suit with a cross through it. It was co-ed with no bathing suits allowed. After my middle of the night hallway incident, I could have walked down to the reception totally nude and no one would have cared.

From bare to Burka, society dictates what goes

May 3

Mattson was in a bad mood. Yes, the golden child was downright ornery. I made him do homework, instead of playing his Game Boy on the way to Salzburg. We argued, and when it became clear I wasn't about to change my mind, the bad mood reared its ugly head. We'd learned to live with Makayla's hormonal mood swings, but a miserable Mattson was foreign territory.

Salzburg was lovely. It was easy to see how Mozart found the inspiration to write his beautiful music, but no matter how spectacular the sites, our day fell flat without our pleasant easygoing Mattson.

Take Mario away and you'll pay

May 4

What would we do without Ken getting us going? The kids and I would have liked to have found out, but Ken, with schedule in hand, turned off the television and informed us there were natural wonders to discover.

The three viewing points for the Krimml Waterfalls couldn't be reached without climbing a small mountain. By the time we reached a scenic lookout cooled by mist from a cascading waterfall, we were more than ready for lunch. Peanut butter and jam took on a whole new flavor on dark Austrian bread. At the local bakery a six foot tall thick boned female clerk (I think?) with grey hair escaping from a tight hair net, stood impatiently pointing to brown bread in various different shapes and sizes. When I finally made my choice, I just about dropped the round dark loaf which was as heavy as a medicine ball. That bread, when converted to sandwiches, chewed like tough steak and the strong taste of rye didn't go well with PB&J. We chewed and chewed until it felt like we'd eaten five sandwiches.

May 5

Sightseeing for the day included an ice cave visit. As I entered the cave my lack of fear came as a shock, after all, dark caves were my nemesis. Feeling cool and calm, we traveled through a pitch black cavern following a narrow tunnel of light created by nothing more than a flash light. Mother Nature, as always, created breathtaking spectacles in the caverns of that cave and for once, I enjoyed her work without a care. Even near the end of the tour, when we walked through a long narrow ice tunnel my heart kept a regular beat. When I stepped out of that cave I knew without a doubt, my war against phobic fear was over. My claustrophobia had vanished as mysteriously as it had come. I wouldn't be heading back to Canada the same girl.

A life without fear is a life with endless possibilities

May 6

Home schooling was winding down. Mattson and Makayla were almost finished the daily assignments on the CDs we'd brought with us, and knowing the end was in sight made them work harder to finish. For all my concerns about their education, it had turned out to be a breeze. It helped to have kids who worked well independently, but undoubtedly their best learning came from our day to day experiences.

In the late afternoon Makayla and I dragged ourselves down to the workout room while Mattson gave in and joined his dad for a wet round of golf. The day passed and in the evening we enjoyed what had become our nightly routine: a swim followed by a rule breaking steam and shower in our bathing suits.

Some rules are meant to be broken

May 7

Pouring rain wasn't a problem: we'd be spending the day indoors at Swarovski's Crystal World in Innsbruck.

Shaking off dripping water, we entered a unique high tech museum featuring hundreds of thousands of glittering Swarovski crystals. Installations depicted scenes where every element, be it a jellyfish or a chair, was encrusted with crystals. This was an artsy place, meant to create an experience beyond the visual. While passing through, if you stopped and took the time to be still, silent and sensitive, all of your senses could take part in the experience. Subtle aromas, sounds from hidden speakers and holographic images floating by created a complex montage. Unfortunately the "still, silent and sensitive" concept was a tough one for the rest of the family. Ken never has been terribly intimate with his senses. When we first met, I closet smoked for months (he didn't like cigarettes) stuffing jelly beans in my mouth to camouflage the smell. By the time I realized I could have blown smoke in his face and he wouldn't have smelled it, I had two new cavities.

Ken and the kids babbled their way through the museum as if on the autobahn, constantly backtracking to find me, violate my moment, and insist I hurry up. It wasn't until we hit the retail shop, filled with sparkling crystal jewelry and embellished clothing that everything changed. Makayla became still as she gushed over a glittering shirt in her size. Ken fell silent hoping no one would ask him for money and Mattson was sensitive to the fact I'd kill him if he asked to leave one more time.

May 8

After a good long drive, we stopped for groceries. I unpacked food while Ken went back for forgotten bottled water. He returned with a large case, wiped sweat from his brow, and settled in to drive. Turning the key while taking a swig from a newly opened bottle creased his brow in disgust. The water was sparkling, not still. Back he trudged, lugging the heavy case for an exchange.

Returning with a new case; he once again slid into the driver's seat and twisted off a cap. Taking a good long chug once again turned his face sour. For the next minute he shook the bottle, examined bubbles and questioned why the label read Aqua natural when it fizzed. A few more sips and shutters of repulsion confirmed what he already knew. "The third time's always a charm honey" I sang out.

After what seemed like forever, we saw Ken slugging along across the parking lot like an overworked donkey. Getting into the camper, he buckled up, swallowed, dropped his head back and cried "nooooo!" A moment of silence passed before Makayla chirped "don't worry dad, I'll go with you to get the right stuff."

Back in the store, Ken and Makayla followed a sales clerk, sick of processing returns, back to the water department. Picking up a case of water, she threw it into Ken's arms and barked "no gas." Pointing her finger back to the shelf stocked with multiple brands of water, another bark spat out "gas." Ken and Makayla obediently followed her finger back and forth as she chanted "gas – no gas – gas – no gas." Pretending to understand, they slunk away.

Buying bottled water in Europe is a gas

Sawarsky Crystal Museum

Church in Austria

GERMANY

May 9

We spent the day at the Dachau concentration camp just outside Munich. After parking and entering the grounds, a sharp penetrating wind made us shiver. Learning about what happened within the walls of that camp ensured we didn't stop. The cold seemed appropriate; oppressive clouds went well with suffering.

Filing past cremation ovens, gas chamber showers and horribly graphic displays of torture made our stomachs turn. I hated exposing the kids to the disgusting side of humanity. I could never explain the how and why of it all. When I'd visited Dachau fourteen years earlier, shaken by my experience, I took solace in a monument located in the courtyard outside the museum inscribed "NEVER AGAIN." After all, the Holocaust happened in a different time. Different from my world – a modern wealthy world, abundant with education and technology. Weren't modern people smarter, wiser, and kinder? I'd thought so that day, but fourteen years later, after living through genocides in Rwanda, Bosnia and Iraq – "NEVER AGAIN" seemed as likely as a quick flight to Mars.

Driving away while processing our day, it dawned on me that for the first time I was able to take the fragmented pieces of history I'd learned in school and fit them together like a puzzle. As the pieces came together, so did an understanding of how the fallout from one tragic historic event ultimately created the poverty, instability and greed leading to another.

I didn't know the ultimate affect Dachau's disturbing pictures and stories would have on my children. Certainly our visit to Dachau, coupled with reading *Anne Frank's Diary*, personalized the Holocaust for them. This was a history lesson they'd never forget.

Rereading the Mother's Day card the kids gave me before leaving for Dachau made me thankful. Thankful to know I'd wake the next day free to love my family and live my life.

May 10

Ken worked while the kids and I spent the day at the Deutsches Museum. Dedicated to technology, its exhibits provided interesting facts about topics ranging from oil and gas to food science. Since we couldn't understand German, we stuck to the visual presentations. When Mattson almost threw up during an open heart surgery video, we welcomed the comic relief. I guess he won't be a doctor when he grows up.

By 5:00 p.m. we were ready for our field trip to end. All day we'd kept an eye out for Ken, who hoped to join us after zipping over to the hospital to drop off equipment. He never arrived. Forced out onto the street as the museum closed, Mattson tried to figure out how zipping into a hospital could take so long. "Dad," he ranted "isn't capable of a zip without a zag."

An hour later we learned what zag snagged him. A detour to search every Wal-Mart shelf for red licorice.

Twizzlers are not sold in Europe

May 11

While sitting across from the kids at breakfast I noticed how scraggly their hair had become. They desperately needed haircuts.

I'd been Ken's stylist ever since a bad professional cut back in our dating days left him looking like Mr. Potato Head – all ears and forehead. Eighteen years and hundreds of haircuts later; I felt like a proficient stylist.

When I confidently told the kids I could do a great job cutting their hair, they weren't believers. Moaning and cringing with every cut, I barely removed a snip of hair before having to pack up to drive to Venice, Italy.

CENTRAL ITALY

May 12

Lost in romantically captivating Venice, a maze of water canals had us trudging over countless footbridges going in circles. Unless you want to go for a very long walk in Venice, stay close to San Marco square. We ended our day there, and like every good tourist, marveled at the thousands of frenetic, fluttering pigeons mooching bird food from tourists. I was setting up for the ever popular picture of birds hanging off your kids like Christmas tree ornaments, when Ken returned with a purchased bag of bird food with hundreds of flocking pigeons in tow. Spastically waving them away, he threw the seed, as if it were toxic, at Mattson. It seemed we'd be adding birds to the list of pets we'd never own.

May 13

A kitchen table, cross-dressing as a bed, wasn't conducive to a good night of sleep. And decorative cushions meant to add a splash of color made lousy pillows. There wasn't much I could do about the bed, other than nag Ken to stay off curbs, but the time had come to go shopping for a nice fluffy feather pillow, no matter the grief I'd get about having "high needs."

We arrived in Florence in time for happy hour pizza at the campsite pizzeria. Canadians needed to rethink their "make fire and roast meat" approach to camping meals. Sitting down at a restaurant and pulling out your wallet was far less work.

A creative work out after dinner must have been entertaining for our neighbors. Ever the creative inventor, Ken fabricated a squat routine by putting Mattson on his shoulders and Makayla on Mattson's shoulders. With his "kid tower" of weight, up and down they went, like a Cirque du Soleil act.

May 14

A kink in my neck, thanks to the loathed decorative pillow, locked my line of vision onto Mattson and Makayla who sat across from me at an outdoor picnic table. They navigated spoons of cereal to their mouths through untrimmed fall-in-your-face hair. The time had come to revisit my scissors.

I roughly adjusted Mattson's moving head, gruffly telling him to hold still. Blonde curls sprinkled with the odd drop of blood, from nicking my finger or his ear, fell to the floor. "Be a man," I commanded; I'd only inflicted a flesh wound, not a Van Gough ear removal.

In the end I was happy with my cut, even when Mattson looked in the mirror and grimly stammered "I look just like dad." So I was a little limited in my style repertoire. "You should be happy to look like your father," I insisted. "He's a very handsome man."

Next victim: Makayla. For days she'd been saying she wanted her hair shorter. The time had come for me to deliver. Not wanting to waste time, I made the initial cut hacking off the requested three inches, then lost another inch or so in the evening up process. To justify taking off more, I told her what my stylist, after giving me a good scalping, always told me. "Going shorter makes the roots healthier so the hair will grow faster." Suddenly, I had to question if the root really knows or cares about its end.

In Florence we toured the Royal Apartments. A string of grandly opulent rooms were decorated in a range of bold colors. The only way I could look up at elaborate murals painted on their ceilings was to rest my sore stiff neck on Mattson's shoulder. Poor kid, not only did he have the hair cut of a middle aged man, he had to be seen making body contact with his mother in public.

May 15

We traveled from Florence to the Tuscan countryside for a memorable home stay in a 12th century restored stone farm house. Talk about charm. This place was sweeter than an Italian Nona. The house sat high on a hill looking down on a frame of cedars surrounding San

Gimignano. If you listened closely, you could hear ringing bells from the quaint village's church towers.

Our hosts, Maria and her husband Micancarlo, served up a tasty home cooked meal complete with tannic local Chianti and flowing conversation. What a warm, authentic introduction to Tuscany.

May 16

We relaxed in the morning, then followed our host's car in our camper to a deserted sandy beach by the ocean. After a tasty lunch of cold risotto salad and homemade biscotti, Maria and her family laid their towels down on the sand for an afternoon siesta. We followed their lead, stretching out and trying to fall asleep. My eyes barely fluttered to a close when the kids started questioning, in a normal voice meant to be a whisper, when we could leave. Five minutes later, four Moores paced the shoreline, back and forth and back and forth, with the rhythmic movement of a Metronome. At four o'clock, when our hosts finally opened their eyes, yawned and suggested packing up, we were loaded and ready to go before they'd stretched and wiped sleep from their eyes.

Instructed to follow their small compact car to our next stop, Ken drove like a maniac on twisting roads attempting to keep up. It was as if they were trying to lose us or something. Whatever the case, Ken wasn't the kind of guy to be left behind.

We eventually arrived at natural hot springs worthy of the crazy drive. Sulfur laced hot water plunged down from the top of a hill into glossy shelves of limestone eroded into spoon-like ladles. Crawling in to soak was like sitting in a hot tub. We'd just gotten comfortable when Ken decided trekking up slippery polished rocks to the highest most forceful waterfall was the thing to do. He was right. Pounding water massaged our backs until the threat of lightening forced us out.

As it started to pour, we bid a quick farewell to our hosts and made a run for the camper. Confined camper air concentrated rotten egg fumes rising up from our bathing suits. With a night of free camping ahead and no place to shower, Makayla, whose twelve year old passion was to constantly smell like some kind of a fruit, was mortified.

May 17

By late morning we made our way to a campground in search of a much needed shower. In a hurry to get clean, I hadn't noticed, while guiding Ken back into a camping spot, the overhead bamboo canopy snaring the ladder on the back of the camper. What to do? Someone had to drive forward for Ken to work us free.

Entanglement put me in a tricky position. I had to get us out yet remain incompetent enough to never have to drive again. Rising to the occasion, I jerked forward enough to free us and immediately stalled. Meanwhile Makayla, in agony over her reeking sulfur laced hair, went straight to the shower. Returning in tears, she reported that it was a dud—tepid water with no pressure wouldn't do. Shredded bamboo hung from our ladder as we made a quick getaway.

Once settled in at a better campground, Ken and I headed to the beach for sunset and wine. We'd discovered a small perforation in the bladder of a box of Chateauneuf du Pape purchased in the South of France (yes, good boxed wine). It was meant to be our summer wine supply back in Calgary, but the leak nixed that. That wine had to be drunk before it oxidized. I was up for the task.

May 18

I bought a pillow. Fluffy and filled with real down feathers, it was my new obsession. I couldn't wait to take it to bed. It was all I thought about during our one hour run and our long drive to Rome.

We did other things, but nothing more memorable than buying my pillow.

May 19

While Ken reported a shower with no hot water, I scratched mosquito bites on my face in our hot and sticky camper, yet I'd never felt better. Well rested from a fantastic sleep on my new pillow, we were heading to Rome, a city I loved.

I could see the Coliseum as we walked up the stairs in the Metro station. The sight of it filled me with nostalgia. We were back at the conception site of The Big Trip.

The kids were preoccupied as I recited the story of how our trip came to be. I hoped to savor a special moment together but – poof – the family instantly vaporized into a pushing crowd.

Things had changed over the years at the Coliseum: increased security, huge line ups and pricey admission fees. We weren't put off – Rome, like a classic movie, captivated no matter how many times you saw it.

May 20

After finding a campground with pressurized hot water for showering, Ken surprised us and suggested we read and relax. Plunking himself down in a lawn chair, he cracked open his novel. Ten minutes later his eye lids drooped. We hopefully watched them slowly fall. When the upper lid met the lower lid, he jerked, snapped open his eyes and popped up to standing.

It was time to break in our new volleyball. This was a new activity for us and it showed. We were terrible. Even Ken, the athletic sportsman, was having trouble. We spent more time laughing and chasing the ball than actually volleying. Ken suggested a daily program to improve our skills but Mattson, with good humor threw the ball towards his dad's head billowing "enough with the programs!"

After dinner Ken and Mattson left for gymnastics training at Rome's Olympic stadium, leaving Makayla and me to pull out the bed, curl up and watch *Lord of the Rings* – yet again!

May 21

Ken received an e-mail calling him to work and forcing the rest of us out for an unexpectedly early day of sightseeing. I was a bit flustered without my usual prep time and forgot to take note of our stop when getting on a bus to the Vatican City. Confessing that it might be a bit tricky getting back home, Makayla glared at me with her critical pubescent daughter eyes while Mattson shrugged it off as if to say "so you made a little mistake, you're still the greatest mother ever." No wonder having a boy and girl is called the million dollar family. The girl knocks you down, the boy builds you up, and somewhere between you hope to find enough mental balance to make the money you'll need to raise them.

Disembarking at Vatican City, we headed for St. Peter's Basilica. Hundreds of tourists cranked their necks back to squint through camera lenses and click off photos of Michelangelo's incredible painted dome. Not paying attention to where they were walking, those tourists crashed into each other like bumper cars at the Calgary Stampede.

On the street, nuns cloaked in black habits and bible toting priests in flowing crisp white robes passed as we made our way to the Vatican Museum. Many blocks from our destination, we ran into a long queue. It would take hours standing under a hot sun to get to the Vatican. The kids turned to protest as I surprised them and agreed we shouldn't wait. And then the most wonderful thing happened; Makayla turned and gave me a "mom you're great" smile and took hold of my hand. And there it was, my special moment, making up for the one I'd missed at the Coliseum.

Before getting on the bus, we stopped at an internet café where Makayla received her dance schedule for the fall. Thinking about home made us pine for family, friends and our favorite things, so much so, we talked about cutting the trip short and heading home early. Silence fell as we pondered the idea. Thankfully it didn't take long to see the light. We had the rest of our lives to socialize and enjoy the comforts of home and only two more months left of the trip of a lifetime.

Finish what you start

May 22

On we went to the southern coast of Italy. At a camp site located on the cratered peak of a volcano, we came to see the remnants of Pompeii. I'd read how red hot lava exploded from out of nowhere and rained down, vaporizing a whole society; truly scary considering we'd be spending the night on the top of that very volcano. They claimed the volcano was dormant and fast asleep, but who are they anyway? Sulfuric steam gushed from cracks in the crater close to our camp site. Maybe the volcano was passing gas, like humans so often do, before they wake up! Ken assured me all was well, but he always said that.

Busy strategically placing my shoes by the door for a quick nighttime getaway, something more serious was erupting. Ken, pulling down our bed for the night, met resistance from Makayla standing in his way. As she delivered a hundred brush strokes to her long hair, Ken ordered her to stop and move. She wasn't big on following orders. Standing inches apart, they stared each other down as Makayla's brush stokes became fast and hard and Ken tried to nudge her aside. Makayla wouldn't move and Ken wouldn't wait. I could almost see steam rising up from their flaring nostrils. Anticipating an entertaining bull fight, Mattson and I sat back and prepared for a good show. It was a scene foreshadowing many a future power struggle between the two carriers of the Moore 'stubborn' gene.

May 23

Somewhere between leaving for and arriving in Naples, the sun moved out and rain moved in. Not just any rain. It was the "I'm not going anywhere and neither are you" type of rain. We bolted from the train station to the familiar Golden Arches of McDonald's for shelter and made ourselves comfortable.

We were in love with McDonald's cones. Let's face it, we couldn't seem to get through a day without one. After placing orders in oh so many countries, we knew – all McDonald's cones aren't created equal. The cheapest cones we licked were in Singapore. At twenty-five Canadian cents with no extra charge for chocolate dipping – they were practically free. In Asia, Australia and New Zealand, they snuck up to fifty cents, but even so Ken stopped at every McDonald's we passed. By the time we got to Europe we had to dish out almost two euros to get a lick. At that point, though, cost was irrelevant – we were hooked.

France won out for the skimpiest portions, while Germany's towering swirls almost fell off their cones. We licked our Naples cones, moderate in size but curvaceous with a well formed curl on top, and speculated on pricing and size in Northern Europe and the United Kingdom.

Finally forcing ourselves up and out, we set out to discover Naples. When our saturated underwear sent tickling streams of water down our legs we finally gave in and bought umbrellas, but only two, keeping with Ken's belief in the financial efficiency of sharing.

Sacrifice in the spirit of sharing can be a worthy cause

May 24

After spending another night on top of the volcano, we set off to explore Pompeii. The sudden violent volcanic eruption in 79 AD covered the city of Pompeii in 3 meters of burning volcanic ash, killing its inhabitants and immediately ending the life of the city. Forgotten until excavations began in the 1700s, today you can walk through the ruins of the well preserved old city to see ancient Roman homes. Murals painted on walls, and original floor tiles in kitchens allow a glimpse of what life must have been like shortly after the time of Christ.

May 25

Running past a grocery store in the morning reminded me we needed chocolate granola. Sending Ken for the cereal, I headed to the electronics section of the store. Makayla's *Lord of the Rings* obsession was starting to worry me. As of late, she spoke more Elvish, the fictitious language of the Elves, than English. Clearly the time had come to buy a new video.

Across the boot of Italy we drove to Brindisi where we would catch a ferry to Greece.

282

Mattson's favorite place

Pigeons hanging off kids like Christmas ornaments

At the Coliseum in Rome

The Duomo in Florence

GREECE

May 26

When our travel book said to arrive early for our ferry crossing, we sat fidgeting in line checking our watches. Surely, there had to be time for a quick tour of Brindisi?

Being the final car to load (good thing the ferry was late) made finding a place to park like squeezing the last bowl into an overfilled dish washer. Ferry workers waved Ken into a tiny nook between vehicles. They turned imaginary wheels in the air singing "right, right, right." Not one to conform, Ken thought it might be better to go left. Those workers gasped and cranked their imaginary wheels as if trying to open the exit hatch in a submarine filling with water. It was enough to make even Ken do what they asked.

We hauled food, books, playing cards and computers up inside the ferry and settled in for an eight hour journey. Time passed, and by early afternoon a search for sunshine led us outside to the ship's tar paper covered deck. Sprawled out under the sun, Makayla turned her head my way and asked if our ferry ride was like taking a cruise. After some thought I responded "you'd have to exchange stale strawberry jam sandwiches for an exotic three course meal; a lounge chair by a sparkling pool for the tar paper and a string quartet for the Greek tunes blaring from a speaker nearby. Despite all of that, the wonderful warmth of the sun would feel exactly the same."

Let luxury be something you can happily take or leave

May 27

Something pulled me up through layers of sleep. Eyes flickered as I made out the shape of Ken's head hovering over me. "It's early, go back to sleep" he whispered. I did just that until the diesel engine of our camper sputtered, coughed and revved like a chain saw. Sneaking away to drive, in what the kids and I considered the middle of the night and Ken called early morning, never went unnoticed.

Grumpily I got up and pulled out the Porta Potty. Getting everything going in the right direction on bumpy roads was tricky. On the bright side, Ken cheerfully informed me after turning off the motor in Meteora, Greece, we had the whole day ahead of us.

Not far from our campground, towering columns of rock emerged from the earth like pegs from a crib board. Back in the fourteenth century, monks seeking solitude claimed the flat tops of those peaks to build monasteries in the clouds. What they went through to find a little peace and quiet was amazing. After the way my morning began, I could identify with their plight.

May 28

Running under the awesomeness of Meteora's majestic rock towers made me philosophical. On The Big Trip, running was initially nothing more than exercise to burn off calories; three kilometers justified one McDonald's ice cream cone. Then came our marathon goal, with the fear of failure as my constant motivator. After months and months of lacing up and running, enjoying beautiful scenery, hashing out world problems with Ken, and people watching in different countries, I'd absolutely, one hundred percent, fallen in love with running. It had become a part of me. I no longer did it to lose weight or boast about going a certain distance. I did it because it made me feel good, clearing my mind from worries of the day and giving me inspirational ideas to improve my life. I was hooked and ready to proudly call myself a runner.

We checked into a fabulous campsite, perched on the side of a mountain, in Delphi, and ate Greek salad with lusciously rich feta. A hilarious game of charades followed. When everyone was played out, I crawled into bed, buried my head into the down feathers of my pillow and wished The Big Trip would never end.

May 29

In the morning we explored ruins from the first Pythonian games dating back to 450 BC. Imagining *Chariots of Fire* under a cloudless Greek sky, a throbbing noon sun sent our sweat glands into overdrive. We needed shade and lunch. Gyros arrived, oozing mustard and mayo and crowned with a ring of French fries. The sauce made the fries soggy but we weren't bothered. True Canadians love their condiments, "eh?"

Waiting for a bus later that afternoon was like waiting to see the green flash. They say it appears immediately after the sun drops into the ocean but stare as you might, it never seems to come. We started walking down a mountain on slippery shale, stopping to ponder two ways to the camper: straight down a steep portion of the mountainside or winding down a switch back path. The girls opted for the path while the guys, manly men, headed straight down.

We all arrived back at the camper at the same time. The girls were dignified and unscathed; the guys scratched and battered. But stories – those boys went on and on about their hardships. Only a B-grade teen horror movie called *Urban Legend* saved us from their banter.

May 30

Visiting Athens a few months before the city hosted the summer Olympics made us feel more like prison inmates than tourists. We pushed our noses between jail-like bars of steel at an Acropolis shrouded in scaffolding. Ken's insistence that DO NOT ENTER really meant PLEASE COME IN ensured a few good snapshots. At the end of the day, we saw enough of Athens to be able to recognize most of the monuments painted on the walls of Greek restaurants back in Canada.

May 31

Finally – warm weather camping. For months I'd been wishing for it, but lying in bed sweating and slapping at mosquitoes, thanks to our Spanish thief's screen slashing, made me pine for the good old chilly days. Buying a new screen was the logical thing to do, but the reality of finding one in a country where few spoke English was more daunting than putting up with bugs.

The highlight of our day, besides a tasty post-Carrefour parking lot picnic featuring Greek salad, fresh bread and juicy roasted chicken, was the exciting purchase of the newly released *Return of the King* disc. This was the last movie in the *Lord of the Rings* trilogy. Makayla cradled the disc like an injured baby bird, then took half an hour during our drive to Corinth to gently peel back the plastic wrap. After reading every printed word on the jacket cover, she finally removed the precious disc she'd so longed for.

We managed one game of volleyball after settling at a campground on the Peloponnese Peninsula before Makayla left us to watch *Return of the King*. The camper was cake oven hot, not having cooled from midday heat, but she didn't care. When it was over, she sat on the edge of our bed looking sad and dejected. "I loved *The Lord of the Rings* so much, I never wanted it to end" she moaned. Plopping down beside her, Mattson told her he knew how she felt. He'd just finished the book *The Power of One* and was also sad to read the last page. Feeling their pain, I lamented about how our trip would soon be over. Ken taking it all in, quietly sighed, and squeezing in between the kids, threw an arm over each of them.

All good things must come to an end

June 1

Under a canopy of blue sky, we explored the ruins of Corinth. Back in the day, that city must have been like Manhattan – chaotically busy with a dark side; St. Paul did spend a great deal of time preaching to the Corinthians. By late afternoon, we felt like a slab of saganaki in a frying pan; "Ola" flaming humans! It was time to cool down at our campsite restaurant. We had fun experimenting with new foods like stuffed vine leaves and rich eggplant moussaka. Every dish swam in a sea of olive oil, but "not to worry" insisted our waiter, a nice cold tumbler of complimentary milky white Ouzo on the rocks would help the oil down. On ice, I had to say, it was quite nice.

June 2

Driving across the Peloponnese to a campground on the west coast, a construction road block and alternative route sign left us confused. Greek words, built on an alphabet different than ours, canceled out the hope of making an educated guess. We certainly understood why the old saying "it's all Greek to me" came to be.

Camping Tholo Beach was a lovely spot located steps from a long deserted fine sand beach. After settling in, Ken headed out to catch a wave while the rest of us stretched out on the beach. And then the most amazing thing happened. Makayla pushing way, way out of her comfort zone, took off her socks - nine months into our trip, she let sand sift through her toes.

Great experiences are worth minor inconveniences

June 3

Our zip zagged when we made a quick stop in town before heading to the beach. It was late afternoon by the time Ken and Mattson caught a wave, Makayla ran her bare feet through the sand, and I willed myself into the ocean. Watching Makayla "do" sand, I told myself I should "do" waves. Fearless "not claustrophobic" me, stood up to go in, but "old me" focused on how big and daunting the waves were. Water did nothing but tickle my toes as another of my internal debates weighing the pros and cons of going in the ocean began.

Disappointing yourself is the worst disappointment of all

June 4

It was a travel day with a ferry ride from Patras to Brindisi. I put on a good thick layer of deodorant as Ken planned our sightseeing itinerary in the mindset we had tons of time before our 4:00 p.m. crossing. Ever try talking an optimist into allotting extra time for construction, wrong turns or unforeseen acts of God? After intense negotiation, I received thirty minutes of grace and rolled on another layer.

We moved through our day in fast forward mode. At the village of Dion flanking Mount Olympus we saw where King Archelaus held nine days of games to honor Zeus and managed to make it to the ferry terminal with time to spare; why do acts of God never happen when you're trying to prove a point?

With a fourteen hour overnight journey ahead of us, we decided to sleep in the camper rather than book an expensive sleeping cabin on the ferry. It seemed like a good idea until hearing the loud grinding noises from metal shifting as the ferry heaved over cresting waves. The time seemed appropriate to break the seal on a bottle of prescription sleeping pills. I'd felt uncomfortable taking that prescription from my doctor, but she was right — in extreme circumstances they come in handy.

Every once in a while, we all need a helping hand

The Acropolis in Greece

Ferry ride to Greece

Ken and Makayla play volleyball

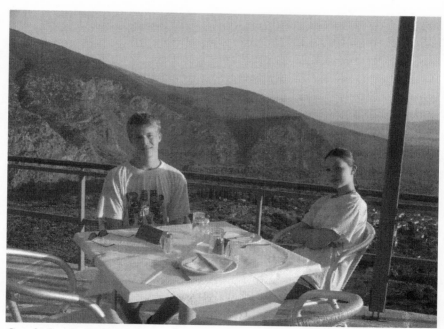

Greek Campsite Dinner

SOUTHERN ITALY

June 5

Reluctantly letting go of deep REM, I made my way up through dense fog to Ken's cheerful "welcome to Italy!" It was a special day. We'd be checking out of the camper and into a condo just south of Naples for another condo getaway. As we drove, Makayla couldn't stop talking about how she was going to "veg out" and watch the National Geographic channel all day long. Depression took hold when the only English channel available was the BBC.

Makayla pouted while Ken grinned like a Cheshire cat. He'd discovered the resort's activities signup sheet. With tennis courts, volleyball, archery, soccer, and water aerobics available for guests, any form of "vegging" seemed highly unlikely.

We stood in front of the sign-up sheets struggling to read Italian when a young staff member noticed our plight and came over to help. Introducing himself as Andreas, the tennis instructor, he was in his early twenties and appropriately good looking; in a tall dark, handsome and hot way. He couldn't speak much English, but we finally deciphered an offer for tennis lessons starting the next morning. The start time was a bit too early, but his dreamy brown eyes had me enthusiastically nodding – yes – like a dashboard hula girl.

June 6

Tennis lessons sounded like a good idea until the morning alarm rang out. Even so I was excited, probably more to drool over Andreas than for the potential improvements to my game. It came as quite a shock when my eye candy turned seriously intense. He ran his tennis lessons like boot camp. We began the morning with nine students. By midmorning, under a blistering hot Southern Italian sun and Andrea's harsh criticism, we withered down to four – yep just the Moores.

Desperately trying to make Andreas happy, we always seemed to be doing something wrong. Undoubtedly, if we survived a week of his lessons, we'd be better players – but could we survive? Keener Ken obviously thought so, swinging his racquet at the end of the session while the rest of us ran for shade and collapsed.

Rain after lunch interfered with Ken's plans for continuous afternoon athletics. He looked disappointedly out the condo window while Makayla suffered the "fifty nine channels with nothing on" blues. To perk them up, I suggested a game of Scrabble. Laughing at her mother's dyslexic inability to spell always improved Makayla's mood.

Still engrossed in the game when dinner time came around, we tried to order pizza. Wouldn't you know – the country inventing pizza didn't deliver. We had plenty of time to complain about irritating Italian customs before picking it up at 8:30 p.m.

June 7

After five long hot hours of tennis, Makayla got her way; we "vegged" for the rest of the day.

June 8

Our tennis court absorbed sunrays like tinfoil. Andreas worked with me on my backhand or bacon, as he liked to call it, boisterously yelling out tips I couldn't seem to implement. He exercised his lungs and shriveled my ego as, in the hot sun, I sputtered and sizzled like real bacon.

With the lesson over, we headed directly to the pool to cool off. As we frolicked in the refreshing water, Ken and I hardly noticed the lifeguard's irritating whistle. When it didn't stop, we looked to see who was in trouble. Following his gaze back to us was a surprise. Not sure what we'd done wrong, the life guard harped about something in Italian and pointed to his head. Pointing to our heads we shrugged, trying to convey our lack of understanding. Repeating his "head point" we did our "shrug and head point" still confused. A bad game of Simon Says continued until he blurted out in butchered English, "no beanie." Looking around, everyone else wore some kind of weird blue and white tight, striped bathing cap on their head. Embarrassed, we slunk back to our room.

June 9

All morning long my backhand made Andreas moan "noooooooooooo, Jennyyyyyyyyfer.......ooooh that baaaaacon." In just a few short days his dreamy brown eyes had turned into burning hunks of coal. He was hot alright. Too hot to handle! Blocking out his billowing, I dreamed of submerging myself in the cool pool until another "noooooooooo Jennyyyyyyyyfer" brought me back to reality.

For only a few Euros we happily bought and donned our beanies to join the rest of the beach ball headed Italians in the pool. Squeezing our heads into them was awkward, but I didn't care; I would have worn a pizza box on my head if that's what it took to cool down. Then came the big question – to tuck or not to tuck? Our ears, that is. I suggested Ken tuck, with his ears out and the tight beanie hugging his head, he looked a bit like a two handed sugar bowl.

We needed our swim to reenergize for our 4:00 p.m. adults-only tennis tournament (Andreas made us go). Almost a week of tennis lessons didn't save us from quick defeat. Walking home with our heads hung low, we stumbled upon the kids playing soccer with other Italian kids. For the first time on the trip, they'd made friends without parental intervention. Maybe they weren't social misfits after all.

June 10

Sore physically and mentally from four days on the tennis court, I opted for a change and signed us up for morning archery. A new skill for us all, little did we know there was a Robin Hood in our midst. Yes, after only a few tries, Ken consistently hit the bull's-eye. Our instructor nicknamed him, The Warrior.

Ken, feeling cocky, decided to sign up for the archery tournament that afternoon. The rest of us, not showing the same talent, headed to the pool for aerobics. Ken returned before dinner with a first place gold medal around his neck. We could no longer blame his bad driving on poor eyesight.

June 11

Rubbing sleep from my eyes on the way to the condo bathroom, it dawned on me – there would be nothing but public bathrooms until we flew home. Heading back to the camper was always tough, but with only 43 more sleeps, I knew we could make it. Time was already erasing the sting of our initial camper hardships. Actually, the life of a camper wasn't so bad after all. I was thinking I might like to do it again someday, as I stepped into a camper that must have been 50 degrees Celsius. The wine I'd so carefully tasted and stored while in France had to be close to a boil. Madly fanning those bottles to cool them down, at that moment I would have been happier to pour them over my head than drink them.

After a very long hot and sweaty hour we stopped at Matera, an ancient Italian town where *The Passion of Christ* was filmed. Wandering its narrow streets lined with small whitewashed cement buildings made you believe you just might run into Jesus and his disciples. Unfortunately, because of the heat, we wouldn't fully appreciate Matera until enjoying photos on a comfortable couch back in cool Canada.

June 12

At a rest stop, after a good night of sleep. I sat up to stretch. Looking out the window, I saw what looked like white concrete rather than sky. The window on the opposite side offered up the same solid white view. Not sure what was going on, I hopped up to look out the window. Making a nose print, a thunderous rumble made the whole camper vibrate. Jumping and gasping as if suddenly released from a stranglehold, it took a few seconds to realize we weren't, in fact, stuck in a block of concrete. Long semi-trucks had backed in on either side of us.

Explaining my gasp to the kids, whose heads instantly popped out from their bedroom curtain, took some creative thinking. I wasn't about to share my encasement misconception, after the abuse I'd taken after the mirror/window situation in Japan. I had no choice but to say

I'd stubbed my toe. Always able to sniff out a blonde moment, their detective eyes searched for incriminating clues, but given the early hour they soon gave up and headed back to bed.

After a quick breakfast, we hit the highway – destination, Bologna, another lovely Italian city most notable for the best gelato ever.

Our swimming beanies

Makayla stretches

Our South Italian condo

Matera where the Passion of Christ was filmed

Mattson and Makayla play soccer and make new friends

Ken the warrior

SWITZERLAND

June 13

With the benefit of hindsight, let me share the workings of two different minds. Ken and I sat in front of a beautiful lake eating breakfast and discussing plans for the day. I said "it's such a nice day we should enjoy it," and Ken responded "you're right, let's do that." We started to drive. I expected to drive for a couple hours, find a camp site and get out of the camper to enjoy the day. Ken thought he'd drive all day long enjoying beautiful scenery from the camper window. We forgot to use our words and later that day the words flew.

A well thought out plan is a well talked out plan

June 14

When Ken wanted to veer off our direct route to Ireland to explore more of Switzerland, the kids and I revolted. We were tired and bored of breathtaking mountain vistas viewed through dirty camper windows. We sat and pouted until Mattson piped up with a suggestion. Why not drive straight through Switzerland to a Six Flags amusement park just outside of Lyon, France? Our day driving would still take us north but the kids would have something to look forward to. The adult in Ken wanted to hold out for more scenery, but the kid in him loved rides. He turned toward France.

After a long day of driving, Ken and I stayed up late venting about frustrations building over the last few days. Work was difficult for Ken. An Italian fellow lining up his meetings named Gianluca was elusive and hard to pin down. We were constantly trying to find phones and internet cafés to send and check for messages from Gianluca. These stops left us waiting impatiently in the camper. After what seemed like the hundredth Gianluca announcement, Makayla went squirrelly, barking like a pit bull "Gianluca, Gianluca, what a stupid name. All you ever do is talk about phoning Gianluca. I'd like to kill Gianluca!" Her violent outburst reinforced the need for amusement park therapy – the kid needed to lighten up.

We closed our discussion with the agonizing topic of what to do about the camper. Yet again it was acting up and occasionally not starting. With a deep sigh, we headed to bed, giving the camper a good kick on the way in.

June 15

Instead of joining the kids on the Six Flags roller coasters, Ken and I embarked on a more emotional roller coaster ride – getting the lousy camper fixed AGAIN"!

The demon was back.

June 16

It was a miracle! Ken connected with Gianluca, making Makayla so happy she forgot it was morning, and smiled. On toward Ireland we drove, passing time with the new used books I'd picked up in Lyon.

How I loved reading. The luxury of long uninterrupted reading time would be difficult to give up when we returned home. Our books, stuffed in every nook and cranny of the camper, somehow migrated throughout any given day. More nights than not, after heading to bed, someone wouldn't be able to find their book. Up Ken would get, walking around our bed and stepping on my blanket covered limbs to search overhead cupboards. All too often, after not finding the book, up we got to fold up the bed. Off in a corner you'd swear it needed legs to get to, there the book would sit.

June 17

In Normandy, we ran on the beach where D-Day occurred. On June 6th 1944, 156,000 allied troops mobilize for a mission to invade France. When that day ended, 4,000-9,000 young men had lost their lives. We stopped for a moment of silence. What a different world it would be if they hadn't successfully opened a passageway to liberate

Paris. As we resumed our pace, I knew my Remembrance Day poppy would be worn so much closer to my heart.

Our Canadian government funded the building of The Juno Beach Center to honor Canadian D-Day troops. Once through the door, we immediately felt at home. Canadian staff spoke our dialect and the maple leaf was displayed proudly. When we left many hours later, we were proud of the sacrifice our soldiers made, proud because they'd been recognized with eloquent dignity and proud to be Canadian.

June 18

Driving, driving, driving, France went on forever; so many chateaus, so many wine varietals. Chateauneuf de Pape, Bordeaux, Burgundy, the camper was filling up with bottles from every region as the kids shook their heads and questioned why. We'd get them home, I promised. I mean really, what was the worst case scenario? They'd have to be drunk before getting on the plane. How hard could that be?

Late in the day we made a short ferry crossing from Calais to Dover. The Cliffs of Dover really are as white as a Canadian in January. It was sad leaving France's well balanced reds and delicate croissants behind for England's ale and bangers and mash, but drive on we did in search of Guinness and family. Ken's folks were flying over to meet us in Ireland.

Makayla skipping

A castle in Geneva

Ice Cave

Mattson without Mario in Salzburg

Juno Beach Centre in Normandy

IRELAND

June 19

Our tortuously long drive ended with a ferry crossing from Holyhead over to Dublin. Upon boarding, we were like deaf mutes miraculously cured. Televisions on the boat showed Tom Cruise's lips arc with Tom Cruise's words. How I loved Tom, and after watching Greek and Egyptian come from that beautiful mouth, it was great to see his words and his mouth in sync.

English is a beautiful language

The ferry crossing passed in a flash as we devoured all things English. What a surprise to find out Julia Roberts had twins! By the time we drove off the boat, I felt like I was back from the twilight zone. It would be nice to have a few things to talk about beyond our travel, when we met Ken's folks later in the day.

After hugs, kisses, and a joyful reunion, six of us sat interlaced in the camper listening to the swish and squeak of windshield wipers pelting away Irish rain. The addition of two people radically changed how we decided what to do next. Our usual "but I want to" changed to "whatever you want to do." As it turned out, being considerate complicates the decision making process. Those windshield wipers swung back and forth, and back and forth, as in time and in turn, we sighed and sang... "I don't care; whatever you want to do."

When all else fails, eat. We drove around looking for a pub Ken's mom wanted to visit. Unfortunately the directions she'd brought along were obscure, leaving us confused and lost. As we prowled up and down poorly lit streets, Phyllis worried about the delay and insisted we abort our mission. We had to laugh. How could she know? Getting lost was like brushing our teeth; we expected to do it at least a couple of times a day.

Eventually finding Scott's Pub, a traditional place more upscale than its name implied, I approached my first Guinness beer with trepidation. Not being a beer lover, I fancied the idea more than the reality of this Irish experience. Surprisingly though, surrounded by all things Irish, it tasted good right down to the last drop.

Taste is all in the ambiance

June 20

In glorious morning sunshine, Dublin looked like an emerald city. Crammed with overly green trees and overly green grass, their pumped up green complimented row upon row of single storey buildings in red, yellow and blue.

After devouring warm bakery scones soaked in jam and cream and washed down with strong bitter coffee, Ken and his parents started working out our sightseeing itinerary. So began another round of "I don't care; whatever you want to do."

Eventually we drove to tour Kilkenny Castle and the Waterford Crystal factory. I happily gave up my co-pilot passenger seat to Ken Sr. and settled in at the kitchen table. With one eye on the Irish countryside and the other in a freshly cracked novel, I listened with one ear to Ken and his dad's conversation and with the other to Phyllis. It didn't take long to realized, I didn't know what was happening in my book; I was clueless about what Phyllis had been talking to me about and the scenery Ken was raving about had passed me by.

Multi-tasking is not an efficient use of time

When our drive took longer than anticipated, I felt the need to apologize to Phyllis. She sat on the edge of her seat with coat fastened and scarf tied, ready to be where we were going. How could she know, Captain Ken's estimated arrival times could be off by days, not just hours.

June 21

So much for sunny Ireland; obviously the rain reigned in this neck of the woods. After learning the intricacies of making Waterford crystal, we carried on, trudging through driving rain in a stiff wind to the famous Blarney Castle.

Inside the dimly lit Blarney Tower, feeling oversized and weighed down in wet clothes, we trudged up a winding staircase that threatened to never end. Stepping back outside into the castles courtyard, we met the Blarney Stone – a rocky gigolo sought after by people from near and far. Like so many before us, we too wanted to pucker up and kiss the Blarney Stone. For legend states "he who kisses the Blarney Stone will acquire the gift of eloquence." All we had to do was lay back and tip our noggins over a deep dark abyss between castle walls to lean in and plant an upside down wet one on the wall (not an easily embraced stone) called the Blarney Stone.

My eyes looked to the sky after being guided down onto my back by castle staff. Dropping my head, prepared to go where so many had gone before, I considered the amount of spit swapping taking place on that wall. I mean, come on! A dentist knows all too well what nasty bugs live in saliva. Even so, I followed the crowd, as we humans so often do. I did try to veer to the right, as if going for the cheek, but the workers holding my feet insisted I keep my body straight. Like it or not, I went for full eloquence.

Later that night, I used my new eloquent words to pipe up and stop indecision in its tracks.

Every group needs an eloquent leader

June 22

Pellets of rain slammed deep into our pores as we stepped out into another overcast morning. Talk about hydration; there was no need for moisturizers in Ireland.

The weather man, claiming conditions would improve throughout the day, made us postpone our drive around the Ring of Kerry until the afternoon. With an unexpected free morning in Killarney, I was happy for time to browse through quaint gift shops. The rest of the gang decided to go to the internet café. After bidding everyone goodbye, Ken Sr. unexpectedly turned back. He wanted to shop with me.

Go figure, Ken's dad a shopper? This man was extremely frugal and certainly not one to shop for clothes. Ever since I'd known him he always dressed the same way: navy pants, a ball cap and a pale blue dress shirt with three ball point pens in the breast pocket. Not one, not two, but always three. Anyway, there I was in lacy-girly-shops selling fragrant soaps, creams and perfumes with my father-in-law, dressed in his usual uniform of course, and he's into it like a good girlfriend. We shop and shop and never once does he seem impatient or bored.

Don't judge a father-in-law by the color of his shirt

Ken Sr. spent most of his time browsing, but did purchase three green ball point pens and a green ball cap with Ireland written across the top. As he proudly replaced his three blue pens with the new green ones and swung his new green ball cap into just the right crease on his forehead, I knew I was witnessing a special moment. Change, he was making a change, and that change had him grinning from ear to ear. His new hat proved he was a traveling man proud of his Irish heritage.

In the afternoon the weather brightened slightly as we started the famous Ring of Kerry drive. The scenery was really lovely, but what I'll also never forget was the actual Ring of Kerry road. Like driving over row upon row of wooden railway tracks it compressed our spinal column in and out like an accordion. Good old Ken, playing Mario as he so loved to do, had a gay old time driving while the rest of us turned green. With my normal seat of influence occupied by Ken Sr. I gave the kids, sitting right behind their dad, a fly swatter and permission to hit his head every time he took a wild pump or turn. If he slowed down, they could reward him with a piece of precious, care package red licorice. Loving his licorice, the strategy worked like a charm.

June 23

In the afternoon we drove to Limerick, an industrial city made famous by Frank McCourt's book *Angela's Ashes*. I'd given up on exerting my gift of eloquence, thinking it might come off a bit bossy, and instead sat back and let Ken and his folks guide their own tour of Ireland. A lengthy family discussion on where to go began; following that came a lengthy family discussion on what to see once there, followed by a lengthy family discussion once there about whether the tour was worth the high price, followed by a lengthy family discussion on what to do after not paying for the tour, and so on, and so on, and, so on.

Flash forward. Later that day standing in a tight decision making family circle outside a castle, we finally hit upon a destination everyone was into; dinner at Durty Nelly's, supposedly the oldest pub in Ireland. Located in a famous old farm house with low ceilings crossed with dark wood beams and miniscule Hobbit sized rooms, we jammed together on bench seats and sipped perfectly headed Guinness trying to decide what to order for dinner, where to go after dinner, where to spend the night and so on and so on.

June 24

Finally, we were greeted by a gorgeous sunny morning. My wet laundry desperately needed sunshine to dry. Buzzing around, searching for anything capable of holding a clothes pin, I'd just clipped my bra to the camper antenna when big dark clouds leaking rain sent our clothes back to the laundry basket for further fermentation.

In the afternoon, we explored a cave dating back millions of years in a geographical area called the Burren. With inky tunnels fit for ground hogs, I crouched down and made my way through – euphorically fearless and free.

June 25

We were off to Newry to trace Ken Sr.'s family tree. After parking, we stood on a street corner looking for long lost relatives as if somehow they'd telepathically know we'd arrived. When family and history didn't rush our way, my Ken suggested a trip to the local library for internet research.

I hoped Ken Sr. wouldn't realize the same research could have been done back home in Canada. Hopefully it would be like drinking Guinness. You could do it anywhere, but doing it in Ireland was just better.

June 26

We talked the kids and Ken Sr. into a walk on the nearby beach. It was fun watching Ken Sr. enthusiastically pick up interesting rocks and shells as we strolled along. He filled his pockets then offered me a handful of his treasures. When I declined, he insisted, and held his hand in place. I tried to explain how I'd learned the hard way to leave beach items untouched, but his outstretched hand remained. Politely declining a few more times, I finally got it. We were in a "Christmas dinner" kind of situation. He'd hold up a plate of food and offer me seconds. I'd say "no thanks" but that plate stayed in position until I gave in and dished out. He simply wasn't one to take no for an answer.

June 27

The two Kens set out in the morning to search for family history. When they didn't return, I wondered if they'd found their history watering the family tree at a pub. Phyllis and I set out to investigate. Sure enough, they shared a table at the pub with four spiky haired young guys sporting studded black leather jackets and skinny jeans. After introductions, nothing would do but for us to join them for a pint. We got acquainted and settled into a detailed conversation about which pub in Ireland served the best Guinness.

Other Irish bartenders had educated us on the ins and outs of a perfectly poured Guinness. They stressed how it had to be dispensed at the correct speed and angle to produce the right thickness of thick creamy head, and how you had to patiently wait for the beer to settle before drinking it. On top of that, the hose running from the keg of beer to the dispensing valve had to be just the right length – the shorter the better.

In the middle of our Guinness chatter, the waiter arrived and asked if we wanted another round. Phyllis, curious about how Guinness was poured in their bar, shouted out "how long is your hose?" just as the roar of bar room chatter took a breath. Not sure how to answer a foreign lady in her late sixties asking about his hose, our waiter stuttered as we all erupted in laughter. Perfectly poured Guinness would have kept flowing had Phyllis and I not extracted the boys from the pub, like so many a good Irish women before us.

June 28

Back in Dublin, we checked Ken and Phyllis into a hotel room, parked the camper down the street and headed off for dinner. Returning and unlocking the camper door later that night, a lady walked by and curtly questioned "I hope you're not leaving your camper there? You're surely to be robbed or vandalized during the night." "No worries" Ken cheerfully replied "We're not going to leave the camper, we're going to sleep in it." The women paused, frowned and shaking her head mumbled "oh, well, yes well then, good luck" and walked on, looking back every few seconds to shake her head.

The ladies warning rolled off Ken's back unnoticed while I took heed and scanned the streets for robbers and murderers. Folding my arms in a, this is serious kind of way, I insisted Ken move the camper. And so, another of our well-worn Big Trip discussions began. Ken argued "nothing bad ever happens to us," and I played my trump card – "How many times have we been robbed?" We moved on.

Good things come from bad

Our last day in Dublin included a whirlwind of historic visits beginning with a stop at The Natural History Museum. Stuffed, real animal scenes of mother and baby didn't sit right with me. The taxidermist was amazing, but dead is dead. On we went to drool over the arched intricately carved dark hardwood ceiling at the Long Hall in Trinity College.

My highlight for the day was seeing the *Book of Kells*, a decorative Irish translation of the gospels dating back to the eighth century. How that book remained in such good condition when the one I was reading looked like a dog chewed on it, I'll never know.

While we did the historic thing, Ken's dad confirmed his love for shopping, buying multiple singing leprechauns from one of the many gift shops he visited that afternoon.

June 29

Waking to a sharp insistent knock on our camper door, I worried we'd over slept. Ken Sr. and Phyllis needed a ride to the airport but according to my watch, it was way too early to leave. Early or not, Ken Sr. stood in our doorway with suitcase in hand. We tried shooing him away, but in true Ken Sr. style, there was no saying no to his need to get going.

Outside the airport, I guarded luggage while Ken helped his folks check in. Lost in a daydream about getting back on the road, suddenly the jingle *When Irish Eyes Are Smiling* rang out, the singer very close at hand. Swirling around with enough momentum to launch a double axel, I saw no one, yet the first two lines of the song repeated over and over again. Breaking through my confusion I connected the music with Ken Sr.'s suitcase. One of his stuffed singing leprechaun souvenirs had accidentally gone off. That little Leprechaun could sing all the way back to Canada and Ken Sr. wouldn't notice. Phyllis would try and tell him about it, but when it came to hearing what she had to say, he often went from hearing impaired to stone deaf.

Back to just the four of us, we let our quirky habits back out of the bag and continued up the road to Northern Ireland. Dunluce Castle sat on crushed velvet green grass high on a hill. Bathing a castle with sunshine, like putting makeup on a beautiful girl, took it from lovely to unforgettable.

Weather is an experience maker or breaker

Down the road, we came to the Giant's Causeway, a perplexing natural rock formation of dark grey hexagonal rock tubes protruding from the earth like bar stools of different heights all pushed together. The rocks, when viewed from the air, meshed together, forming what looked like large stepping stones heading out to sea. According to legend, giants used the stones to walk across to Scotland.

We felt like insignificant ants sitting on those bar stools. Watching the setting sun bail out crimson and gold, we dreamed of how such a place came to be.

June 30

After getting a chilly nine holes of golf over with, it was time to do the same with my public morning shower. The coffin-sized stall drizzled tepid water. I shivered, lathered my hair and realized I'd forgotten my towel.

Trying to yank my jeans, which suddenly felt three sizes too small, over wet skin, left me off balance. I bounced off the shower's confining walls bruising myself on all sides like an evenly tanned roasted marshmallow, before marching back to the camper – cold in a wet T-shirt with arms crossed high. I might forget tokens, shampoo or underwear, but never again would I forget my towel.

After checking out, we drove to the Carrick-a-Rede Bridge, touted by our travel book as sure to thrill, but rated by Mattson as boring enough to kill. We were more than ready to leave the dark grey clouds of Ireland behind to make our way to Scotland.

Ken and Jen at the Cliffs of Moher

Ken and Ken Sr. at Durty Nelly's Pub

Ken and Phyllis enjoy a Guinness

Jen goes for eloquence kissing the Blarney Stone

Mattson and Makayla at the Giants Causeway

Castle in Ireland

SCOTLAND

July 1

A short ferry ride deposited us in a little town called Straner. Driving down skinny streets lined with quaint stone cottages, we searched for a grocery store to find new and unusual foods.

The family wasn't sure about the Scottish egg I insisted they try. Big and round like an ostrich egg, it was brown and covered with some kind of unknown fuzzy substance. We all gathered round the camper table, leaning forward to inspect the egg while pushing it about with chopsticks as if it were toxic. Stepping up to begin a dissection, I grabbed a sharp kitchen knife and neatly sectioned the egg into quarters. Inside the quarter of an inch thick brown covering was a hardboiled egg. Looking up into faces contorted in disgust, everyone knew what had to be done. Reluctantly, we pounded back our sections like a shot of tequila. To our surprise, it wasn't bad at all.

July 2

More rain; "might as well head to Edinburgh" Ken sang out, flaunting his ever even nature. We drove and talked as stunning countryside, even more heavily treed and lush than Ireland, passed by. Once in Edinburgh, its amazing architecture made it one of our favorite cities, and rich and creamy sticky toffee pudding ensured we'd be back.

On the way back to the campsite, Scottish Highland cows had us stopping to take a closer look. Their curved horns and long shaggy red hair covered huge brown eyes. To get a picture of their adorable faces, we whistled and called out "here little cows, come on little cows, look over here little cows." Scots driving past probably shook their heads at the crazy antics of tourists.

July 3

Ken, up early to golf, wanted me to come along. "You're in the birth place of golf," he pleaded "you should come." Placing birth and golf in the same sentence seemed appropriate; as far as I was concerned they were both painful. Groggily pulling the covers over my head I croaked "away with you laddie."

Heading back to Edinburgh for a second look we explored various museums and confirmed, once and for all – we truly were "museumed out." I had so many historical facts swimming around in my head I couldn't keep my Jacobites from my Orange men. It was enough to send you into a gift shop.

While shopping, I stayed true to my promise to never again fill my house with unnecessary stuff, until coming across the cutest hand-painted Highland Cow coffee mug ever. I had to have it. Every time I lifted that cup to my lips, I'd be back in Edinburgh.

Go for travel mementos that don't accumulate dust.

July 4

It was late morning by the time we aimed the nose of our camper for St. Andrews. During the drive our conversation focused on "back to reality" decisions. Makayla had just learned her dance teacher was moving to a studio on the other side of the city. To follow her would mean a two hour commute, six days a week. Ken flat out said no, sending our emotionally delicate pre-teen into a spin and my mind into overdrive figuring how I could make things right. The stresses of resuming life back in Calgary began to seep into our peaceful travel world.

On we went to St. Andrews. Ken drooled over the golf course, but to me, it looked shabby and disjointed. When I told him so, he blurted out "It's a links course," looking at me as if that should mean something. "As in a large cat?" I innocently questioned, not understanding why, if the course was so famous, they couldn't at least cut the grass.

That night, we celebrated the kids' home schooling graduation, inhaling warm ginger cake with creamy custard and patting ourselves on the back for a job well done.

July 5

Did you know you can play ninety-nine holes of golf at St. Andrews? Ken did, and since he couldn't play them, he wanted to at least see them during our morning run. We jogged through drizzling rain while he scrutinized fairways and greens and I wondered how long our tour would take. Ninety-nine holes covered a lot of ground. Focused on ninety-nine, my mind clicked back to the old beer drinking song *99 Bottles of Beer on the Wall*. Giving it a tweak I sang out "99 holes of golf and a ball, ninety nine holes of golf. Keep your head down, chase it around, 98 holes of golf and a ball." I got down to 25 holes of golf and a ball, when Ken agreed to leave the rain and the rest of St Andrews ninety nine-holes behind.

Later that day, we made our way to London.

ENGLAND

July 6

The Crystal Palace campground had clean showers and trees. Located right in the middle of London, you could walk right out the front gate and find public transportation downtown. Back in Canada, you'd have to climb a mountain, cross a river and fight off a few grizzlies before getting anywhere close to a bus stop. We happily hopped on our bus and transferred to the Tube (underground train system) to find half-price theater tickets in Covent Garden. I looked to Ken with big needy eyes, hoping to get as many musical theater fixes as possible. Like a good sugar daddy he pulled out his wallet.

July 7

Getting Makayla moving in the morning was painful; extracting her from the camper was like watching a snail crawl out from under its shell. Mattson badgered her to hurry up but that just slowed her down more. Despite Makayla, we made it to the changing of the guard at Buckingham Palace. Ken helped move us up and past a view of backs and heads by hoisting us, in turn, up onto his shoulders. The people behind us probably weren't impressed, but we'd learned in Asia, aggressive selfishness is the only way to operate in a crowd.

July 8

With amazing sites on every corner, we loved London. This was my perfect city. No language barrier, lots of theater and Pizza Hut. Normally I wouldn't place pizza on a sophisticated cities list of highlights, but all you could eat salty meaty cheesy pizza and a full salad bar all for just 6 pounds affordably filled our bellies.

The only part of London I didn't like was the Northern Line Tube ride, taking us back and forth from Covent Garden. The oldest of their lines, the train was a cigar tube stuffed with people. I concentrated on every printed detail on my theater tickets to take my mind off the acrid hot breath coming from some guy pressed into me so tightly we may as well have been slow dancing.

Our Theater Review:
Chicago- fantastic, even better than the movie
Anything Goes- an old-fashioned musical with a simple fun story
Fame- Makayla's favorite. Modern, loud and racy
Blood Brothers- a powerful tear jerker
Les Miserables- dramatic and moving for the parents, sleepy for the kids

July 9

    While driving Mattson to gym in gridlock traffic, striking rain splintered across our windshield and marred my view of trench coat wrapped Londoners. Briskly strutting past row upon row of red brick brownstones, they skillfully tilted their umbrellas to agree with the gusting wind. When I tried for that sweet spot the wind beat me down. It sucked up and flipped out my umbrella until it looked like a bowl of metal wire covered with a shredded napkin. Watching Londoners pass by, I daydreamed about what it would be like to be one of them.

To discover a city, look beyond its tourist traps

July 10

    My husband was driving me crazy. Sharing a small camper with kids for five months was a bit hard on the love life. Now, with our return to Calgary and privacy on the horizon, Ken realized his drought was almost over and buzzed around me like a big old black fly. A playful pinch here, a gentle grope there with a good swat only temporarily driving him away. No amount of rain dancing would open the flood gates, but he tried. Oh how he tried.

    It was time to leave the UK. We caught an afternoon ferry back to France, then drove and free camped near a Six Flags Amusement Park in Belgium. We had a two week pass allowing unlimited visits to any Six Flags park. The last stretch of our Big Trip was going to be, quite literally, one big long roller coaster ride.

326

BELGIUM

July 11

As we ran through the fields of Flanders, with blood red poppies bobbing in the wind, I was reminded of John McCrae's poem '*In Flanders fields where poppies grow, beneath the crosses row by row...*' The thought of it iced my bones, even after I broke a sweat.

The thought of war and death made me consider how losing Mattson to war would feel. Coupling that thought with the anticipation of riding terrifyingly huge roller coasters made me cranky. I tried to chase the family off to the amusement park without me, but Mattson wouldn't have it. He relentlessly pleaded for me to come until I finally gave in. As we teetered at the top of a mammoth roller coaster, I so regretted his powers of persuasion. My stomach moved into my throat as the nose tipped and our car dived. The jolt of the fall, like shock therapy, turned my fearful scream to a crazed cackle and knocked me out of my bad mood.

Mattson vibrated with enthusiastic energy as we disembarked, grabbing my hand and pulling me toward the next ride. "Wasn't that awesome, mom?" he cheered, "come-on, let's sit together in the very front car this time!" Laughing, and skipping, off we went. Our Big Trip high flying grand finale had begun.

To really feel alive, do something scary

July 12

Another day, another amusement park (getting our money's worth of course), Ken drove day and night to make it happen, but no one, except maybe me, complained.

Mattson's rollercoaster passion raged on while my enthusiasm waned. I tried putting in another amusement park day but by mid-afternoon my brain felt crushed and blended. I had to free myself from Mattson's grip and get back to the camper for Aspirin and stable ground. I'd just popped the pills, brewed a cup of tea and settled in for some journal writing when Ken burst through the camper door looking like a hungry lion ready to pounce on fresh kill. I was surprised to see him giving up his rides. He was, after all, a boy at heart but as he came toward me, it was obvious he'd changed into his big boy pants. Good thing my Aspirin was kicking in.

Eventually heading back to find the kids, I endured a few more loops and inversions watching a mostly upside down sunset before heading for dinner in Brussels. On the way in we discussed a new technological advancement called wireless internet. The concept of free e-mailing in the comfort of our camper seemed too good to be true.

In the city center we began a search for a wireless signal. Ken got out of the camper and walked around with the computer held to the sky. When power bars lit up, I marked the spot and Ken parked as close as possible. Crowding around the computer, Mattson signed onto a wireless network. It was the most amazing thing.

July 13

The Big Trip turned me into an addict. Every night I'd finish off my bed time routine stuffing and screwing the best ear plugs ever invented into my ears. They were lemon yellow, made from a soft plastic, and looked like little Christmas trees. I loved them. Those beauties blocked the irritating noise of Mattson's snoring, Makayla's twitching, and whatever other racket might be going on during any given night.

I'd started the trip with three pairs, but two had mysteriously disappeared, leaving me with one last precious set. Although I guarded them with my life somehow, even under my watchful eye, they'd gone missing. Sick with worry I interrogating the family insisting someone must have moved them. Everyone swore innocence. I tore the camper apart to find them all the while muttering like my mother so often used to do "you kids must have taken them, I know where I put them and now they're gone. Do you think they just got up and walked away?"

Not finding them, Ken tried making me feel better by patiently explaining I really didn't need them; the notion was all in my head. His advice stung like peroxide on an open cut. He was right though, it was all in my head, and my head was full of it until well past 3:00 a.m. when I found myself down on hands and knees searching through the slime of our garbage. Without a doubt I was flat-out addicted to ear plugs.

DRIVING BACK TO AMSTERDAM

July 14

The situation was rapidly deteriorating in the camper; sinks were plugged, the holding tank stunk and the quilts on our beds were dirty. A rattle here, a stall there, we lived in fear of another huge camper repair bill.

I sat at our kitchen table after a sleepless night chasing chocolate granola with a spoon while blankly staring at a wall of grey clouds. How would I survive another two weeks in such a smelly disgusting place with no ear plugs and no sleep? Dropping my hands from my lap in a depressed slump, I felt something hard between the seat cushions. There was my plastic container holding my ear plugs. How they got there I'll never know, but finding them gave me the boost I needed to pleasantly carry on.

When the kids got up and complained about the plugged sink, I was able to crisply point out, as good mothers should – they were lucky they didn't live in a slum like so many other poor underprivileged children.

With a new lease on life I gleefully embraced a rollercoaster-free day at Movie Land (yet another Six Flags park).

July 15

Continuing our extended roller coaster ride, up and down we went at another amusement park. When it closed, the ups and downs continued. The excitement of going home took us up and strange noises coming from the camper took us back down.

July 16

We'd spent the night free camping a few blocks from a hospital and in the morning decided to just stay put, while Ken went to work. Makayla looked disgustedly repulsed as I pulled out the Porta Potty. You'd think after all of our travel she'd be a bit more flexible when it came to waste elimination, but no, like a prissy princess she lifted her cute upturned nose and declared "I don't have to go."

We'd parked for the night around 8:00 p.m.; she held tight until 2:00 p.m. the next day when body language hinted she might not be quite the camel she hoped to be. Sitting in the camper quietly drawing portraits of each other, she started to squirm. By late afternoon, when Ken still wasn't back, she lost her composure and begged me to find her a bathroom. I held my ground and pointed to the Porta Potty while continuing to sketch. An hour later, after hearing one creative reason after another why the Porta Potty was impossible for her, she wore me down. Mother and desperate daughter burst through the hospital emergency room doors. Red faced after a long run, we attracted the attention of concerned doctors quickly mobilizing for a medical emergency.

Germany has good health care

Circled by doctors, it was a bit embarrassing to explain all we really needed was the bathroom.

July 17

After Ken finished work, we drove to Berlin. This European city, bombed to rubble in World War II and rebuilt after the war, was modern and futuristic. Old Europe we'd figured out. Twentieth century Berlin left us baffled.

We followed Ken and got horribly lost. Trudging along, we all complained about everything and anything until Ken threw up his hands, refusing to lead such a miserable group. Makayla, seeing an opportunity, grabbed the map and took over. Twenty minutes later, we sat in a Thai restaurant happily slurping Tom Yum Goong soup. It was a good thing The Big Trip was drawing to a close. Cocky Makayla's success left the smell of mutiny in the air.

July 18

We drove to Berlin's city centre on express freeways with sparse traffic, pulled into an oversized parking spot steps from a huge park and appreciated the efficiency of modernization.

At a flea market in the park we dispersed. I found an area with household stuff and lovingly caressed formal china. It wasn't something I'd ever wanted before, but nostalgic thoughts of big family Sunday dinners made those dishes so luscious I wanted to lick their beautiful gold rim. Dragging Ken over to take a look, he should have flat out said no. I shouldn't have told him how much more they'd cost back in Canada. We bought a full set of china with extra serving plates and placed them carefully in the camper beside our towering stack of wine.

Be practically impulsive

Later in the day, driving on to Hamburg, we settled into a campground. We ate outside in warm sunshine using my new elegant gold-rimmed china, and after dinner, ignoring Renee's advice to keep computers out of sight, watched a movie outside. It was well after dark when I made my final jaunt to the campground bathroom. On my way back, I was startled by a man standing in the shadows near a mobile home parked beside our camper. He was just leaning against the trailer and smoking, but for some reason, he made the hairs on the back of my neck stand up.

July 19

Ken gently shook me awake, sighed and said the dreaded words I'd heard too many times before. Once again we'd been robbed. A thief entered our camper during the night while we slept and took both laptops and Ken's wallet.

Thanks to my lemon yellow Christmas tree ear plugs and the rest of the family's ability to sleep deeply we'd heard nothing. My skin erupted in goose bumps imagining what would have happened if we'd woken up to an intruder at the foot of our bed.

I say guy, because instantly I remembered the guy in the shadows from the night before. Now comes the really sad part, the torturous part I beat myself up for.

The creepy feeling that guy gave me prompted me to lock the door of the camper before going to bed. The door was tricky to lock. You had to bend down and mess with a latch that was sticky and finicky. We usually didn't bother with it when in a campground. It just seemed ludicrous that anyone would break into the camper when we were in it, but because of the hairs on the back of my neck, I locked the door. I stood up and then I reconsidered.

Ken would be leaving for work early in the morning and would expect the door to be open. He was already asleep and I didn't want to wake him to tell him I'd had an uncomfortable feeling and locked the door. If I locked it, he'd be yanking on the door and fiddling with it in the darkness of early morning. He'd be noisy and wake us up. In a quest for more sleep, I bent back down, unlocked the door and went to bed.

Oh how I replayed that moment in my mind wishing I could hit stop before bending back down.

Trust your intuition

I hadn't backed up my computer for over two weeks;

Ken hadn't backed up his computer for months. His detailed trip budget and work documents were gone. I felt like throwing up; Ken appeared mildly put out. The police came. We learned others had been robbed. Tents had been slashed. He had a knife.

And so I slipped into post robbery emotional turmoil. Was I angry at the thief? No – I was angry at myself. We'd been told, way back when, when we bought the camper, not to leave valuables in it, not to leave wallets on dash boards and not to let anyone see our technology. We'd done all three, and three times we'd been robbed.

Ouch. I felt like a little kid, doing something your parents told you not to do. When you don't listen, you pay – oh how you pay. The scary thing was, I knew we should have learned a lesson, but our trusting nature would have us making the same mistakes over and over and over again.

The police came but didn't want to hear about the creepy guy in the shadows from the night before. They gave us no hope we'd ever get our stuff back.

Ken stood dejected as the officers drove away, but perked up as a plan to get into the bad guy's mobile home and rescue our stolen property unfolded. Filled with renewed optimism, he assured me all would be well and set off for work. I sat at the camper's kitchen table numbly chewing tasteless cereal and pressed stop and rewind, over and over again, in my mind. I imagined myself beating Ken to the guy's door to forcefully take back our things. I chewed. I blindly stared into space. I didn't move.

Eventually I mustered the willpower to move. Marching up to the campground reception, a horsey German lady about thirty-five years old stood at the counter staring blankly down at me while I told my sad tale. When I asked what she knew about my suspected robber, devoid of emotion, she spat out "I can't help you, call the police." Her words, hardened with a heavy German accent, stung. I'd never before thought of myself as a racist but at that moment I wanted to punch that big fat homely German lady in the face. I wanted to spit on the German police and every other lousy German in that country. I hated their stupid language, their sausages, and their beer. I wanted to be anywhere but in their awful country.

Anger isn't a rational emotion

The kids took the robbery reasonably well. With no forced sign of entry and their Game Boys safe, it didn't impact them like our other robberies had. Ken was disappointed when knocking on the bad guy's mobile home door and politely asking for our stolen property got him a slammed door in the face, but he got over it quickly. I continued to fester.

Three robberies, a blown motor, and ongoing mechanical trouble was messing with my assumption that we Moores, good and nice people, were immune to all things bad. It's just that things usually worked out for us. Seeing our "special" status slip away was disturbing. If we weren't in fact special, more bad things could happen.

I stared out the window and watched a smashed camper being towed down the highway, realizing that camper could be ours. We could get in a terrible accident, total the camper and end up in some German hospital facing physical and financial ruin.

When you go to the dark side living can get really scary

July 21

Ken drove while I kept my eyes peeled for potential disaster. Watch that car, don't drive too fast, stay in your lane, he'd heard it all before, but not with the same frequency and intensity.

We had three days before selling the camper back to Renee in Amsterdam. Three days to avoid disaster. I wondered how I'd managed one night of sleep during the trip. There were so many WHAT IFS I hadn't considered.

After Ken left for work I wanted to sleep the day away. My computer was gone. My desire to write was gone. I willed my body to shut down, but my over active stomach cramped like it had the stomach flu – and so I ran. I don't know where or for how long, the thief took my watch, but I ran until I remembered I had children and then I ran home. Forcing a smile, I woke them up. We drew and colored a cow copied off the back of a milk carton. It was a long day and when Ken came home and we resumed driving, my disaster watch continued.

July 22

With another amusement park day planned, we free camped in the parking lot by the roller coasters to ensure admittance the minute the gates opened. I didn't want to go. I didn't want to do anything but be miserable, but I did go and I did do my best to rain down on everyone.

Ken's ability to brush off our tragedy irritated me. He was so insensitive. Not wanting to be alone in my misery, I tried dragging him down to my level. Attempt number one: arguing in favour of Makayla's dance commute. I was quickly shot down. Attempt number two: why did we have to go to so many amusement parks when everyone knew I didn't really enjoy them? No matter how hard I tried, Ken wouldn't play my game. He'd just run off with the kids, leaving me to brood, and brood I did, for half the day, until Mattson finally rescued me from myself.

Insisting I ride what he claimed was the best roller coaster in the whole world, I screamed with terror, then with anger, then with frustration. I screamed until screaming turned to laughter and when the laughter came it changed everything.

Forgive yourself for the mistakes you make

July 23

After closing down the amusement park and forcing down another pasta and red sauce dinner (I was starting to look like a piece of macaroni) we drove on to Amsterdam. Our camper journey had come full circle; just one last day before trading it back in.

Everyone else in the family was more than ready to go home. Certainly, I too was sick and tired of so many of our Big Trip challenges, but still, I could have happily continued our loop around the world. Let me clarify – IN A HOTEL ROOM, NOT A CAMPER! I loved the thrill of waking up to new adventure every day. No two travels days were the same. Once home our tight family unit would disperse and we'd be right back into scheduling chaos and day to day routine. Still, Calgary felt safe, and when you're down on your luck and paranoid, safe is a good thing.

The day felt like a week as we impatiently waited for Ken at multiple stops. When the ignition key turned to off at our last campground, we'd done it. We'd traveled for just short of a year on the trip of a lifetime. We had money in the bank and still liked each other. We should have celebrated, but there was work to be done. I boiled water for pasta while we all started to clean the camper.

July 24

Once the cheque for the camper was in hand, I felt the curse of bad luck vaporize. We were free, unburdened.

Giddy, we headed to our last sightseeing tour. We'd all read *The Diary of Anne Frank*, and wanted to visit the house where she hid from the Nazis. While waiting in line, we quizzed each other on what we looked forward to the most once home: Tim Hortons donuts, Dairy Queen ice cream, seeing family and friends. We drooled, laughed and joked until entering the Anne Frank house and in the blink of an eye, our moods turned.

That house summarized all the uncomfortable places we'd visited on the trip: memories of nuclear annihilation in Hiroshima, brothers killing brothers in Korea, killing fields in Cambodia, napalm in Vietnam, concentration camps in Germany, and rows of crosses in France. Each one slowly ripped away our armour of ignorance. Ann was like a friend to us; imagining her dying alone in a concentration camp after displaying such heroic optimism throughout her miserable confinement seemed wrong on so many levels. Anne was our face of injustice. She was our face for the tormented and persecuted throughout history. Anne left us once again questioning why.

July 25

There was no visible carpet in our room at the Crown Royal Airport Hotel. In the mad rush to return the camper we moved our things, out and up into our room, until we backed ourselves out the door. How would we ever get organized? I sat on the bed willing myself to jump in and get packing, but instead sat paralyzed. I couldn't wrap my head around resuming life as we once knew it.

Focused on the T.V., commercials with sexy waifs tossing their long shining locks about and singing praises for Herbal Essence shampoo had me running my fingers through my ratty, dark-rooted, untrimmed hair. The next commercial was a weight loss advertisement, reminding me of the repercussions of too much pasta, red wine, chocolate and gelato. Stumbling to the bathroom, I stared in the mirror at my reflection. Was it time to start worrying about appearance again or had travel taken me beyond such concerns? A moment passed before a voice in my head called out "WHAT EVER!" I wasn't Jennifer Moore from September 2003. I was well traveled Jennifer Moore; a girl okay with herself morning, noon and unmade-up. A girl with the flexibility to let go of what she was leaving behind to fearlessly tackle the challenges of the future, and most importantly, a girl who'd lived a dream and knew without a doubt she would live another. Smiling at myself, I moved on to help Ken with the momentous task at hand and somehow, long after midnight, we managed to pack up all of our things right down to a full set of dishes and way too much wine.

The cab was waiting as I hung back and searched the room for forgotten items, a check I'd done so many times before. This was it; the Big Trip was over. Slowly closing the hotel room door, I suddenly stopped and couldn't resist looking back. Transfixed, the special moments of our trip flipped through my head. It wasn't over at all. Our Big Trip would never end. It would live on in our minds and play out again and again in our stories. Those stories would grow and take on a life of their own, but in them there would always be – the four of us, working as a team to experience the world.

Memories are the best part of travel

EPILOGUE

Returning to normal life back in Calgary seemed strange. I just didn't feel quite "normal" any more. Even so, our day to day lives reset to pre-trip speed. At social functions, I gushed about our remarkable trip insisting it changed my life, but getting more specific about it would have been impossible.

A few years after the trip I decided to revise my travel journal. Writing, and looking back, sent me on another journey of self-discovery filled with as many ups and downs as the trip itself. It was like looking into a reflective mirror of truth showing me who I really was. As I worked my way from the beginning to the end, I could see how our Big Trip experiences changed me.

After being back home for a few years, we started to long for the daily adventure and physical activity enjoyed on the Big Trip.

Back in Ken's college football days, when he played for the University of Hawaii, the spirit of Aloha got into his blood. Adventure and activity could certainly be found on a Hawaiian island. WHAT IF we could live in paradise? I poured a glass of wine and we once again started to dream and scheme.

Once Makayla graduated from grade twelve and long before Ken thought about selling his company and retiring, steps were taken to make a life in Hawaii possible. We bought a house in Kona and Ken announced he'd run his company, for six months of the year, from the Big Island.

Ten years have passed since our Big Trip. I retired from dentistry in 2010, and in 2011 Ken sold his company to his international distributor. We continue to live six months of the year beside the ocean in Kona Hawaii and the other six months in Canmore Canada nestled in the Rocky Mountains. Amazing experiences in both of our incredible homes keep our lives exciting and full.

Mattson graduated from Mechanical Engineering in 2013 and that same year won a bronze medal in pummel horse at Canadian National Gymnastics competition. He currently works in the oil and gas industry in Calgary. As always, Makayla remains our little singing, dancing, drama queen. She graduated from the musical theater program at Capilano University in 2014 and has landed multiple roles in professional musical theater shows. In no way, did their year away from school, gymnastics and dance, hold them back.

Our trip wasn't always easy, but the memories we laugh about the most happened during our hardest times. I tell anyone who will listen to take the time for a family sabbatical. It doesn't have to be somewhere exotic, or even far away; all you really need is time together. The adventure of it, and the memories collected along the way, will be the glue strengthening your family bond for years to come.

Everyone's lessons learned on the road will be different, but their impact as a catalyst for personal growth will hold the same power. Just go. One way or another, it will all work out as it should.

Thanks to travel, I get into the ocean whenever I can. I go to the bathroom on airplanes and I no longer live life on the side-lines. How did travel change my life? It led me to the mantra I now try to live by:

Live fearlessly,
love enthusiastically,
lighten up to laugh – and dream;
dream wondrous limitless dreams and make them happen

Acknowledgements

This book would never have come together without the help of many. I have to first and foremost thank my daughter Makayla for putting up with me when she'd arrive home from school to find me writing (Mattson had moved away from home). Total submersion in my words ensured late dinners and a distracted mother. My family stuck with me even when it seemed my revisions would never end. Thanks to my husband, mother, sister and aunt for taking the time to read through my stories and give helpful advice.

A special thanks to my good friend Maggie Pringle who patiently worked through an early revision and gave me hope that others might enjoy reading about our adventures. That encouragement, and the mentoring generously offered by Diane Tullson, gave me the push I needed to publish The Big Trip Revealed.

I also want to acknowledge my editors Barb Green and Kelli Taylor. Thank you for your meticulous hard work.

Jennifer Moore was born in 1960 in Regina Saskatchewan. She graduated from the University of Saskatchewan dental school in 1990 and practiced dentistry for 22 years. Ken and Jen met while Ken played for the Saskatchewan Roughriders CFL football team. They married in August of 1987.

Since retiring from Dentistry, Jennifer runs their family owned vacation rental business with properties in Canmore, Alberta and Kona, Hawaii. Ken and Jen continue to travel the world and bring Mattson and Makayla along whenever they can pry them away from their careers.

Having learned the importance of following your passions, Jen dedicates her time to write and explore the world of art through painting. For more about their travel, see www.thebigtriprevealed.com

Made in the USA
Charleston, SC
28 January 2015